The European Social Model and an Economy of Well-being

NEW HORIZONS IN SOCIAL POLICY

Series Editors: Patricia Kennett and Misa Izuhara, *University of Bristol, UK*

The New Horizons in Social Policy series captures contemporary issues and debates in social policy and encourages critical, innovative and thought-provoking approaches to understanding and explaining current trends and developments in the field. With its emphasis on original contributions from established and emerging researchers on a diverse range of topics, books in the series are essential reading for keeping up to date with the latest research and developments in the area.

Titles in the series include:

Housing Wealth and Welfare
Edited by Caroline Dewilde and Richard Ronald

Social Investment and Social Welfare
International and Critical Perspectives
Edited by James Midgley, Espen Dahl and Amy Conley Wright

Social Services Disrupted
Changes, Challenges and Policy Implications for Europe in Times of Austerity
Edited by Flavia Martinelli, Anneli Anttonen and Margitta Mätzke

Social Policy After the Financial Crisis
A Progressive Response
Ian Greener

Social Policy in the Middle East and North Africa
From Social Assistance to Universal Social Protection
Edited by Rana Jawad, Nicola Jones and Mahmood Messkoub

The Small Welfare State
Rethinking Welfare in the US, Japan, and South Korea
Edited by Jae-jin Yang

Poverty, Crisis and Resilience
Edited by Marie Boost, Jennifer Dagg, Jane Gray and Markus Promberger

The European Social Model and an Economy of Well-being
Repairing the Social Fabric of European Societies
Giovanni Bertin, Marion Ellison and Giuseppe Moro

The European Social Model and an Economy of Well-being

Repairing the Social Fabric of European Societies

Giovanni Bertin

Professor of Comparative Welfare States, Department of Economics, Ca' Foscari University of Venice, Italy

Marion Ellison

Professor of European Social Policy and Sociology, Department of Psychology, Sociology and Education, Queen Margaret University, Edinburgh, UK

Giuseppe Moro

Professor of Sociology and Social Policy, Department of Political Science, University of Bari Aldo Moro, Italy

Foreword by Romano Prodi, *former prime minister of Italy and former president of the European Commission*

NEW HORIZONS IN SOCIAL POLICY

Cheltenham, UK • Northampton, MA, USA

Published by
Edward Elgar Publishing Limited
The Lypiatts
15 Lansdown Road
Cheltenham
Glos GL50 2JA
UK

Edward Elgar Publishing, Inc.
William Pratt House
9 Dewey Court
Northampton
Massachusetts 01060
USA

A catalogue record for this book
is available from the British Library

Library of Congress Control Number: 2020952044

This book is available electronically in the **Elgar**online
Sociology, Social Policy and Education subject collection
http://dx.doi.org/10.4337/9781800378070

ISBN 978 1 80037 806 3 (cased)
ISBN 978 1 80037 807 0 (eBook)
Printed and bound by CPI Group (UK) Ltd, Croydon, CR0 4YY

Contents

Figures

Tables

Foreword

The welfare state was the greatest achievement of the twentieth century. Devised and developed in Europe, it is for us Europeans a source of great pride as it is a cornerstone of our way of understanding life, and relationships between people and between people and institutions. The welfare state, in its various national forms, is certainly not perfect, and as society changes, the social model needs modernizing and reforming. But it should be preserved because of its unique ability to combine social justice with economic growth.

First, the European social model has contributed to economic growth by ensuring that the large majority of the population, including the elderly and the unemployed, could take part in economic life.

Second, it has made for social cohesion and political stability, without which it would be impossible to modernize our economy.

Third, it promoted social justice by redistributing wealth. If market forces alone distributed wealth, a large percentage of all households in Europe would find itself below the poverty line. Europe's tax and protection systems saved hundreds of millions people from that fate. For this reason, the differences within Western countries tended to decrease up until the 1980s. Subsequently, on the strength of Ronald Reagan and Margaret Thatcher's policies, the market was left without limits, and the growing weight of finance in the economy and a reduced redistributive role of the state produced increasing differences in all countries.

The long economic crisis and major structural changes arising from the increasing pace of globalization have hit Europe and its people hard. As a result, considerable sections of the European population are living under difficult, grievous conditions. The overall gap between rich and poor is the largest in 30 years.

And the concerns increase even more as our observation widens from the viewpoint of strictly economic inequalities to include the complex of social conditions (school, health, family, justice, security) that determine the possibility of developing and exploiting one's own abilities. This is adversely affecting human well-being, social cohesion and economic growth.

To successfully respond to the current situation and future challenges, robust and innovative initiatives must be devised and implemented in the social sphere. For some time now, the welfare systems and organization of labour have slowly been adapting to the new risks and realities in people's lives. However, they are clearly not going fast enough, and progress is being made at very different speeds in different regions of Europe. Our social models need to adapt continuously and invest massively in human capital and inclusive resilient communities. One reason we need to modernize the welfare state is the problem of aging populations.

Health care is changing radically due to the emergence of increasingly aging populations. This poses the often-dramatic issue of long-term hospitalization, family assistance and care for the terminally ill. With respect to matters concerning health and well-being and care for the elderly, Europe reserves the right to call itself a civil society.

Europe is one of the regions where people live longer and have fewer children. Therefore, Europe will have a much larger number of people in the 80-plus and 65-plus categories. The old age dependency ratio, which is defined as the ratio of the population aged 65 and over to the population aged 15 to 64, is expected to rise from 29 per cent in 2015 to 52 per cent in 2080.[1] While the increase in people's life expectancy is partly due to improved nutrition and healthcare, in old age people often become frail and develop multi-morbidity conditions. This creates the need to make affordable integrated chronic health and social care accessible. Addressing this issue calls for different ways of organizing our communities and cities as well our health, social and long-term care services and housing.

This means the cost of health care and pensions will rise continuously in the coming years. At the same time, of course, the proportion of the population actually working and paying income tax will decrease, as will the numbers of schoolchildren and students.

Furthermore, Europe's social model financing is coming under serious strain because fewer people now contribute to the public pursue through work, while more people are becoming dependent on social benefits. In the future, the few who are working will have to support the many that are not.

So, the EU must find ways of meeting these increasing health care and pension costs while at the same time putting a lot of resources into education and training for the working population. While continuing to care for our senior citizens, we need to invest much more heavily in our young people.

A further concern regards the world of work, which is alarmingly segmented. Among those who have an occupation and enjoy efficient protection of their rights and others who are seeking or have lost theirs, no longer being able to return to the active world of work, there exists a category of temporary workers. Almost all of these are young people who are largely undefended and unable to create for themselves secure employment which will safeguard their future.

Secondary and vocational education is no longer sufficient in today's service and new-technologies economy. Even our universities, as they are currently structured and conceived, appear largely insufficient and incapable of ensuring adequate work opportunities for the educational investments made by students and families. Nor do they appear to be able to guarantee the level of excellence necessary to allow Europe to excel in innovation and compete on an equal footing with the more developed countries.

A key demographic component that must be considered when assessing the generational aspect of poverty is the NEET group (a young person who is not in education, employment or training). Without a suitable education, it is becoming increasingly difficult for young people to be employed and become productive members of society.

Finally, family policies are proving to be increasingly inadequate when compared to current social phenomena that see the expansion of single-parent families, increasingly larger groups of lonely elderly people without family support, and women who pay for their work by accepting or by choosing not to have children or by deciding to reduce the number of their offspring to one.

The overriding objective of social investment policies is to break the intergenerational transmission of poverty, through social reforms that help 'prepare' individuals, families and societies to respond to the changing nature of social risks in advanced economies. This can be achieved through investing in human capabilities from early childhood through to old age while improving work–life balance provision for working families, rather than merely pursuing policies that 'repair' social misfortune after times of economic or personal crisis.

If Europe does not want to jeopardize its future, these tears in the fabric of its society must be repaired, a task rendered more profound and complex during and after the current Covid-19 pandemic. A core challenge is to ensure full and equal access to new technologies that will give all who live and work in Europe comprehensive technological connectivity within this new world. Equipping people with the right to full and equal access to digital skills and resources will facilitate the inclusive and effective operation of the labour market, education system and social services. In my opinion, this right to technological connectivity, so critical to the future of our society, is now a human right; as fundamental as equal access to water and freedom.

These are the real problems of the community in which we live, the priority of which European institutions have not always recognized. However, we must recognize that the crisis and its consequences have raised an awareness of these problems. Never before has the drama of inequality and the need for greater social protection entered the European agenda. We just have to hope that in the next legislature this attention will not only continue but be underscored.

We must never forget that Europe is not just about money; it is about people. The EU exists for European citizens and must serve their interests. European integration is about creating a peaceful, democratic society in which all the peoples of the 'old continent' can live together in security and freedom, justice and equality. A Europe where human rights are respected and the rule of law prevails.

Romano Prodi

NOTE

1. *The 2018 Ageing Report. Economic & Budgetary Projections for the 28 EU Member States (2016–2070).* European Commission Institutional Paper 079. Brussels: European Commission. Brussels. https://ec.europa.eu/info/publications/economic-and-financial-affairs-publications_en.

1. Introduction: healing the divisions – restoring the foundations for a 'Social Europe'

Marion Ellison, Giovani Bertin and Giuseppe Moro

For the 113 million people living and working in European societies who are at risk of poverty or social exclusion, including 43 million people living in severe material deprivation, the concept of a European Social Model, however defined, is no more than an elusive dream (Eurostat, 2019). The everyday struggles and long-term scars caused by income poverty, low pay, poor-quality work and social exclusion have been evidenced as contributing to growing levels of mental and physical illness across European societies (Elliot, 2016; Marmot, 2020; OECD, 2019). In 2018, mental health problems, such as depression, anxiety disorders and alcohol and drug use disorders, affected more than one in six people across the European Union (EU) in any given year (OECD, 2019). Inequalities within social, economic and physical environments underly the complex and multi-dimensional factors contributing to mental and physical health problems (Marmot, 2020; Stafford, 2020; Urali and Oyebode, 2004; World Health Organization, 2020).

This has been made more profound by the health emergency that European societies and societies across the world now face as a result of the Covid-19 pandemic, a crisis that jeopardizes the social, cultural and economic fabric of all of our lives. As recent epidemiological evidence reveals, the impact of Covid-19 is directly related to levels of poverty and related health inequalities within each society (Bedford et al., 2020; Marmot, 2020; ONS, 2020; PSE, 2020; World Health Organization, 2020). Moreover, inadequate public health infrastructures and public pharmaceutical capabilities have also been revealed by the differential impact of the pandemic and concomitant strategic response in different European countries (EAPN, 2020; Marmot, 2020; Mavragani, 2020). Infodemiology has emerged as a critical tool merging new approaches to disease surveillance to facilitate the preparedness of public health care and pharmaceutical systems at a regional level in Europe (Emiliani, 2020; Mavragani, 2020; Saglietto et al., 2020).

It may be argued that recent evidence relating to the differential impact of the Covid-19 virus in Germany and the United Kingdom (UK) underlines the importance of an adequate public health infrastructure, particularly with regard to testing capacity at local level (Stafford, 2020). It may be strongly contended that the unprecedented challenges we now face across Europe demand a dual approach encouraging significant investment in public health infrastructures, and a strong drive towards more equitable economic and social conditions within European societies (Cheng and Khan, 2020; Emiliani, 2020; Marmot, 2020; Saglietto et al. 2020). This, it may be argued, forms the fundamental basis of the European Social Model.

The complex contours of inequality across European societies have given rise to socio-economic and health inequalities across and within European societies. These health inequalities have contributed to the differential impact of the Covid-19 pandemic on European societies. Widening divisions between the top and bottom of the income distribution are clearly evident within European countries (Blanchet, 2019; Eurostat, 2019; Marmot, 2020; OECD, 2019). Equally, evidence relating to widening trends in inequality, poverty and social exclusion between different countries is so capacious that the notion of a single European Social Model is difficult to conceptualize or justify, particularly in the light of the current health crisis (Emiliani, 2020; European Commission, 2019b; Vlachos and Bitzenis, 2019).

Definitions of the European Social Model are located within a highly contested terrain (Ellison, 2011; Fletcher et al., 2016; Grewal, 2018; Grimmel and Giang, 2017; Jaroszynski and Rolstone, 2019; Kauppi, 2018; Wiener et al., 2019). More broadly, the notion of a 'Social Europe' is usually counter-poised against the concept of free-market, neo-liberal models of Europe. The uncertainty relating to the specific meaning and contribution to European integration of the European Social Model relates to both its proposed intent and effect across Europe.

Historically, the EU was established as an economic organization with the central aim of fostering integration through frictionless trade whilst retaining trade barriers against countries outside the EU (Amato et al., 2019; Antoniolli et al., 2019; Ellison, 2011; Olsen, 2020). Growing awareness of the way in which economic conditions within the 1970s gave rise to widespread economic and social insecurity among EU citizens led to the establishment of the Charter of Fundamental Social Rights of Workers, which provided a minimum set of social rights for all EU citizens (Council of the EU, 2008). The Charter constituted a non-binding political declaration. Critically, in 1992 the Charter was annexed as a social protocol within the Treaty on European Union. The Charter could not be established within the main body of the text due to opposition from the UK Conservative Government. As a result, the UK opted out from provisions within the Treaty leading to the adoption of a body of European directives concerning social and employment policies. These directives related to areas such as maternity rights, working time and the regulation of collective redundancies (Council of the EU, 2008). These social and employment rights were fortified by the incorporation of the provisions within the main body of the Amsterdam Treaty. Article 11 provided a range of competencies directed at the reduction of social exclusion and maintaining stable industrial relations (European Union, 1997). Thus, whilst there is ambivalence relating to the definition of the European Social Model it is undoubtedly the case that employment and social rights have been established as a core intent of European solidarity. Reinforcing this, the European Pillar of Social Rights (EPSR), established in 2000, recognizes the intrinsic relationship between social and economic rights (Vanhercke, 2020).

Whilst employment and social rights across Europe remain subject to a range of policy interpretations and inconsistent implementation, it is nevertheless the case that most European nations have expressed a unified approach to values relating to the promotion of social protection and social dialogue (Amato et al., 2019; Baubôck, 2019; Ellison, 2014; Moro and Pacelli, 2012). Critically, however, whilst there is a clear consensus regarding the intent of the European Social Model, the establishment of a 'Social Europe' has faced many challenges. The pervasive move towards a neo-liberal Europe in recent years has led to increasing unease within and across European societies (Baubôck, 2019; Chiocchetti and Allemand, 2019). In particular, reductions in public expenditure as a ratio of gross domestic product (GDP) in key areas such as education, social protection, health care and social services, together with the decreasing role of collective bargaining within industrial relations and perceptions of declining national political influence in EU decision making, have led to the rise of populism within a number of European countries (Ellison, 2017; Theodore, 2020; Wôhl et al., 2020). Indeed, this is perhaps most clearly evidenced by the withdrawal of the UK from the EU, as the UK is identified as having one of the most neo-liberal policy agendas in Europe (Cafruny and Ryner, 2003; Clarke and Newman, 2017; Taylor-Gooby and Leruth, 2018; Taylor-Gooby et al., 2017). The acceleration and deepening of austerity measures and deregulation of labour markets has characterized policy approaches across a number of European countries since the financial crisis of 2007–2008 exacerbating social and employment conditions (Avram et al., 2012; Bargain et al., 2017; Baubôck, 2019; Farnsworth and Irving, 2017; Gaisbauer et al., 2019). The tension between a 'Social Europe' and a 'Competitive Market Economy Europe' is clearly evident today. As Farnsworth and Irving (2017) argue, austerity is

> not simply about expenditure cuts, it more accurately describes an intention towards and reconfiguration of economics and welfare states that cannot be measured or

assessed simply by reference to social spending as a proportion of gross domestic product (GDP). While the intension is to dissolve the bonds of solidarity that characterized the post-war period of the welfare state building, because for neo-liberalism they have always represented constraints on freedom. It is the reconfiguration of the welfare state that is expected to achieve this outcome. (p. 103)

Underlying this, as the devasting impact of the Covid-19 virus itself reveals, the interaction between public health, work, capital, poverty, formal care and informal social care lies at the axiom of the relationship between economy and society in Europe. Calls for a new focus on a well-being economy which recognizes the centrality of the economy of care have arisen (Bauhardt and Harcourt, 2018; Chertkovskaya et al., 2019; Addati et al., 2018; Marmot, 2020). This focus on a well-being economy was at the forefront of the Finnish Presidency of the Council for the EU between 1 July 2019 and 31 December 2019. The central focus of the Presidency was upon building a European 'Economy of Wellbeing' which fully supports the development of the welfare economy contributing to a socially, economically and environmentally sustainable Europe (Finnish Government, 2019). Fundamental to this approach was the view that the formulation of macro-economic policy requires the comprehensive analysis of its implications upon the well-being of citizens, particularly with regard to the quality of social and health care services and the prevalence of social exclusion among vulnerable groups (Bauhardt and Harcourt, 2018; Chertkovskaya et al., 2019; Addati et al., 2018; Marmot, 2020).

The financial crisis of 2007–2008 led to deepening levels of income inequality across many European countries (Bargain et al., 2017; Callan et al., 2018; Whyman et al., 2014). The adoption of fiscal austerity policies designed to increase economic competitiveness across a wide range of European countries exacerbated levels of inequality within and between European nations, with a devasting impact on the well-being of citizens, particularly in countries such as Greece, Portugal, Ireland, Cyprus, Spain and the UK (Castells, 2018; Eurostat, 2019; Morlino and Sottilotta, 2020). The intensity of the austerity measures has also undermined economic growth in both the medium and long term, particularly in those countries benefitting from support from formal 'bail out' measures such as Greece, Ireland, Spain, Cypris and Portugal, which were forced to adopt stringent macro-fiscal austerity policies (Castells, 2018; de la Porte and Heins, 2016; Morlino and Sottilotta, 2020).

Whilst there is clear evidence of the differentiated nature of austerity and welfare reform across European nation states, it is undoubtedly the case that austerity and welfare reforms have weakened the capacity of public health social protection systems to respond to the current Covid-19 crisis, especially in national settings with pre-existing high levels of economic, social and health inequalities, such as the UK (Chapman, 2017; Marmot, 2020; Viens, 2019).

Here it may be argued that austerity policies and welfare reforms legitimated as a response to the financial crisis of 2007–2008 have exacerbated social and health inequalities for vulnerable groups across Europe in recent years. It is critical that the response to the current Covid-19 crisis does not follow the same pattern. Recent epidemiological evidence has revealed that inequities in health have exacerbated the impact of the Covid-19 virus pandemic (Ahmed et al., 2020; Chapman, 2017; Krouse, 2020; Marmot, 2020; Viens, 2019). This underlines the critical need to invest in social and fiscal policies directed at reducing levels of social and health inequalities across European welfare settings.

There is also clear evidence of welfare retrenchment across European settings in recent decades. At the same time, several European countries have instituted tax and transfer policies since the crisis which have reduced levels of income inequality and relative poverty (Bargain, 2017; Callan et al., 2018; Funke et al., 2016; Whyman et al., 2014). Critically, analysis of fiscal and policy outcomes also reveals that some welfare systems are more effective than others at reducing income inequality through redistributive instruments. The Nordic countries are revealed as being the most equal European countries, but Central Eastern European countries (Slovenia and the Czech and Slovak republics) also exhibit lower levels of income inequality (Eurostat, 2019). Western European countries, such as France, Germany and the Netherlands, are close to the European average. Income inequality is above average in all Southern European countries. The highest levels of income inequality in Europe are evident in the UK and the Baltic States (Eurostat, 2019).

The value of effective fiscal and welfare systems in reducing socio-economic inequalities is also evidenced by the most recent European Quality of Life Survey, which found that in some European countries, the quality of public services had improved since the financial crisis, leading to perceived improvements in areas such as healthcare and childcare since 2011. Critically, however, the 2016 European Quality of Life Survey also revealed substantial differences between European countries (Eurofound, 2017). Demonstrating this, the UK was identified as the worst place to live in Europe for quality of life. Significant indicators underlying this were the third lowest spend on health as a percentage of GDP, below-average government spending on education, and the fourth highest retirement age in Europe. At the same time UK households face a high cost of living, with food and fuel prices being the highest in Europe. Given these variations, the influence of differential welfare regimes on outcomes for people living and working in Europe is significant.

Despite these differences the commitment of the EU Commission to a unified European Social Model is evidenced by the overarching aim of the Lisbon Treaty (2007), which was to create a more equal society, ending poverty and low pay and guaranteeing fundamental human rights (EU, 2007). These fundamental social rights, legally enshrined within the Charter of Fundamental Human Rights, included social protection delivered through highly developed universal systems and wealth distribution measures such as progressive taxation and minimum income (European Parliament, 2000). These rights also included fair working conditions, equality and non-discrimination and the right to conclude collective agreements. All legislation enacted by the EU must comply with the Charter. The Court of Justice for the EU[1] has the power to remove legislation that does not comply with the Charter (Hoevenaars, 2018; Horsley, 2018; Krenn, 2018; Schmidt, 2018; Shaw, 2018).

Reinforcing this judicial capacity, the European Court of Human Rights has jurisdiction to make decisions with regard to complaints submitted by individuals and states related to violations of the Convention for the Protection of Human Rights and Fundamental Freedoms.[2] This convention focuses on civil and political rights of individuals living and working in Europe. Recent studies have revealed a strong correlation between the degree of compliance with judgements made by the court and the quality of democratic governance in member states (Lang and Bell, 2018; Von Staden, 2018). Changes to laws, policies and practices required by judgements made by the European Court of Human Rights are very much reliant on the quality of democracy within each member state. In particular, diverse liberal democracies may exploit all available options to minimize the domestic impact of court judgements on their own framework of law, policies and practices (Lang and Bell, 2018; Von Staden, 2018). This diversity is illustrative of the limits of Europe-wide effective judicial governance over human rights across the EU. Nevertheless, it remains the case that when taken together the European Court of Justice and the European Court of Human Rights do represent the judicial institutionalization of principles of social, economic, civil and political rights for people living and working in Europe. As such they provide legal protections and legal redress for people who live and work in Europe. At this critical juncture in the history of the EU itself, reinvestment in and reinvigoration of the European Social Model is reliant on the judicial effectiveness of both of these institutions.

More broadly, the advancement of a Social Europe has also been facilitated by the soft instruments of governance of the Open Social Method of Coordination (OMC). Founded on the concept of social solidarity within and between nations, the OMC has been designed to encourage the coordination of policies directed at social protection, pensions, health, social care and social inclusion of people who live and work in Europe. At the same time social policy in the EU is built on the notion of subsidiarity, rendering the effective implementation of the European Social Model reliant upon adequate levels of social solidarity within and across European nation states (Barcevičius et al., 2014; Ellison, 2011; Sirovátka and Mareš, 2011).

More broadly, the effectiveness of the OMC has been significantly weakened by the tensions between the concepts and principles underpinning notions of a 'Social Europe' and free-market, neo-liberal models of Europe. Critically, however, recent contributions have evidenced the significant role that the OMC has played in encouraging flexible kinds of policy-making and cooperation between EU-level, national and sub-national governments across European welfare systems (Vanderbroucke, 2017). Indeed, the OMC has strengthened the influence of the European Social Model by enabling monitoring and benchmarking of welfare policies across different welfare systems. In addition, the OMC facilitates the coordinated use of EU funding instruments aimed at rebalancing economic and social inequalities between wealthier and poorer regions and groups within the EU.

Superseding the Charter of Fundamental Human Rights, the EPSR provides the legal framework for the operationalization of EU funding instruments designed to address these imbalances. Established in 2017, the EPSR addresses 20 central principles and rights designed to support fair and well-functioning labour markets. These principles and rights are embedded within three chapters: equal opportunities and access to the labour market; fair working conditions; and social protection and inclusion. Despite these principles, recent evidence has pointed to a growing liberalization of the European Social Model, particularly with regard to increased emphasis on flexible labour markets; wage moderation; a reduction in relative pension levels and social security entitlements; reductions in expenditure on public health care services, social services and education; and the privatization of social and health care services over the last three decades (Amato, 2019; Callan et al., 2018). These tendencies have been accentuated since the financial crisis of 2007–2008. In particular, the adoption of social measures and programmes imposed upon countries in Southern Europe as a result of bailouts provided by the Troika[3] has led to a significant rolling back of welfare provisions and the privatization of public services in countries such as Greece, Portugal and Ireland (Balbona and Begega, 2015; Heins and de la Porte, 2015; Karger, 2014; Morlino and Sottilotta, 2020).

Critically, however, there is also clear evidence of attempts to respond to economic crises and financial constraints through the hybridization of welfare arrangements with an emphasis upon social innovation within the context of meta-governance of social policies across European states (Bassi and Moro, 2015; Bertin and Ellison, 2019). This is demonstrated by the adoption of distinct policy and governance approaches directed at improving the level and quality of social protection, pensions, health, social care and social inclusion of people who live and work in Europe. Exemplifying this, the EU Youth on the Move initiative advocates that each European member state implement a Youth Guarantee which ensures that all young people between the age of

16 and 25 are guaranteed a place on either a training, educational or employment programme. Whilst the UK opted out of this measure, all of the other 28 EU nations have developed a range of measures, often highly innovative and funded partly by European Social Fund (ESF) and European Regional Development Fund (ERDF) funding within distinct governance and welfare arrangements. In many cases hybrid arrangements are adopted at local level to ensure relevance to local priorities (Ellison et al., 2017). In Scotland, for example, a sophisticated place-based community planning and partnership approach is a statutory requirement of all 32 local authorities. A critical component of this is that local communities are given the power to select local priorities under the Community Empowerment Act (2015). A range of national and local public and third-sector organizations are then required by law to work in partnership with local communities and local authorities and businesses to respond to these priorities in partnership (Bertin and Ellison, 2019; Ellison, 2020).

This book adopts a network governance theoretical lens. This is centrally based upon the notion that there is emerging evidence across European welfare states of communities and organizations at local level initiating processes which have contributed to the construction of a shared idea of social rights and welfare policies from the bottom up. Thus, the relationship between the European Social Model at EU level and welfare measures developed at national and local level is informed by the analysis of distinct processes which have arisen within specific national contexts.

Emerging from this, the book focuses on organizational processes which are pursued in attempts to achieve these shared welfare policies. Here we argue for a move away from standardizing logic systems that claim to build a single welfare model from the top down towards an investigation of the processes experienced by people at community level with distinct regulatory forms and integrative dynamics which are embedded into local cultures. Developing this, we utilize international comparative methods to interrogate the construction of learning opportunities which are based upon concrete experiences. Within this it is clear that the EU continues to play a central role in enabling the growth of network governance by facilitating the sharing of effective forms of partnership and hybrid welfare arrangements within well-established forms of dialogue and community initiation of projects.

These specific forms of network governance are currently facilitated by key instruments of European funding such as the ESF and ERDF enabling the development of new forms of local community-initiated welfare arrangements by redistributing investment to less developed[4] and transition regions.[5] It is nevertheless clear that the scale of regional inequalities and inequalities at individual and household level across European settings reveals the immense social and economic challenges that lie ahead. As recent research reveals, whilst austerity measures and welfare reforms have exacerbated these inequalities it is the fundamental reconfiguration of the relationship between economics and society which is driven by neo-liberal economics that has undermined the social and political fabric of Europe in recent years (Bailey, 2017; Caterino and Hansen, 2019; Della Porta et al., 2017; Farnsworth and Irving, 2017; Kamali and Jönsson, 2019; Palley, 2018; Taylor-Gooby et al., 2017; Tett and Hamilton, 2019). As has been argued, the current Covid-19 health pandemic has exposed the depth and extent of health inequalities in Europe (Marmot, 2020). The relationship between economy and society in Europe has stimulated a growing literature in the field in recent years (Büllesbach et al., 2017; Burroni et al., 2012; Taylor-Gooby et al., 2017).

We argue that investment strategies should support the effective governance of welfare measures developed as part of bottom-up, place-based, collaborative strategies. This requires the transition from a logic of hierarchical regulation to a process of network governance. These processes require a focus on the concept of community and the construction of its capacity to be resilient. The logic of social investment, and the need for measures and arrangements that facilitate the mobilization of individual and collective resources within distinctive welfare cultures and systems, are central to this process. In arguing for a cross-sectoral, horizontal approach to governance we also underline the central importance of the effective judicial implementation of the EPSR. The EU itself is strongly committed to this in principle:

> To strengthen its economic and social performance, the EU must fully deliver on the principles of the European Pillar of Social Rights. While the economic recovery helped to improve employment and social outcomes across Europe, action is needed to ensure the enjoyment of social rights and to counter the risks posed by a growing social divide. (European Commission, 2019a, p. 10: Section 5, Fairness)

Critically, however, a growing number of commentators argue that the fundamental source of the growing social divide in Europe is neo-liberalism itself (Farnsworth and Irving, 2017; Taylor-Gooby et al., 2017). There is growing literature relating to alternative, economic models offering a progressive, just and environmentally sustainable way forward (Dubb, 2016; Kristensen, 2016; Stiglitz, 2020). A unifying characteristic of these models is the promotion of cross-sectoral, horizontal approaches to the governance and mobilization of social investment measures that facilitate the realization of individual and collective resources within distinctive welfare cultures and systems. New organizational forms, such as social enterprise ownership at the urban community level, community development corporations and community development financial institutions and employee stock ownership plans (ESOP), provide the basis for a more comprehensive strategy for shared well-being at local level.

The actualization of individual and collective resources at community level also relies on social investment measures which recognize the critical importance of progressive government policies such as accessible and equitable lifelong worker training and education, and investment in social care and child care for the well-being of citizens (Bonoli et al., 2017; Cantillon et al., 2017; Ellison, 2014; Hemerijck, 2018; Kristensen, 2016).

A unifying theme across these economic proposals is the importance of balanced, democratic and sustainable social economies. Illustrating this, Joseph Stiglitz (2020) argues for the construction of a balanced social economy that advances the well-being of people who live and work in distinct societies. A fundamental pre-requisite of this is the conceptualization and operationalization of prosperity as a symbiotic relationship between social, economic, political and environmental activity, requiring equilibrium among social, public and private sectors of society. Crucially, Stiglitz (p. 8) argues that

> the economy is not an end in itself but a means to an end to improving living standards and well-being of the people within the country in ways that do not impose harm on people outside the country.

Ecological economic approaches endorse this view by promoting alternative economic models which centre on human development and ecological regeneration (Hanaček et al., 2020; Milani, 2000; Muradian and Pascual, 2020; Spash, 2020). Milani (2000) articulates a fundamental premise of ecological economic models in his re-definition of the concept of wealth itself. In essence, he says, wealth is conceptualized in qualitative terms as individual and community well-being and ecological regeneration rather than the quantitative accumulation of money and material objects.

In summary, the central premise of this book is that an effective and sustainable relationship between public health, work, capital, formal care and informal social care is the central generating mechanism of a well-functioning well-being economy. In light of this, we argue that to repair the social fabric of Europe we need to invest substantially in locally driven welfare strategies which address inter-regional inequalities as well as inequalities faced at individual level by people who live and work in Europe. Here we argue for the development of place-based approaches involving collaborative networks and partnerships between different sectors and organizations in society which are designed to respond to priorities identified by people within local communities in distinct European societies.

At the same time, the book clearly evidences the scale and depth of economic, social and health inequities and the intersectional vulnerabilities suffered by a substantial number of people who live and work in Europe. We also recognize the need to address issues of economic democracy and the effectiveness of the judicial processes in supporting economic and social rights of people living and working across Europe. In particular, the book argues that the effectiveness of place-based network governance strategies is dependent upon the recalibration of work and well-being in knowledge-driven, environmentally sustainable economies of well-being. Equally, the effectiveness of network governance is contingent upon substantial investment in coherent, locally relevant and cross-sectoral, interorganizational services and labour market measures. More broadly, the book evidences the symbiotic relationship between the architecture of the European Social Model, characterized by redistributive, place-based network governance and innovative alternative economic infrastructures such as the 'foundational economy'. Here it is argued that the relevance and effectiveness of the European Social Model within post-Covid-19 European societies is contingent upon the equitable and sustainable delivery of universal public services and measures vital to the health and well-being of all who live and work in Europe.

NOTES

1. The Court of Justice for the EU operates as the supreme court of the EU in all matters of EU law. It is considered by many to be 'the most powerful and influential international court that is realistically possible'.
2. The European Court of Human Rights is an international court which was established by the European Convention on Human Rights.
3. The Troika was the decision-making group comprising the European Commission (EC), the European Central Bank and the International Monetary Fund (IMF). The use of the term came to the fore during the financial 'bailouts' of Greece, Cyprus, Portugal and Ireland, which were made necessary by potential economic insolvency within these states caused by the financial crisis of 2007–2008.
4. That is, where GDP per inhabitant is less than 75 per cent of the EU average.
5. That is, where GDP per inhabitant is between 75 per cent and 90 per cent of the EU average.

REFERENCES

Addati, L., Cattaneo, U., Esquivel, V., and Valarino, I. (2018). *Care Work and Care Jobs for the Future of Decent Work.* Geneva: International Labour Organization.

Ahmed, F., Ahmed, N., Pissarides, C., Ahmed, F., and Stiglitz, J. (2020). Why inequality could spread Covid-19. *Lancet Public Health,* **5** (5), E240.

Amato, G., Moavero-Milanesi, E., Pasquino, G., and Reichlin, L. (2019). *The History of the European Union: Constructing Utopia.* New York, NY: Hart Publishing.

Antoniolli, L., Bonatti, L., and Ruzza, C. (2019). *Highs and Lows of European Integration: Sixty Years after the Treaty of Rome.* Cham: Springer International.

Avram, S., Figari, F., Leventi, C., Levy, H., Navicke, J., Matsaganis, M., Militaru, E., Paulus, A., Rastrigina, O., and Sutherland, H. (2012). The distributional effects of fiscal consolidation in 9 EU countries. Social Situation Observatory Research Note 01/2012.

Bailey, D. J. (2017). *Beyond Defeat and Austerity: Disrupting the Critical Political Economy of Neoliberal Europe*. Abingdon: Routledge.

Balbona, D. L., and Begega, S. G. (2015). Austerity and welfare reform in south-western Europe: a farewell to corporatism in Italy, Spain and Portugal? *European Journal of Social Security*, **17** (2), 271–291.

Barcevičius, E., Weishaupt, J. T., and Zeitlin, J. (2014). *Assessing the Open Method of Coordination: Institutional Design and National Influence of EU Social Policy Coordination*. Basingstoke: Palgrave Macmillan.

Bargain, O., Callan, T., Doorley, K., and Keane, C. (2017). Changes in income distributions and the role of tax-benefit policy during the Great Recession: an international perspective. *Fiscal Studies*, 38, 559–585.

Bassi, A., and Moro, G. (2015). *Politiche sociali innovative e diritti di cittadinanza* (Innovative social policies and citizenship rights). Milano: FrancoAngeli.

Bauböck, R. (2019). *Debating European Citizenship*. Berlin: Springer.

Bauhardt, C., and Harcourt, W. (eds) (2018). *Feminist Political Ecology and the Economics of Care: In Search of Economic Alternatives*. Abingdon: Routledge.

Bedford, J., Enria, D., Giesecke, J., et al. (2020). Covid-19: towards controlling of a pandemic. *The Lancet*, **395** (10229), 1015–1018. www.ncbi.nlm.nih.gov/pmc/articles/PMC7270596/.

Bertin, G., and Ellison, M. (2019). Social innovation and metagovernance of welfare policies. *Salute e società*, 2, 40–56.

Blanchet, T., Chancel, L., and Gethin, A. (2019). Income inequality in Europe, 1980–2017. World Inequality Database. https://wid.world/document/bcg2019-full-paper/.

Bonoli, G., Cantillon, B., and Van Lancker, W. (2017). Social investment and the Matthew effect: limits to a strategy, in A. Hamerijck (ed.), *Social Investment Uses*. Oxford: Oxford University Press.

Büllesbach, D., Cillero, M., and Stolz, L. (2017). *Shifting Baselines of Europe: New Perspectives beyond Neoliberalism and Nationalism*. Bielefeld: Transcript-Verla.

Burroni, L., Keune, M., and Meardi, G. (2012). *Economy and Society in Europe: A Relationship in Crisis*. Cheltenham, UK, and Northampton, MA: Edward Elgar Publishing.

Cafruny, A. W., and Ryner, M. (2003). *A Ruined Fortress? Neoliberal Hegemony and Transformation in Europe*. Lanham, MD: Rowman & Littlefield.

Callan, T., et al. (2018). Inequality in EU crisis countries. How effective were automatic stabilisers? Institute of Labour Economics. www.iza.org/publications/dp/11439/inequality-in-eu-crisis-countries-how-effective-were-automatic-stabilisers.

Cantillon, B., Chzhen, Y., Handa, S., and Nolan, B. (eds) (2017). *Children of Austerity: Impact of the Great Recession on Child Poverty in Rich Countries*. Oxford: Oxford University Press.

Castells, M. (2018). *Europe's Crises*. Cambridge: Polity Press. http://public.ebookcentral.proquest.com/choice/publicfullrecord.aspx?p=5188194.

Caterino, B., and Hansen, P. (2019). *Critical Theory, Democracy, and the Challenge of Neoliberalism*. Toronto: University of Toronto Press. https://doi.org/10.3138/9781487532147.

Chapman, A. R. (2017). *Global Health, Human Rights, and the Challenge of Neoliberal Policies*. Cambridge: Cambridge University Press.

Cheng, S. O., and Khan, S. (2020). Europe's response to Covid-19 in March and April 2020: A letter to the editor on 'World Health Organization declares global emergency: A review of the 2019 novel coronavirus (Covid-19)' (Int J Surg 2020; 76:71–6). *International Journal of Surgery*, 78, 3–4.

Chertkovskaya, E., Barca, S., and Paulsson, A. (2019). Towards a Political Economy of Degrowth. London: Rowman & Littlefield.

Chiocchetti, P., and Allemand, F. (2019). *Competitiveness and Solidarity in the European Union: Interdisciplinary Perspectives*. Abingdon: Routledge.

Clarke, J., and Newman, J. (2017). 'People in this country have had enough of experts': Brexit and the paradoxes of populism. *Critical Policy Studies*, 11, 101–116.

Council of the European Union (2008). *Charter of Fundamental Rights of the European Union*. Paris: Editions BIOTOP.

De la Porte, C., and Heins, E. (2016). *The Sovereign Debt Crisis, the EU and Welfare State Reform*. London: Palgrave Macmillan.

Della Porta, D., Andretta, M., Fernandes, T., O'Connor, F., Romanos, E., and Vogiatzoglou, M. (2017). *Late Neoliberalism and its Discontents in the Economic Crisis: Comparing Social Movements in the European Periphery*. Cham: Palgrave Macmillan.

Dubb, S. (2016). Community wealth building forms: what they are and how to use them at the local level. *Academy of Management Perspectives*, **30** (2). https://journals.aom .org/doi/10.5465/amp.2015.0074.

EAPN (2020). Putting social rights and poverty reduction at the heart of the EU's response to Covid-19. Europe Anti-Poverty Network. www.eapn.eu/wp -content/uploads/2020/05/EAPN-EAPN-Assessment-of-2020-Country-Reports -with-alternative-CSRs-4405.pdf.

Elliott, I. (June 2016). *Poverty and Mental Health: A Review to Inform the Joseph Rowntree Foundation's Anti-Poverty Strategy*. London: Mental Health Foundation.

Ellison, M. (2011). *Reinventing Social Solidarity across Europe*. Bristol: Policy Press.

Ellison, M. (2014). No future to risk? The impact of economic crises and austerity on the inclusion of young people within distinct European labour market settings, in K. Farnsworth, Z. Irving, and M. Fenger (eds), *Social Policy Review 26: Analysis and Debate in Social Policy*. Bristol: Policy Press.

Ellison, M. (2017). Through the looking glass: young people, work and the transition between education and employment in a post-Brexit UK. *Journal of Social Policy*, **46** (4), 675–698.

Ellison, M. (2020). The construction of public knowledge within community plan- ning partnerships: reducing structurally embedded inequalities at local level, in E. Scandrett (ed.), *Public Sociology Education*. Bristol: Policy Press.

Ellison, M., Sergi, V., and Giannelli, N. (2017). *An In-Depth Analysis of the Relationship Between Policy Making Processes, Forms of Governance and the Impact of Selected Labour Market Innovations in Twelve European Labour Market Settings*. Urbino: University of Urbino, Faculty of Economics. https://eresearch.qmu .ac.uk/bitstream/handle/20.500.12289/4744/4744.pdf?sequence=1&isAllowed=y.

Emiliani, T. (2020). *How Relevant? The EU's 'Geopolitical' Commission and the Response to the Covid-19 Pandemic*. Bruges: College of Europe. www.coleurope .eu/system/files_force/research-paper/emiliani_cepob_4-2020.pdf.

Eurofound (2017). *European Quality of Life Survey 2016: Quality of Life, Quality of Public Services, and Quality of Society*. Luxembourg: Publications Office of the European Union.

European Commission (2019a). Communication from the Commission to the European Parliament, the Council, the European Central Bank, the European Economic and Social Committee, the Committee of the Regions and the European Investment

Bank. Annual Sustainable Growth Strategy 2020. https://eur-lex.europa.eu/legal -content/EN/TXT/PDF/?uri=CELEX:52019DC0650&from=EN.

European Commission (2019b). Implementation of the new European Consensus on Development – addressing inequality in partner countries. Brussels, 14.6.2019 SWD (2019) 280 final.

European Parliament. (2000). *Charter of Fundamental Rights of the European Union.* Luxembourg: Office for Official Publications of the European Communities.

European Union (1997). Council of the European Union: Treaty of Amsterdam Amending the Treaty on European Union, The Treaties Establishing the European Communities and Related Acts, 10 November 1997. www.refworld.org/docid/ 51c009ec4.html.

European Union (2007). *Treaty of Lisbon Amending the Treaty on European Union and the Treaty Establishing the European Community*, 13 December 2007, 2007/C 306/01. www.refworld.org/docid/476258d32.html.

Eurostat (2019). Europe 2020 indicators: poverty and social exclusion. https://ec .europa.eu/eurostat/statistics-explained/pdfscache/29306.pdf.

Farnsworth, K., and Irving, Z. (2017). The limits of neoliberalism? Austerity versus social policy in comparative perspective, in B. Jones and M. O'Donnell (eds), *Alternatives to Neoliberalism: Towards Equality and Democracy*. Bristol: Policy Press.

Finnish Government (2019). High-level Conference on the Economy of Wellbeing: Finland strives for better cohesion between wellbeing and economic growth in the EU. Finnish Government, Ministry of Social Affairs and Health. https:// valtioneuvosto.fi/en/article/-/asset_publisher/1271139/hyvinvointitalouskonferenssi -suomi-haluaa-lisata-hyvinvoinnin-ja-talouskasvun-yhteenkuuluvuutta-eu-ssa.

Fletcher, M., Herlin-Karnell, E., and Matera, C. (2016). *The European Union as an Area of Freedom, Security and Justice*. Florence: Taylor & Francis. https://public .ebookcentral.proquest.com/choice/publicfullrecord.aspx?p=4748626.

Funke, M., Schularick, M., and Trebesch, C. (2016). Going to extremes: politics after financial crises, 1870–2014. *European Economic Review*, **88** (C), 227–260.

Gaisbauer, H. P., Schweiger, G., and Sedmak, C. (2019). *Absolute Poverty in Europe: Interdisciplinary Perspectives on a Hidden Phenomenon*. Bristol: Policy Press.

Grewal, S. (2018). *Habermas on European Integration*. Manchester: Manchester University Press.

Grimmel, A., and Giang, S. M. (2017). *Solidarity in the European Union: A Fundamental Value in Crisis*. Cham: Springer.

Hanaček, K., Roy, B., Avila, S., and Kallis, G. (2020). Ecological economics and degrowth: proposing a future research agenda from the margins. *Ecological Economics*, **169**, p.106495.

Heins, E., and de la Porte, C. (2015). The sovereign debt crisis, the EU and welfare state reform. *Comparative European Politics*, **13**, 1–7.

Hemerijck, A. (2018). Social investment as a policy paradigm. *Journal of European Public Policy*, **25** (6), 810–827.

Hoevenaars, J. (2018). *A People's Court? A Bottom-up Approach to Litigation before the European Court of Justice*. Utrecht: Eleven International.

Horsley, T. (2018). *The Court of Justice of the European Union as an Institutional Actor: Judicial Lawmaking and its Limits*. Cambridge: Cambridge University Press.

Jaroszynski, P., and Rolstone, L. (2019). *Europe: Civilizations Clashing from Athens to the European Union*. Berlin: Peter Lang.

Kamali, M., and Jönsson, J. H. (2019). *Neoliberalism, Nordic Welfare States and Social Work: Current and Future Challenges*. London: Routledge.

Karger, H. (2014). The bitter pill: austerity, debt, and the attack on Europe's welfare states. *J. Soc. & Soc. Welfare*, 41, 33.

Kauppi, N. (2018). *Toward a Reflexive Political Sociology of the European Union: Fields, Intellectuals and Politicians*. Cham: Springer.

Krenn, C. (2018). *Legitimacy in the Making: The Procedural and Organizational Law of the European Court of Justice* (Doctoral dissertation, Johann Wolfgang Goethe-Universität Frankfurt am Main).

Kristensen, P. H. (2016). Constructing chains of enablers for alternative economic futures: Denmark as an example. *Academy of Management Perspectives*, **30** (2). https://doi.org/10.5465/amp.2015.0152.

Krouse, H. J. (2020). Covid-19 and the widening gap in health inequity. *Otolaryngology–Head and Neck Surgery*, **163** (1). https://doi.org/10.1177/0194599820926463.

Lang, R., and Bell, M. (2018). *Complex Equality and the Court of Justice of the European Union: Reconciling Diversity and Harmonisation*. Leiden: Brill.

Marmot, M. (2020). *Health Equity in England: The Marmot Review 10 Years On*. London: Institute of Health Equity. www.health.org.uk/sites/default/files/upload/publications/2020/Health%20Equity%20in%20England_The%20Marmot%20Review%2010%20Years%20On_full%20report.pdf.

Mavragani, A. (2020). Tracking Covid-19 in Europe: infodemiology approach. *JMIR Public Health and Surveillance*, **6** (2), e18941. DOI: 10.2196/18941.

Milani, B. (2000). *Designing the Green Economy: The Postindustrial Alternative to Corporate Globalization*. Lanham, MD: Rowman & Littlefield.

Morlino, L., and Sottilotta, C. E. (2020). *The Politics of the Eurozone Crisis in Southern Europe: A Comparative Reappraisal*. Cham: Palgrave Macmillan US.

Moro, G., and Pacelli, D. (2012). *Europa e società civile. Esperienze a confront.* (Europe and civil society. Comparing experiences.) Milan: Franco Angeli.

Muradian, R., and Pascual, U. (2020). Ecological economics in the age of fear. *Ecological Economics*, **169**, p.106498.

OECD (Organisation for Economic Co-operation and Development) (2019). *Health for Everyone? Social Inequalities in Health and Health Systems*. OECD Health Policy Studies. Paris: OECD Publishing.

Olsen, J. (2020). *The European Union: Politics and Policies*. Abingdon: Routledge.

ONS (Office of National Statistics) (2020). Number of deaths registered each month in England and Wales, including deaths involving the coronavirus (Covid-19), by age, sex and region. ONS. www.ons.gov.uk/peoplepopulationandcommunity/birthsdeathsandmarriages/deaths/bulletins/deathsinvolvingcovid19englandandwales/deathsoccurringinapril2020.

Palley, T. I. (2018). *Re-Theorizing the Welfare State and the Political Economy of Neoliberalism's War against It*. Forum for Macroeconomics and Macroeconomic Policies Working Paper 16. www.boeckler.de/pdf/p_fmm_imk_wp_16_2018.pdf.

PSE (Poverty and Social Exclusion) (2020). The coronavirus (Covid-19) has had a proportionally higher impact on the most deprived areas. PSE. www.poverty.ac.uk/editorial/coronavirus-covid-19-has-had-proportionally-higher-impact-most-deprived-areas.

Saglietto, A., D'ascenzo, F., Zoccai, G. B., and De Ferrari, G. M. (2020). Covid-19 in Europe: the Italian lesson. *The Lancet*, 395, 1110–1111.

Schmidt, S. K. (2018). *The European Court of Justice and the Policy Process: The Shadow of Case Law*. Oxford: Oxford University Press.

Shaw, K. (2018). *The Court of Justice of the European Union: Subsidiary and Proportionality*. Boston, MA: Brill.

Sirovátka, T., and Mareš, P. (2011). Solidarity at the margins of European society: linking the European social model to local conditions and solidarities, in M. Ellison (ed.), *Reinventing Social Solidarity across Europe*. Bristol: Policy Press.

Spash, C. (2020). *Greenhouse Economics: Value and Ethics*. Abingdon: Routledge.

Stafford, N. (2020). Covid-19: why Germany's case fatality rate seems so low. *BMJ*, 369, m1395. https://doi.org/10.1136/bmj.m1395.

Stiglitz, J. (2020). *Rewriting the Rules of the European Economy: An Agenda for Growth and Shared Prosperity*. New York, NY: W. W. Norton & Co.

Taylor-Gooby, P., and Leruth, B. (2018). *Attitudes, Aspirations and Welfare: Social Policy Directions in Uncertain Times*. London: Palgrave Macmillan.

Taylor-Gooby, P., Leruth, B., and Chung, H. (2017). *After Austerity: Welfare State Transformation in Europe after the Great Recession*. Oxford: Oxford University Press.

Tett, L., and Hamilton, M. (2019). *Resisting Neoliberalism in Education: Local, National and Transnational Perspectives*. Bristol: Policy Press.

Theodore, N. (2020). Governing through austerity: (Il)logics of neoliberal urbanism after the global financial crisis. *Journal of Urban Affairs*, **42**(1), 1–17.

Urali, V., and Oyebode, F. (2004). Poverty, social inequality and mental health. *Advances in Psychiatric Treatment*, 10, 216–224.

Vandenbroucke, F. (2017). Comparative social policy analysis in the EU at the brink of a new era. *Journal of Comparative Policy Analysis: Research and Practice*, **19**(4), 390–402.

Vanhercke, B. (2020). From the Lisbon strategy to the European Pillar of Social Rights: the many lives of the Social Open Method of Coordination. Social Policy in the European Union 1999–2019: the long and winding road, p. 99.

Viens, A. M. (2019). Neo-liberalism, austerity and the political determinants of health. *Health Care Analysis*, 27, 147–152.

Vlachos, V., and Bitzenis, A. (2019). Post-crisis growth prospects in the European Union, in V. Vlachos and A. Bitzenis (eds), *European Union: Post Crisis Challenges and Prospects for Growth*. Cham: Palgrave Macmillan, pp. 1–16.

Von Staden, A. (2018). *Strategies of Compliance with the European Court of Human Rights: Rational Choice within Normative Constraints*. Pennsylvania, PA: University of Pennsylvania Press.

World Health Organization (2020). *Mental Health and Psychosocial Considerations during the Covid-19 Outbreak, 18 March 2020* (No. WHO/2019-nCoV/Mental Health/2020.1). Geneva: World Health Organization.

Whyman, P. B., Baimbridge, M., and Mullen, A. (2014). Revisiting the European Social Model(s) debate: challenges and prospects. *L'Europe en Formation*, **372** (2), 8–32.

Wiener, A., Börzel, T. A., and Risse, T. (2019). *European Integration Theory*. Oxford: Oxford University Press.

Wöhl, S., Springler, E., Pachel, M., and Zeilinger, B. (2020). *The State of the European Union: Fault Lines in European Integration*. Wiesbaden: Springer.

2. Moving forward together? European welfare regimes and the differentiation of welfare policies

Giovanni Bertin

INTRODUCTION

In the latter half of the twentieth century all European countries developed social protection systems (Hemerijck, 2013), albeit according to different rationales. Esping-Andersen (1990) studied these systems during their phase of maximum expansion (1990) then proposed a classification based on the concept of welfare regimes. His proposal distinguishes three types of welfare state, described as social democratic, liberal and corporate (or conservative), respectively. Ferrera (1996) used the same definitions, adding a fourth category defined as Mediterranean or family solidarity welfare.

While this remains a benchmark for comparative studies of welfare systems, in time the literature revealed a number of criticalities. Moreover, Powell and Barrientos (2004) have pointed out that this classification was drawn up by analysing the expansion phase of the welfare states prior to the emergence of critical factors responsible for profound changes to their structures. Current comparative research must take into account at least two other factors: the strong social and economic transformation process that has affected all European countries from the latter half of the twentieth century onwards, and the European Community's efforts to reinforce the European Social Model (ESM). The future resilience of the ESM has been made obvious and urgent by the current Covid-19 health pandemic. These dynamics of change raise the problem of the stability and reproducibility of welfare regimes. In other words, we need to discover whether these changes represent a transformation that is coherent with the political and cultural matrices that gave birth to these welfare systems, or whether it has tended to distort them.

For this reason, the analysis of welfare systems and their differences must focus on three areas:

1. The critical review of the classification of welfare regimes.

2.   The analysis of processes influencing the development of welfare systems.
3.   A critical consideration of the processes of differentiation and hybridization of welfare systems across Europe.

THE DEBATE ON WELFARE REGIMES AND THE CRISIS OF CLASSIFICATION SYSTEMS

The unique welfare regime classification put forward by Esping-Andersen (1990) was greeted positively by the scientific community, and his seminal work has transformed research into welfare systems over the past 30 years. However, numerous studies have questioned his classification and interpretation system (Powell et al., 2020; Lynch, 2019; Johansson and Panican, 2016; Barrientos, 2015; Vrooman, 2013; Emmeneger, 2010; Bonoli, 2007; Powell and Barrientos, 2004; Arts and Gelissen, 2002). The ensuing debate drew attention to a number of critical aspects that we can attribute to the theoretical method used by the author and to the methodological choices underpinning his empirical analysis. The criticisms of the theoretical method used in the definition of these welfare regimes regard three key aspects.

How the Concept of 'Regime' is Used

The use of the concept of 'regime' does not meet with unanimous consensus in the scientific community. In this case the topic of debate concerns the links between the culture of welfare systems and the characteristics of the regimes used in Esping-Andersen's classification. In regard to this Vrooman (2013) maintains that 'the connection between welfare structure and culture may differ between countries and it may change over time though typically not always in a single direction and not without a struggle' (p. 448).

While also critical of the concept of regime, other authors (Barrientos, 2015; Emmeneger, 2010) emphasize the interpretational hypotheses of the processes giving rise to the different welfare systems. According to these authors there is not enough empirical evidence to corroborate the theory of a strong relationship between the cultures of welfare regimes and the characteristics of the religious traditions in the single countries. Rice (2013) suggests taking another look at the cultures that have contributed to the consolidation of welfare regimes, linking these cultures to two factors: the religious heritage of the countries (present also in Esping-Andersen's works) and the type of relationship between Church and state (based on alliance or friction).

The Choice of Criteria Used to Define Regimes

One of the main criticisms made in this regard concerns the lack of attention paid to the problem of social risks (Bonoli, 2007), and of the capacity of the single welfare systems to provide responses to the risks that individuals will encounter during the course of their lives. However, during his subsequent research Esping-Andersen (2002) responded to this criticism by paying greater attention to this dimension of the empirical analysis.

The Clarity of the Concepts Used

Powell (2015) underlines the absence of a precise definition of the concept of de-commodification. The concept of de-commodification has been used by numerous other authors in their comparisons of welfare systems but the imprecise definition of the concept has led to it being used in a non-uniform manner in subsequent studies (Powell et al., 2020; Talme, 2014; Bambra, 2006). This belief is shared by Sgruggs and Allan (2006), who state that 'decommodification indices are not strong elements of regime classification. Our benefit generosity index also suggests that Esping-Andersen's index provides an inaccurate picture of actual cross-national variation in "decommodification"' (p. 69).

A second type of criticism concerns the methodological choices made in the empirical research underpinning the definition of welfare regimes. Bambra (2006; 2007) suggests that there is not sufficient clarity concerning the type of data used and the statistical analyses that led to the definition of the three welfare regimes. Vrooman (2013) maintains that the number of indicators was inadequate and Powell (2015) criticizes the lack of indicators relative to social risks. While praising the heuristic approach seeking to keep together all dimensions of welfare, Powell and Barrientos (2015) follow Jensen (2011) in suggesting that Esping-Andersen's classification of welfare regimes is penalized by the fact that not all welfare sectors are represented in the same manner. Moreover, they also maintain that 'welfare regime analysis remains largely focused on cash benefits, with limited development of conceptual and measurement […] issues relating to services' (p. 244).

These criticisms have accompanied a series of research studies that have either confirmed the welfare-regime-based classification or proposed more or less significant changes (Powell et al., 2020; Powell, 2015; Powell and Barrientos, 2015; Alcock and Craig, 2009; Hudson and Kühner, 2009; Wood and Gough, 2006; Powell and Barrientos, 2004; Gallie, 2004; Arts and Gelissen, 2002). Arts and Gelissen (2002) have attempted to compare the classifications available in the literature by selecting the ones that they believe to have a relatively robust empirical analysis. The classification of systems into only three types is already questioned – at least as far as verifying the theory is concerned – in the title of their study. The comparison of the studies considered reveals the complexity of such analyses and the dis-homogeneity of research approaches. The terms used to define the single types are: liberal, conservative, social democratic, radical, corporatist, and European. Interestingly, some states are classified in very different ways by the authors. For example, Finland is classified among the social democratic systems by Kangas (1994) and by Shalev (1996), while Ragin (1994) believes it has the traits of a corporatist system, and Obinger and Wagschal (1998) refer to a European system. These differences can be explained by the different ways in which such terms are conceived, by the use of different indicators and also by the differing types of policies examined by these researchers. It is no coincidence that in the handful of cases in which their analyses concur in defining the type of welfare state, the system concerned was one that had immediately evolved towards a universalist approach hinging on the role of the state as funder and supplier of welfare services.

Powell and Barrientos (2004) built up their classification of welfare regimes on the basis of a number of criticisms of Esping-Andersen's work. According to these authors this classification does not take into consideration a key element that will play a major role in the future: that is, the presence or absence of active labour market policies (ALMPs). The other element taken into consideration in the construction of this analysis model concerns the mix of market, state and family aid in the supply of welfare services. Based on these two aspects – welfare mix and ALMPs – the two authors have identified a group of indicators that can be useful for comparing national welfare systems. Data was processed by means of a cluster analysis, making it possible to construct a classification model that is rather different to the welfare regimes proposed by Esping-Andersen.

Hudson and Kühner (2009) also base their analysis on the need to consider the rationale pursued by policies in the classification of welfare state systems. With this in mind they state that the focus has been on protective policies intended to deal with potential risks creating hardships for people. However, they state insufficient attention has been paid to productive policies that would reduce risks and the likelihood of people finding themselves in situations of social distress.

Wood and Gough (2006) maintain that the analyses of the welfare models developed so far are based on the perspective of Western countries, particularly with regard to the focus on the role that the state has played, and plays, in the management of welfare policies. The globalization process affecting the economy today makes it necessary to extend the analysis beyond these countries and to assume a perspective comparing all countries that are economically linked. Starting from this viewpoint, the authors add the dimension of globalization to the analysis, introducing the following as classification criteria: the

Table 2.1 Comparison of welfare system classifications (from the end of the Golden Age of Welfare)

Esping-Andersen (2002)	Powell, Barrientos (2004)	Hudson, Kuhner (2009)
US, Canada, Australia, UK	US, Australia, UK, Switzerland, Japan	US, New Zealand
	Canada, New Zealand,	Canada
		Australia, UK
Germany, Austria, France, Netherlands	Germany, Netherlands, France	Germany, Belgium
Italy, Spain, Portugal, Greece	Italy, Spain, Austria	Greece, Ireland, Switzerland, Italy, Korea
	Greece, Belgium, Portugal	Spain, France, Czech Republic, Japan, Portugal, (United Kingdom)
Sweden, Denmark, Norway	Finland, Norway, Denmark	Sweden, Netherlands, Austria, (Finland)
	Sweden	Finland
		Denmark, Norway

Note: Country clusters are characterised by specific welfare models denoted by each theorist.

formalization of rights; service allocation processes; and 'de-clientelization'. The assumption of a global perspective shows that a classification based on the role of the state is reductive and that the response to social risks is always the combined result of the different dynamics of market, state and community.

The comparison of the research studies presented reveals that the choices underlying the Esping-Andersen classification need to be re-examined in the light of the processes that have characterized, and that continue to characterize, the transformation of welfare systems.

In fact, Table 2.1 shows that the more recent studies do not confirm the existence of similarities between different welfare systems. If we consider the liberal regime, for example, we can see that only Australia and the UK remain in the same cluster in all the studies considered (that is, they continue to have similar characteristics), while the other states reveal marked differences. The same situation emerges with regard to the social democratic regime, which shows that only Denmark and Norway belong to the same type in all the classifications considered. It is interesting to note that these regimes are distinguished by more cohesive models with more distinct political connotations. The other two welfare regimes appear to be even less homogeneous and stable. This situation is particularly evident in the case of the Mediterranean regime, which was residually inclusive from its very first formulation. The states included are also distinguished by non-systematic elements typical of other regimes. Beginning with the classification of Italy, we should note that the analysis developed by Powell and Barrientos (2004) groups together Italy, Spain and Austria but not Greece and Portugal, while the research study of Hudson and Kühner (2009) puts Italy, Greece, Ireland, Switzerland and Korea in the same cluster while excluding Spain and Portugal.

The difficulties inherent in confirming a classification based on three welfare regimes is revealed by a meta-analysis of classifications present in the literature and referring to the period between the end of the last century and the beginning of this century. Figure 2.1 is a multidimensional scaling of research studies classifying social care systems based on research studies that analyzed social care services. The research transformed the single classifications by constructing a matrix of similarities to which multidimensional scaling was applied. The figure represents the homogeneity of the classifications; in other words, whether the different studies considered classify the single states in the same way. The closer the states lie in the Cartesian space, the greater the consensus in the literature in attributing them to the same cluster. This analysis reveals that only the Scandinavian system withstands this meta-analysis. Denmark, Sweden and Norway are very close to each other, revealing the homogeneity of their classification in the different studies. Moreover, Finland is not very distant and is certainly closer to the other Scandinavian states than to the other states considered in this comparison. On the other hand, Spain and Greece are also close, and Portugal can also be included in this group, while Italy resembles Ireland and the Netherlands more than the other countries in southern Europe. These distances can be linked to the different indicators and models of statistical analysis used in the single studies. What I wish to point out here is that even in the first review phase of the welfare systems, international literature did not adopt a homogeneous approach in its classification of the single national welfare systems.

A further critical element mentioned by the literature (Bertin and Carradore, 2016; Kazepov, 2010) concerns the decision to consider national levels as a unit of analysis. In fact, the problem of defining nations as the units of analysis of comparative studies is not exclusive to welfare systems, but also arises in other comparative analyses. In this regard Sassen (2007) maintains that the national dimension is always less useful in analyzing social phenomena and that cities are a dimension of reference for the analysis of social dynamics. Global and local have therefore become two dimensions that must be taken into account by comparative studies analyzing processes of change. An analysis of the situation in Europe reveals regions with different levels of economic and social development within the same state as well as social protection

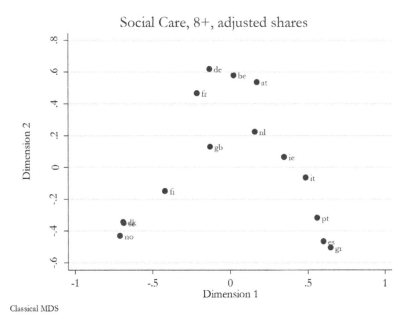

Figure 2.1   *Multidimensional scaling of research studies classifying social care systems*

systems with corresponding degrees of consolidation. As far as the comparison of welfare systems is concerned, this choice is dictated by two factors, namely:

1. The origin of the works classifying welfare systems, which are built upon the basis of the assumption that there is substantial homogeneity within the single states.
2. The limits set by the constraints arising from the information sources that may be used in the construction of empirical research designs. Most of the data that is processed and communicated has a national dimension and only rarely do researchers have access to indicators on a sub-national scale.

These observations suggest that the process of development of welfare systems has not followed a linear (rational) path linked to a specific socio-political matrix and that the actors, dynamics and processes of change have been conditioned by multiple factors at international, national and local level.

EVOLUTION AND CHANGE IN WELFARE SYSTEMS

Jensen (2011) analyzed the process of change in welfare systems in Western countries after the so-called 'Golden Age'. From the 1980s onwards, the growth of social protection slowed down and became stable. However, the recession of 2007–2008 led to the implementation of austerity policies and welfare reforms which have seriously undermined the level and quality of social protection and social inclusion measures across many European welfare states. The analysis of the dynamics conditioning the change processes of welfare systems is key to our understanding of the stability of the single welfare regimes and the processes of differentiation and homogenization that have accompanied the transformation of welfare systems in European countries.

The debate about the interpretation of the dynamics of this change is characterized by three main analytical perspectives, including (Jensen, 2011):

1. The 'ideological' perspective that traces back the change to the confrontation between the value systems and to the ideologies of welfare actors.
2. The neo-institutional perspective emphasizing the capacity of institutions to consolidate the roles and aims of the systems.
3. The neo-functionalist perspective that interprets change in relation to the capacity to adapt to the evolutionary dynamics of socio-economic systems.

Ideologies of Welfare and Political Dynamics

Häusermann (2012) analyzed the political dynamics between the actors who contributed to the development of welfare systems, drawing attention to the way that the de-industrialization process and development of post-modern rationales have blurred the traditional positions of the political parties in relation to processes of reform. In other words, this confrontation cannot be reduced to opposing positions: liberalism versus social democracy. Liberalist policies cannot be automatically linked to rationales intended to reduce the level of social protection just as social democratic policies should not always be associated with the intent to increase social protection. In her analysis of the role played by political parties in the welfare transformation process, Häusermann (2012) considers the dynamics of confrontation-conflict in relation to the level of social protection consolidated during the expansionist phase of welfare (old policies) and to the new policies activated to deal with new needs/risks emerging during the passage to post-modernity. We also need to consider the fact that in each of these families of policies – old and new – actors may play a role that either reduces or expands the welfare system. Bearing this in mind we can hypothesize a four-dimensional space of attributes that can be used to define the political actions of the single actors. This approach allows us to describe individual ideological approaches to welfare as aiming to:

1. Renegotiate the level of social protection created and consolidated during the development of welfare systems. This scenario comes into being when there is a breakdown in the social contract between taxation (withdrawal of resources) and redistribution through the supply of services and benefits.
2. Consolidate and maintain the forms of social protection that have developed in time, taking care to prevent such actions from targeting new social risks.
3. Redefine welfare systems by renegotiating the established levels of social protection in order to allocate resources to new social risks. This zero-sum process demands the construction of a new social contract in which the most protected subjects are called upon to give up part of their acquired rights in order to re-balance the degree of social protection among people exposed to a different type of risk. In this case social dynamics require a high degree of solidarity and legitimization of the stakeholders (the public) called upon to manage this process of social change.
4. Consolidate and expand social protection. Welfare systems tend to consolidate acquired rights by responding to the normal evolutionary tendency of the traditional demand for social protection (risks linked to the aging population, to the increase of chronic illnesses, and so on) but also by activating resources to tackle new social risks.

Although schematic, this ideal-typical classification of the possible directions of the reform process underlines the plurality of the possible reforming thrusts that have guided the changes in the single welfare systems.

Using this classification of political tendencies, the author suggests that typically conservative currents tend to promote the overall reduction of welfare policies while the traditional left seeks to defend old acquired rights and to maintain social protection from the risks that have characterized the development phase of welfare systems. The new Leftist currents tend to pursue welfare policies intended to balance the new demand for social protection that emerged during the transition towards post-modernity with the acquired rights of the history of social protection policies. Finally, the more liberal forces actively support this process of transition to post-modernity and tend to focus on discussing acquired rights and the incentivization of forms of protection from new social risks related to new socio-economic changes.

This classification, though possibly a little schematic, makes it possible to represent the confrontation taking place and to consider the presence of negotiation processes between the various forces on the ground in the light of their negotiation capacity, their power, systems of alliances and representation constructed over time, as well as the capacity to build consensus. Here it may be argued that these dynamics lead to the development of concrete policies produced by mediation processes emerging in a disconnected manner rather than within a stable coherent ideological framework.

THE NEO-INSTITUTIONAL PERSPECTIVE AND REPRODUCTIVE CAPACITY OF INSTITUTIONS

The approach to public policies based on neo-institutionalism reminds us that institutions have a great self-preservation capacity and a huge ability to influence the development of systems beginning with their history and their consolidated characteristics. Starting from this approach, Jensen (2011) states that the stakeholders of 'vested interests have emerged with the expansion of welfare programmes and that their preferences are to ensure further expansion of their individual policy areas. Vested interests may include both the service providers and the recipients, and often a coalition will form between these two groups' (p. 126).

The tendency to preserve characteristics acquired by welfare systems during their expansion phase becomes a critical factor at times of great social change. These processes match the relationship between the dynamics involved in building political consensus and the choices guiding policies. Weaver (1986, p. 371) states that 'Politicians are motivated primarily by the desire to avoid blame for unpopular actions rather than by seeking to claim credit for popular ones.' Politicians, convinced of the negative impact that criticisms of actions going against expectations have upon their consensus and upon their votes, end up behaving conservatively as far as maintaining the status quo is concerned. If we consider these different aspects, it is safe to say that in the end, although they affect a large number of individuals the new social pressures are less able to influence public decisions with respect to the demand to maintain acquired rights, even if these rights consolidate disparities in the guarantee of social safety and concern a relatively small segment of the population. These dynamics contribute to the reproduction of bureaucratic systems. According to Bonoli and Natali (2012) preservation processes have had a particularly strong impact upon the welfare systems of countries whose social expenditure structures are rigidly oriented towards old needs (like Italy, for example) as well as having a considerable influence upon the reform processes in European countries.

The Systemic Perspective and the Capacity to Adapt to Changes

A trend going in the opposite direction is the one that literature associates with the capacity to interact and adapt to change (Hudson, 2019; O'Donovan, 2019; Taylor and Bronstone, 2019; Nguyen, 2010; Westlund, 2006). Taking up the work by Iversen and Stephens (2008), Jensen states that 'market economies in social democratic welfare states will generate a social demand for high levels of childcare (as well as active labour market policies and education) because it supports the kind of specialized, knowledge-intensive economy found in these countries' (2011, p. 127). Social democratic countries are currently more dependent on specialized training and knowledge historically and 'it is well established that the entire world economy from the 1990s has entered a stage where human capital formation is more central than previously' (Jensen, 2011, p. 127).

The passage to post-modernity is one of the criticalities affecting welfare systems, and the characteristics of this change suggest that measures require recalibration. These changes concern the following key factors:

1. The de-standardization of the life cycle. The use of the concept of 'life cycle' represents the life of people broken down into a number of stages that reproduce themselves in a standardized, generalized manner. Each stage of life is characterized by given social risks that are typical and exclusive to that particular existential moment. By now, the transformation processes affecting our social system reveal the difficulties involved in using these logical categories and demand a review of the concepts used. In this sense, the literature (Dewilde, 2003; Wells and Gubar, 1966) recommends considering other concepts such as the life course concept, which replaces a vision of the linear development of existence with a more complex vision maintaining that the social changes characterizing people's lives originate in the events and experiences encountered during their existence. Such events may re-occur and recreate the conditions in which personal experiences have already taken place. The risks therefore are no longer specific to life phases but are linked to critical events that may be recursive and may re-occur on numerous occasions during the course of people's lives.

2. Family dynamics. Here we should bear in mind the increase in divorces and separations, in couples living together and in families with children born from previous relationships. We should also remember that the instability of the labour market and of couples has led to an increase in young adults returning home after leaving – the so-called 'boomerang generation' – because of the breakdown of their personal and/or professional relationships. An increasing number of families with children live

together with grandparents who are no longer able to live on their own. By introducing the concept of life spirals, Combrinck-Graham (1985) reinforces the need to consider changes in the situation of an individual as the result of inter-relations and inter-dependencies in the chains linking the life of that person to the events of the context and the instability characterizing the evolution of families. In fact, family dynamics can no longer be represented by means of the concept of 'family life cycle' but involve a spiral process in which the phenomena of change (construction of the family, the arrival of children, the time when they leave home, the break-up of families) can occur on several occasions in a person's life, building different links and causing inter-generational solidarity to become less stable.

3. The demographic trend and strong increase in the elderly population. This demographic dynamic has a strong impact both on the health and welfare system and on the pension system. We should remember that the elderly are the main 'consumers' of resources (both public and private) dedicated to the production of welfare. The imbalance in the population structure also has a marked impact on the ratio between the generations, thus causing the elderly person's potential family network to shrink. We are already in the era of the so-called 'sandwich generation', which sees a single adult (in the vast majority of cases, a woman) caring for grandchildren, a partner and elderly parents (Di Nicola, 2013; Naldini and Saraceno, 2011).

4. Changes in the employment market. The speed of technological developments and the globalization of competition have tended to reduce the demand for manual employment and have made many of the skills necessary to remain in the employment market obsolete. On the other hand, the increased demand for professionals has strengthened the link between training and employment. It has also led to a request for greater training to enter the labour market, thus delaying entry as well as creating a training–job–training cycle. In other words, entry to the labour market no longer coincides with the conclusion of the training phase. The labour market is characterized by less stable 'trajectories', leading to a more variable relationship between personal paths and the creation of stable conditions in which people can plan their lives and consolidate personal and relational links. It also makes the moment in which people exit the labour market less definite (and less definitive). Another aspect concerns the transformation of the production model in the post-industrial society, which has revealed several aspects of instability. Just consider, for example, the short life span of technologies and knowledge and their rapid obsolescence or the rapid emergence of new professions lacking a clearly defined status and a clear and predictable potential income. Another aspect

concerns the marked increase in the number of women with access to the labour market compared to a drop in male employment. The criticalities that this phenomenon induces in the current welfare system are caused in particular by women with low skill levels who find it difficult to balance the demands of their paid work with the burden of care that continues to rest mainly on their shoulders. This leads to a vicious circle because the burden of care borne by families (therefore, by the woman) is particularly heavy in families with a low income and low family social capital. In these cases families without access to public services or a social network cannot afford to purchase assistance (caregiver, babysitter, creche, and so on) in the market at critical times. Their inability to cope with emergencies leads to job insecurity and reduces their disposable income, thus reinforcing a vicious circle between job insecurity – critical events – increased care burden and increased job insecurity.

5. The transformations of cities and consequent difficulties in constructing identity together with the rarefaction of social relations. The process of social transformation underway, the dynamics of globalization and the rapid technological changes brought into being by the 'web society' are all having a significant impact upon the structure of our cities. Referring to a work by Graham and Marvin (2001), Bauman (2007) states that 'virtu-ally all cities across the world are starting to display spaces and zones that are powerfully connected to other "valued" spaces across the urban land-scape as well as across national, international and even global distances. At the same time, though, there is often a palpable and increasing sense of local disconnection in such places from physically close, but socially and economically distant, places'. (p. 73)

The process of construction of identity undoubtedly also comes about by seeking cultural factors and aspects reflecting personal history. Identity is a mechanism of social integration but, at the same time, also a factor of diversification and social exclusion. Different cultures are often experienced as a threat, as elements from which to defend ourselves, and communities with similar identities tend to attract each other and distinguish themselves (also geographically) from cultures held to be different and perceived as a threat to the social order. Social marginality may promote the construction of alternative identities and the interruption of processes of acceptance of norms. Bearers of different cultures, those living by their wits and thanks to micro-criminality, and those living in poverty may all be perceived as deviants and as an equal threat by those living in affluence. Such processes give rise to vicious circles reinforcing mechanisms of social exclusion, creating vital worlds comprising those lacking economic and relational resources and social capital as well as the capacity to use cognitive and informative instruments. These conditions of exclusion consolidate identities based on the negation of social rules and can provoke illegal behaviour and micro-criminality.

6. Globalization is another factor that has influenced the transformation of welfare systems. Clayton and Pontusson (1998) state that globalization could cause workers in sectors affected by delocalization processes to construct cross-class alliances with employers representing these very industries in order to reduce welfare measures and costs to ensure greater international competitiveness. Other authors (Timonen, 2001; Rodrik, 1998) maintain that this kind of impact is rather improbable and that if anything the opposite case is true: delocalization processes would increase job insecurity and thus the demand for social protection.

7. A final factor of the neo-functionalist category is the role of women. 'It is well known that women are among the key beneficiaries of extensive social care service provision because it allows them to enter the labour market as care for children and elderly family members is left to the public' (Jensen, 2011, p. 128). The profound changes in the demand for social protection provoked by these dynamics mean that the various services need to abandon their 'one size fits all' approach in order to develop welfare policies and facilities capable of tackling the risks posed by the social transformation currently underway.

COMPLEXITY AND HYBRIDIZATION OF WELFARE SYSTEMS

All these factors influence the process of transformation of welfare systems, highlighting their complexity, fragmentation and discontinuity. Hemerijck (2013) emphasizes that the changes affecting welfare systems hinge on attempts to resist and maintain the imbalances that have characterized the consolidation of social protection in the latter half of the last century, and on the need to respond to the new risks produced by the social and economic changes underway. The result is a complex process of transformation taking different forms in response to the nature of existing welfare systems, to the dynamics between the social stakeholders in local contexts and to the socio-economic conditions in which such dynamics have evolved. Hemerijck concludes by stating that the analysis of processes currently underway shows that this change, which is not guided by a clear reforming intent, is unpredictable in nature and involves multiple actors and levels. 'For this reason, it is imperative to study the politics of changing welfare states, not as models, but, more dynamically, as open systems caught up in processes of path-dependent evolutionary social and economic reconfiguration' (Hemerijck, 2013, p. 12).

The complexity of welfare systems is also highlighted in Jensen's studies (2011). He has attempted to use a multidimensional approach in his analysis of the processes of change. In his work he has analyzed 18 Western nations (Australia, Austria, Belgium, Canada, Denmark, Finland, France, Germany, Ireland, Italy, Japan, the Netherlands, New Zealand, Norway, Spain, Sweden, the UK and the USA) during the 1980–2001 period. His comparison takes into account a number of possible factors of change related to: the negotiation ability of left-wing parties, the dynamics of defence of existing interests, the social demand by women, globalization and de-industrialization processes. The complexity of the process of change is also underlined by Häusermann (2012), who states that 'the actor configurations in the new policy space of the European welfare state are characterized by complex multidimensionality, which makes the result of reform processes highly contingent' (p. 122).

Another study contributing to this debate is by Ferrera (2013, 2016), who suggests that we consider the current phase as the evolutionary result of the encounter between the crisis being experienced by the liberalist ideology that has characterized the last 30 years in many European countries (neo-liberalism) and the drive to maintain the levels of social protection consolidated in the second half of the past century. The use of the term 'new liberal welfarism' is intended to remind us that this is an approach that seeks to keep together, by hybridizing, the welfare state culture coming to the fore in social democratic regimes and the neo-liberalist rationale expressed in liberal regimes and their revised versions. This balance represents the mid-point between the tensions generated by pairs of values such as freedom versus equality, competition versus cooperation, individual versus society, personal responsibility versus collective responsibility, merit versus need, choice versus coercion, globalism/cosmopolitanism versus localism/communitarianism. According to Ferrara, the balance between these pairs, which refer to either the liberal ideology or welfarism, is favoured by three factors guiding the reorganization of the new welfare system: in other words, productivist or 'flexible' solidarity, active inclusion and social promotion. From this perspective, we could possibly interpret liberal neo-welfarism as being the result of the economic and value crisis and problems of legitimization affecting the main ideologies encountering each other in the process of construction and redefinition of welfare systems. This crisis reduced the ideological content inherent to the contrast between models, allowing them to be recalibrated with the aim of building a new ideology capable of finding a balance between freedom, equality and social justice.

Donati's studies (2014) into the Lib–Lab approach also contribute to the analysis of liberalist and social democratic welfare dynamics. The *Lib–Lab approach* refers to a working arrangements between the Liberal Democrats (also previously known as the Liberal Party) and the Labour Party in the UK. There have been four arrangements of this kind at national level in the UK, and these arrangements have also been implemented at local level in the UK. Donati draws attention to the criticalities underlying the encounter between the liberalist and the social democratic perspective. He reminds us that the social dynamics underpinning the social protection system cannot be exclusively limited to the encounter between state and market dynamics. While this approach merely leads him to propose a number of very partial corrective actions to be carried out upon welfare systems in crisis, the central question concerns the dynamics of solidarity as processes guiding people's actions regardless of whether this is personally advantageous.

Underlying these considerations is an extremely important debate reflecting the relationship between the economy and society from the time of Hobbes to the present day. Reflecting on whether human behaviour is naturally guided by a utilitarian or rather by a cooperative principle is key to the examination of the responsibilities of the different social stakeholders (individuals, communities and societies). Sennett (2012) undoubtedly makes an important contribution to this debate by dismantling the belief that we have a natural propensity towards utilitarian behaviour that is driven to maximize individual interests. In fact, it is our culture that offers us this type of model. According to Sennett, the rediscovery of the dimension of solidarity and cooperation plays a vital role in allowing us to rethink the relation between economy and society, providing a foundation for the development of new approaches to social protection.

These observations reveal that the resolution of the criticalities emerging from the crisis of the liberalist and social democratic models on the one hand, and the need to rethink the relationship between economy and society on the other, requires an in-depth analysis of the complex and multidimensional features of solidarity and competition within specific welfare settings. With the dynamics of cooperation and solidarity placed at the axiom of this relationship these considerations have also formed the backdrop to the debate on the redefinition of welfare policies across Europe.

An across-the-board analysis of these research studies reveals a number of factors playing a key role in the transformation processes of welfare systems, in which the focus is on:

1. The capacity of institutions to resist change.
2. The neo-functionalist perspective that interprets change in relation to the capacity to adapt to the evolutionary dynamics of socio-economic systems.
3. The socio-economic drive towards change – in particular, the effects of globalization.
4. The characteristics of the local socio-economic context.
5. The concrete action systems rooted in segments of the welfare system and the ideologies of the opposing forces.
6. The social dynamics influencing the permanence of the culture of solidarity.

These factors of complexity confirm the idea of a fluctuating change process linked to dynamics between the ideology-bearing social actors and systems of different and distinct welfare systems. In many cases, the power relations between social actors change over time, producing mutable paths of change. However, while changing power relations may cause shifts in the orientation of decision-makers, they certainly will not reset existing systems. The result is a combination of policies that may even stem from different rationales, ideologies and cultures. The combined effect of these processes is the reduction of the burden of the political and cultural matrices that gave rise to the welfare regimes and to the launch of the hybridization dynamics eroding their differences.

Referring to the hybridization of welfare systems means assuming that we are not in the presence of an evolutionary process that changes the arrangement of systems in relation to changes in demand, but rather that we are dealing with a series of fragmented, multidimensional and multi-actor paths determined by changing power dynamics and cultural transformation processes.

Moreover, the very term 'hybridization' requires some clarification in order to be used as a cognitive instrument for the interpretation of the changes underway. This concept is widely used in the literature dealing with the regulation processes of welfare systems. In this case, the focus is on the coexistence of regulatory rationales long considered as alternatives (hierarchy, competition, cooperation). Going back to this approach we can refer to hybrid systems if:

1. The welfare system is characterized by the coexistence of several features denoting different regimes, making differentiating elements harder to distinguish.
2. The policies developed integrate characteristics typical of different regimes to the point of producing new forms that are hard to include in the categories traditionally defining them.

This hybridization process tends to blur the boundaries between the cultural matrices determining the transformations of the single welfare systems.

CONCLUSION

In conclusion, this chapter has evidenced the way in which national welfare systems in Europe have been shaped by a series of fragmented multidimensional and multi-actor paths determined by changing power dynamics and cultural transformation processes. Critically, however, collaborative policy responses to the Covid 19 health emergency have emerged both within and across European welfare settings. These dynamics of cooperation and solidarity between European nation states may potentially lead to a strengthened

ESM. The move towards a more coordinated and responsive European Welfare System emerges from concrete actions involving mutual support between health systems in European countries. Crucially, however, it may be argued that given the influence of dominant ideological forces within European welfare systems, a critical factor determining the future shape of the ESM will be the degree to which social and cultural dynamics influence the development of a transnational culture of solidarity across European welfare settings.

REFERENCES

Alcock, P., and Craig, G. (2009). *International Social Policy Welfare Regimes in the Developed World.* Basingstoke: Palgrave Macmillan.

Arts, W., and Gelissen, J. (2002). Three worlds of welfare capitalism or more? A state-of-the-art report, *Journal of European Social Policy,* **12**, 137–158.

Bambra, C. (2006). De-commodification and the worlds of welfare revisited, *Journal of European Social Policy,* **16** (1), 73–80.

Bambra, C. (2007). Going beyond *The Three Worlds of Welfare Capitalism*: regime theory and public health research, *Journal of Epidemiology and Community Health,* **61** (12), 1098–102.

Barrientos, A. (2015). A veritable mountain of data and years of endless statistical manipulation: methods in the *Three Worlds* and after, *Social Policy and Society,* **14** (2), 259–270.

Bauman, Z. (2007). *Liquid Times.* Cambridge: Polity Press.

Bertin, G., and Carradore, M. (2016). Differentiation of welfare regimes: the case of Italy, *International Journal of Social Welfare,* **25**, 149–160.

Bonoli, G. (2007). Time matter, post-industrialisation, new social risk, and welfare state adaptation in advanced industrial democracies, *Comparative Political Studies,* **40**, 495–520.

Bonoli, G., and Natali, D. (eds) (2012). *The Politics of the New Welfare State.* Oxford: Oxford University Press.

Clayton, R., and Pontusson, J. (1998). Welfare-state retrenchment revisited: entitlement cuts, public sector restructuring, and inegalitarian trends in advanced capitalist societies, *World Politics,* **51**, 67–98.

Combrinck-Graham, L. (1985). A developmental model for family systems, *Family Process,* **24**, 139–150.

Danforth, B. (2014). Worlds of welfare in time: a historical reassessment of the three-world typology, *Journal of European Social Policy,* **24** (2), 164–182.

Dewilde, C. (2003). A life-course perspective on social exclusion and poverty, *British Journal of Sociology,* **54** (1), 109–128.

Di Nicola, P. (2013). Il lavoro di cura tra defamilizzazione e mercificazione, *Sociologia e Politiche,* **1**, 49–62.

Donati, P. (2014). Beyond the welfare state: trajectories towards the relational state, in: Bertin, G., and Campostrini, S. (eds), *Equiwelfare and Social Innovation,* 4–21. Milan: FrancoAngeli.

Emmeneger, P. (2010). Catholicism, job security regulations and female employment: a micro-level analysis of Esping-Andersen's social Catholicism thesis, *Social Policy & Administration,* **44** (1), 20–39.

Esping-Andersen, G. (1990). *The Three Worlds of Welfare Capitalism*. Cambridge and Princeton, NJ: Polity and Princeton University Press.

Esping-Andersen, G. (2002). *Why We Need a New Welfare State*. Oxford: Oxford University Press.

Ferrera, M. (1996). The 'southern' model of welfare state in social Europe, *Journal of European Social Policy*, **6** (1), 17–37.

Ferrera, M. (2013). Neowelfarismo liberale: nuove prospettive per lo stato sociale in Europa, *Stato e Mercato*, **97**, 3–35.

Ferrera, M. (2016). *Rotta di collisione*. Bari: Laterza.

Gallie, D. (2004). *Welfare Regimes and the Experience of Unemployment in Europe*. Oxford: Oxford University Press.

Graham, S., and Marvin, S. (2001). *Splintering Urbanism*. London: Routledge.

Häusermann, S. (2012). The politics of old and new social policies, in: Bonoli, G., and Natali, D. (eds), *The Politics of the New Welfare State*, 111–134. Oxford: Oxford University Press.

Hemerijck, A. (2012). When changing welfare states and euro crisis meet, *Sociologica*, **1**, 1–42.

Hemerijck, A. (2013). *Changing Welfare States*. Oxford: Oxford University Press.

Hudson, J., and Kühner, S. (2009). Towards productive welfare? A comparative analysis of 23 OECD countries, *Journal of European Social Policy*, **19**, 34–46.

Hudson, R. (2019). *Co-Produced Economies: Capital, Collaboration, Competition*. Abingdon: Routledge.

Iversen, T., and Stephens, J. D. (2008). Partisan politics, the welfare state, and the three worlds of human capital formation, *Comparative Political Studies*, **41**, 600–637.

Jensen, C. (2011). Determinants of welfare service provision after the Golden Age, *International Journal of Social Welfare*, **20**, 125–134.

Johansson, H., and Panican, A. (2016). A move towards the local? The relevance of a local welfare system approach, in: Johansson, H., and Panican A. (eds), *Combating Poverty in Local Welfare Systems: Work and Welfare in Europe*. London: Palgrave Macmillan.

Kangas, O. E. (1994). The politics of social security on regressions, qualitative comparisons and cluster analysis, in: Janoski, T., and Hicks, A. M. (eds), *The Comparative Political Economy of the Welfare State*, 346–364. Cambridge: Cambridge University Press.

Kazepov, Y. (2010). *Rescaling Social Policies: Towards Multilevel Governance in Europe*. Farnham: Ashgate.

Lynch, J. (2019). *Regimes of Inequality: The Political Economy of Health and Wealth*. Cambridge: Cambridge University Press.

Naldini, M., and Saraceno, C. (2011). *Conciliare famiglia e lavoro: vecchi e nuovi patti tra sessi e generazioni*. Bologna: Il Mulino.

Nguyen, T. T. (2010). *Knowledge Economy and Sustainable Economic Development: A Critical Review*. Munich: De Gruyter Saur.

O'Donovan, N. (2019). From knowledge economy to automation anxiety: a growth regime in crisis? *New Political Economy*, **25** (2), 248–266.

Obinger, H., and Wagschal, U. (1998). Das Stratifizierungkonzept in der cluster-analytischen Uberprufung, in: Lesseniche, S., and Ostner, I. (eds), *Welten des Wohlfahrtskapitalismus: der sozialstaat in vergleichender perspektive*, 109–135. Frankfurt: Campus Verlag.

Powell, M. (2015). A re-specification of the welfare state: conceptual issues in *The Three Worlds of Welfare Capitalism*, *Social Policy and Society*, **142**, 247–268.

Powell, M., and Barrientos, A. (2004). Welfare regimes and the welfare mix, *European Journal of Political Research*, **43**, 83–105.

Powell, M., and Barrientos, A. (2015). Introduction: twenty-five years of the welfare modelling business, *Social Policy and Society*, **142**, 241–245.

Powell, M., Yörük, E., and Bargu, A. (2020). Thirty years of *The Three Worlds of Welfare Capitalism*: a review of reviews, *Social Policy & Administration*, **54**, 60–87.

Ragin, C. (1994). A qualitative comparative analysis of pension systems, in: Janoski, T., and Hicks, A. M. (eds), *The Comparative Political Economy of the Welfare State*, 320–345. Cambridge: Cambridge University Press.

Rice, D. (2013). Beyond welfare regimes: from empirical typology to conceptual ideal types, *Social Policy and Administration*, **27** (1), 93–110.

Rodrik, D. (1998). Why do more open economies have bigger governments? *Journal of Political Economy*, **106**, 997–1032.

Sassen, S. (2007). *A Sociology of Globalization*. New York, NY: W. W. Norton.

Sennett, R. (2012). *Insieme. Rituali, piaceri, politiche della cooperazione*. Milano: Feltrinelli.

Sgruggs, L., and Allan, J. P. (2006). Welfare state decommodification in 18 OECD countries: a replication and revision, *Journal of European Social Policy*, **16** (1), 55–72.

Shalev, M. (1996). *The Privatization of Social Policy? Occupational Welfare and the Welfare State in America, Scandinavia and Japan*. London: Macmillan.

Talme, L. (2014). Do capitalist welfare states still consist of 'The Good, the Bad and the Ugly?' Revisiting Esping-Andersen's *Three Worlds* studying welfare regimes of the 21st century. Lunds universitet/Statsvetenskapliga institutionen. http://lup.lub.lu .se/student-papers/record/4229151.

Taylor, A., and Bronstrone, A. (2019). *People, Place and Global Order: Foundations of a Networked Political Economy*. Abingdon: Routledge.

Timonen, V. (2001). What explains public sector restructuring? Evaluating contending explanations, *Journal of European Social Policy*, **8**, 43–59.

Vrooman, J. C. (2013). Regimes and cultures of social security: comparing institutional models through nonlinear PCA, *International Journal of Comparative Sociology*, **53** (5–6), 444–477.

Weaver, K. (1986). The politics of blame avoidance, *Journal of Public Policy*, **6**, 371–398.

Wells, W. D., and Gubar, G. (1966). Life cycle concept in marketing research, *Journal of Marketing Research*, **3**, 341–348.

Westlund, H. (2006). *Social Capital in the Knowledge Economy: Theory and Empirics*. Dordrecht: Springer.

Wood, G., and Gough, I. (2006). A comparative welfare regime approach to global social policy, *Word Development*, **34** (10), 1696–1712.

3. Is there a European Social Model? Theorising the relationship between economics and society

Giuseppe Moro

INTRODUCTION

The European Social Model (ESM) can be defined as an attempt by a number of European countries, albeit in different ways, to reach an innovative form of compatibility between the realities of the market economy and social state and the goal of ensuring economic competitiveness and social solidarity and cohesion (Cavalli and Martinelli, 2015). In short, it is based on several key elements (individual rights, solidarity, freedom of negotiation, and so on) and a number of conventional institutional features such as welfare's universalist tendencies, a regulation of work markets and a system of industrial relations.

However, the ESM is also a concept which presents a number of ambiguities; so many meanings overlap that social Europe has been considered 'one of the most elusive concepts in European studies and political debates on the process of integration' (Ferrera, 2016, p. 105). It can be considered from either a legislative or positive/interpretative point of view (Montanari et al., 2008, p. 788).

In the first case, the hope is that an agreement on a single model for institutions overseeing social welfare in different European countries can be made. In the second case, however, it can be seen that the different institutional models in Europe will progressively merge to ensure the same type and level of welfare services. On the other hand, from an analytical point of view the term 'European Social Model' sees the overlap of at least two elements (Hermann, 2009), the first of which is institutional. It is believed that, aside from national differences and so-called welfare regimes, European state social welfare systems share a large number of similarities: the common nature of welfare, the key role of the state in managing the economy (also by direct intervention and ownership of banks, industries and service infrastructures, to the extent that the term 'market social economy' could be applied) and the role of developed models to regulate work and industrial relations.

The second feature is political and is probably somewhat more ambiguous; over the previous few decades, the ESM was initially identified as a social democratic vision of society to oppose the neo-conservative ideologies predominant in the 1980s, above all in the United States and United Kingdom. However, the ESM subsequently became characterised for its process of alignment among European countries towards a welfare model which addressed the principles of economic sustainability and the competitiveness of economic systems on a global scale, even if this contradicted the traditional social democratic approach to welfare.

Lastly, the ESM assumes a separate meaning as a form of identity representation. It embodies one of the key features of the so-called European identity, helping to distinguish it from other social models, above all that of the United States. Compared to the United States, the European Union (EU) is defined by lower disparity in incomes and greater redistribution of revenues through higher progressive taxation and free access to public services.

CRITICISMS OF THE EUROPEAN SOCIAL MODEL

The innate ambiguity within the ESM has led some analysts to reject its validity. The existence of a European social model is questioned by those who believe that social integration had been largely subordinated to economic integration and has been characterised by a great deal of talking but only a limited impact on the everyday lives of Europeans. According to this viewpoint (Barbier, 2013), the development of Europe was based almost exclusively on economic criteria and this characteristic is still relevant today, with a clear division in the jurisdiction which grants states virtually exclusive authority on social issues, including education.

Over the course of the European integration process, a fundamental asymmetry developed between policies supporting market efficiency and those promoting social protection and equality (Scharpf, 2002). Indeed, while at national level these policies compete at the same constitutional level, during the process of integration economic policies are increasingly Europeanised while social policies remain a national concern. As a result, national welfare states are constitutionally limited and directed by the supremacy of European rules on economic integration, liberalisation and competitiveness. This has led to fiscal competition between countries with a consequent reduction in the financial base of welfare policies as well as a decrease in the cost of work. This decoupling of economic policies from social policies in promoting the integration process has thus reduced the capacity of member states to influence the progress of their own economies or achieve autonomous socio-political objectives. The only permissible choices within European regulations have been tax reduction, deregulation and work flexibility, growth of salary gaps and welfare cuts. In fact, countries have had to compete against each other to make these options even more extreme in order to attract investment and discourage businesses from moving abroad.

Prevalent economic logic dictates that economic and social rights are never treated in the same way and that an underlying asymmetry between the two remains. Thus, for example, freedom of movement and residency in an EU country constitutes a right which is legally overarched to national legislation as this is seen as helping improve the performance and competitiveness of the single market. On the other hand, social rights at European level are only taken into consideration when these are seen as conditioned by the performance of the single market and can, in turn, influence it. Consequently, the Europeanisation of social rights is extremely limited and the legal bases of social protection and regulation of the labour market are defined almost entirely at national level. Those who support this theory argue that the alignment of different European countries towards a homogenous and uniform model of social protection is purely superficial and that European legislation has not created new, far-reaching laws. On the contrary, the process has only been negative in its attempt to remove the obstacles to freedom of markets and competition which social legislation at national level has created.

Even during a ten-year period from the end of the 1980s, the so-called 'golden era' of social Europe, no move was made to go beyond the coordination of ideas and cognitive frameworks which were to influence only marginally the social status of citizens. As a result, in areas such as pensions, health and social inclusion, national programmes and policies (despite their partial coordination at European level) remained determining variables, with no noticeable change to the variety of national institutions and models. Similarly, the minimum level of coordination set up during this period was to be brushed away halfway through the first decade of the new century, culminating in the great economic crisis of 2007–2008. A series of events such as the extension of the EU to Eastern European countries, the rejections of the new constitutional treaty in Holland and France and the Treaty of Lisbon in Ireland and the Greek debit crisis marked the 'near collapse' of the European social context (Barbier, 2013, p. 105).

It can be seen that deep-seated causes are behind the weaknesses of a social Europe. In particular, there is the prevalent tendency to identify individuals as citizens of a specific country and that as a result, support is only given to other members of the same community. In other words, there is still a strong link between national citizenship, solidarity and social justice, while these same sentiments are not shared at a European level. Clear signs of such a lack of solidarity are evident in how the crisis affecting southern European states was managed, in particular Greece, as well as the increasingly hostile sentiment of public opinion in northern and eastern European countries towards foreign immigration. The same holds true for immigration within the EU, including the example of Brexit, the outcome of which was heavily swayed by British hostility to seeing equal social rights extended to other European citizens.

Furthermore, the process of differentiated integration joins a context which is already characterised by an acute differentiation between the three models of welfare capitalism identified by Esping-Andersen (1990). This distinction has recently deepened given the extension of EU membership firstly to southern European countries and subsequently to those from the north and east. The diversification between these groups of countries is not only operative at the level of social welfare, but above all applies to the different regulatory concept of the roles the state, financial markets and family have to fulfil in generating social welfare. Each of these models boasts a strong consensus at the level of individual national public opinion, not only as they are deeply rooted in their respective cultural traditions, but also because citizens have planned their lives on the basis of existing social protection schemes and oppose any changes which could radically alter these plans.

Thus, using social insurance as an example, there is no evidence of a progressive alignment towards a single institutional model and the processes of benefit adjustment or limits do not produce a redefinition of the organisational aspect of social insurance present in any one country (Montanari et al., 2008, p. 801). Similarly, there is no concrete proof of any agreement on social insurance procedures in case of unemployment or injury. On the contrary, in the periods of economic crisis which have blighted European countries in recent years a wider degree of differences has been visible. This can be explained by the fact that even if social aid has been reduced in all countries, those with traditionally higher replacement rates have made less drastic cuts than states with less generous systems. It would appear that path dependency prevails, a product of an agreement with political support to keep social laws that have already been passed.

Similar measures were proposed at the turn of the twenty-first century to support a 'weak' alignment between European social policies, in particular the Open Method of Coordination. However, these only encouraged the adaptation of existing social welfare systems to market forces and tax obligations derived from European treaties. Even at the level of desired political objectives, such strategies were only able to identify the minimum standards acceptable for all member states.

Finally, questions have been raised regarding the validity of comparisons showing a European social model that is different from social policies common in Anglo-Saxon countries, in particular the United States. It is evident that the United States and Europe have far more in common than the traditional differences between residual welfare and redistributive institutional welfare which characterise their two widely differing models of social policies (Alber, 2010). Indeed, the entire social spending of the United States is not so dissimilar to the European average when one considers tax benefits for the poorest and tax obligations for private businesses to provide social benefits for their employees. The character of social spending is also comparable, with a predominant (and growing) share set aside for pensions and healthcare. More specifically, the United States spends a share of gross domestic product (GDP) on healthcare which is equal to that of many European countries (also given the greater cost of medical care in the United States), and while these are not universal as in European health services, their level of coverage has shown a sharp rise in recent years. If one takes into account the contrast between the demographic composition of the United States and that of many European countries (with a lower percentage of elderly people in the former), both pension spending and average pension levels are higher in the United States. Therefore, the American welfare system is not so radically different from its European counterpart, but is organised in a different way; the use of instruments such as fiscal credit and minimum wage is more common and more use is made of private health and pension schemes, work performance benefits and selective and specific assistance schemes. Yet even these traditional differences have shrunk over the last decade or so, since recent European social policy reforms have adopted a number of features from the American welfare system. These include an emphasis on individual responsibility and activation strategies for those of working age as well as a growing interest in the private provision of services and freedom of choice for service users. At the same time, the policies set out by the Obama administration appeared more 'European' than those adopted on the other side of the Atlantic. Health reform extended public health cover, and in a broader sense expansive economic policies were implemented following the 2007–2008 economic crisis. Meanwhile, Fiscal Compact regulations in Europe resulted in a reduction in social spending.

THE POLITICAL VALUES OF THE EUROPEAN SOCIAL MODEL

There are clearly grounds for such critical observations and these views are useful above all in providing an evaluative analysis of some of the more recent changes in social policies throughout European member states. However, if a long-term approach is considered, it would be reductive to see the ESM as little more than a slogan or rhetorical device to provide cover for neo-liberalist policies influenced by Anglo-Saxon models, particularly the United States'. Colin Crouch (1999) has found that since the middle of the twentieth century a process of alignment has been underway in most western European countries towards a social model based on compromise and balance between four key features:

1. Industrialisation as the bedrock of employment and economic production.
2. Capitalistic organisation of property.
3. Liberal institutional structures which, in a certain way, set the limits for traditional community institutions.
4. An across-the-board recognition of citizens' rights.

One of the most important institutional symbols of this agreement, particularly as regards the concept of mass citizenship, was the welfare state. This represented possibly the most significant tool in guaranteeing social stability and economic prosperity as it was able to support tensions between all four areas of the social compromise outlined above (Benassi and Mingione, 2019; Moon, 2019; Pestieau and Lefèbvre, 2018). Thus, in the mid-twentieth-century European model, social citizenship reigned supreme. It limited the negative impact of market capitalism and industrialisation through traditional methods of solidarity (above all for families) and reduced social inequalities through progressive taxation, which helped fund the social state itself. The existence of powerful social states was also due to the strong impetus of political organisations whose background was distinguished by specific religious or class identities. These groups supported the extension of widespread social protection, despite somewhat differing institutional features. Above all, the involvement of class-based political bodies gave the lower classes greater capacity for activism to pursue their own interests. Historically, this also led to a decrease in inequality following state intervention.

The result was a social system in which any differences were ordered, limited and structured, a model clearly different from the far more pluralistic and disjointed American set-up held together by the economic market and a vast national framework. It is safe to say, therefore, that a European social model was built whose relevance goes well beyond the clearest welfare aspects of the ESM, which is portrayed as merely a combination of political priorities centred on welfare, social consultation and mixed economy. A wider analysis of the European model, which also takes into account this more restrictive view, focuses on the political values and policies which were to become the heritage of democratic Europe. For example, in 2003, a round table was organised by the then-president of the European Commission Romano Prodi to consider the viability of a European development model. Experts identified four key areas of the European social model: the inviolable nature of human rights, culture as a means of liberation, sustainable development and a peaceful vision of international order (Strauss-Kahn, 2004). As can be seen, this manifesto goes beyond the vision of a European social model as building a structure which includes social security and public health and education systems based on progressive taxation. It assumes that Europe can propose its own original political, economic and social project as part of a new globalised society (Delanty and Rumford, 2005).

These two interpretations of the ESM are not contradictory; on the contrary, one view clearly supports the other. It can be said that there has been an agreement on common ethical and political values throughout different periods of history among the different founding countries of the EU. These include democratic procedures, individual rights, equal opportunities, freedom of negotiation and solidarity (Cavalli and Martinelli, 2015, p. 246). According to Giddens' account (2007), the following can also be added: a division of risks and opportunities in society, solidarity and social cohesion, protection of the most vulnerable members of society, conciliation in industrial relations and the recognition of a wide range of economic and social rights to benefit the entire population.

Several common traits of the European welfare system were founded on these values. These include non-residual welfare, which earmarks a significant proportion of GDP for social spending; regulation of the labour market, which attempts to match the interests of business with workers' rights; and finally an institutionalised system of social relations.

This alignment was not only based on values but also on the long process of post-World War Two national welfare expansion, which saw western European countries sharing a number of common features (Hermann and Hofbauer, 2007). Firstly, European welfare systems are universal, meaning that citizens are entitled to care in case of need on principle. Moreover, the level of social protection is higher than other, non-European countries, in particular the United States, where a large proportion of the population has no right to any form of benefit whatsoever.

Secondly, the state plays a key role in providing citizens with services, not only those most closely linked to social assistance but also those which promote well-being in a broader sense, such as health, public transport and education. This combination of universal access to benefits and provision of public services creates a third feature of European welfare which Esping-Andersen (1990) has termed 'decommodification': ensuring the well-being of European citizens by making them less dependent on the market compared to citizens from other countries. The current Covid-19 pandemic has amplified the criticality of adequate public health and welfare systems.

BUILDING THE EUROPEAN UNION AND THE EUROPEAN SOCIAL MODEL

Such common attributes are the result of a process of an alignment which, although never formally predetermined, was an almost inevitable consequence of the establishment of the EU.

It could be argued that the idea for a European social model had been around since the signing of the Treaty of Rome and that it was reinforced over time due to two factors; firstly, to meet the social costs of the integration process and secondly, because it was almost inevitable that social citizenship would join civil and political citizenship as a right of all European citizens to have equal access to services, resources and work opportunities.

It is clear the relationship between European integration and the welfare state has been redefined and developed over time. In the first thirty years of the integration process, the EU was unable to promote a common social policy which reflected the evolution taking place simultaneously in different member states. The articles in the Treaty of Rome which covered European social legislation (48, 51) were only measures to guarantee European economic and social rights for people as citizens of member states, not to strengthen or promote them. One could say that care was taken to keep social rights at the lowest possible level (Juhàsz, 2006). Thus, in the initial phase from the signing of the Treaty of Rome to the 1980s, there was a marked growth in welfare within member states without any clear role played by the Union, even though the economic resources needed for this welfare expansion derived from the economic growth that was favoured by the freedom of trade in a common market. An initial compromise between founding member states seemed to work in this period as they entrusted the Union with the tasks of creating a combined market and promoting economic freedom and member states with fostering political freedom and social cohesion. Simultaneously, Europe enjoyed an economic miracle and the creation of increasingly universal welfare. Maurizio Ferrera (2016) is right when he states that this division of labour between Brussels and member states was the 'original sin' which hampered efforts to draw up a general, symbolic framework of a European social mission to complement the one fostered for economic freedom and a common market. However, it is also true to say that from the very beginning, the construction of Europe was always a much wider-scale project than simply economic union.

The second phase, from the 1980s to the first part of the 1990s, was characterised by a clear acceleration of the integrated economy, above all in monetary terms, culminating in the introduction of the euro in 1999. The almost exclusive attention given to this process, together with the ideological strength of New Right thought and the full development of a globalised economy, pushed social policies into second place, even if neo-liberalism was unable to undermine the foundations of the different forms of welfare state.

Moreover, Crouch (1999), writing at the end of the twentieth century, made the acute observation that the European model seemed to be on the point of disintegration following the failure of the institutions which had made European social order possible. As negative elements, he identified the process of secularisation, the decline of notions of class and the collapse of traditional social hierarchy. Emerging phenomena included the changes caused by economic globalisation, the growth of financial capitalism and the pervasion of an unlimited ethic of individualism. To this end, he warned against a tendency towards an Americanisation of European society with a resulting increase in substantial inequalities. This was facilitated by European integration only in its negative sense, such as the removal of obstacles to free trade and the abolition of certain organisational structures which were not closely linked to the economic market.

Yet paradoxically, clear discussion about the ESM in European political debate only began in the years which saw traditional European social compromise (which had been reached after the Second World War) under threat. This may have been a reaction to the ideological attacks of the New Right on the welfare state; whatever the cause, the term officially entered the EU agenda in the mid-1990s (EU Commission, 1994). The core value of the ESM was identified as the solidarity shown between different members and groups within society, encouraged by policies on redistribution of revenue and opportunities which allowed for the development of welfare states characterised by highly developed social protection programmes.

The third phase of the relationship between the process of European integration and the ESM began in the 1990s. Its clearest example was the Lisbon Strategy at the turn of the new millennium, but this had been preceded by the inclusion of a Social Chapter in 1997's Amsterdam Treaty, the European Strategy for Employment in 1998 and the Nice Treaty of 2001, which saw the adoption of the Charter of Fundamental Rights.

The ESM represents an integral part of European identity and its agreements. In the Lisbon Strategy, the social policies implemented were considered an essential factor in competitiveness, which no longer stood in opposition to social inclusion. Article 12 of the Treaty of Lisbon (European Union, 2007) states that

> today the European Social Model, developed through significant Community *acquis* over the past 40 years, includes indispensable references to a large number of issues such as free movement of workers, gender equality in employment, health and workplace safety, work and employment conditions and most recently the fight against all forms of discrimination.

It is true to say that this phase saw the emergence of an understanding that social protection programmes required modernisation in order to be considered as a productive factor rather than simply a cost. Numerous proposals were drawn up by European institutions, but the key political players in what can be considered a new lib–lab vision of welfare were the centre-left parties and coalitions governing various European countries, from the United Kingdom to Germany and from Italy to Spain. Ferrera (2017) has proposed the term 'Liberal Neo-Welfarism' as a definition of this new vision, containing as it does typical elements of liberal tradition (protection of negative liberty, equal opportunities, non-discrimination, individuality, market efficiency) as well as those of social democratic ideals (solidarity, redistribution, inclusion, universalism).

Recognition of the fact that the ESM was a fundamental pillar of European identity was not so much the result of a 'natural' evolution of the idea of an EU as much as that of a specific political project which wanted to establish an alternative to the laissez-faire model of globalisation. Accordingly, it offered the aim of building a social Europe at exactly the same time in which the welfare systems of European countries, founded during the so-called Glorious Thirty Years, appeared most at risk.

A similar concept of the ESM was coined by Jacques Delors, president of the European Commission from 1985 to 1995, and represented the core of his social democratic vision of a united Europe in a globalised world. According to this vision, following the abolition of capital control and the internationalisation of the monetary market which marked the end of the Bretton Woods Agreement, it was impossible to establish progressive, Keynesian economic policies at national level (Hermann and Hofbauer, 2007). It was, however, feasible at European level to build an alternative to the laissez-faire capitalism predominant in Anglo-Saxon countries which were governed by neo-conservative groups during the 1980s. Europe was to be more than just a simple economic association, and social development and economic progress were to be two equally important objectives.

In the same way, a Union which had achieved so much at an economic level should also have a strong socio-political agenda, social standards and European workers of a high level. Indeed, only in this way would it be possible for citizens to fully accept the European project. In the words of Delors himself (Notre Europe, 2005): 'You cannot fall in love with a common market.' In a certain way, the EU would be heir to the direct state intervention policies on economic development which came in for so much criticism at national level (Wilde, 2007). It should be remembered that the white paper 'Growth, Competitiveness, Employment', published in 1993, prefigured considerable public investment in transport, energy, and computer and environmental networks with the aim of creating millions of new jobs in a period when employment prospects were few. The institutionalisation of social dialogue, which began in the period when Delors was the president of the Commission, was a clear signal of the commitment to establish a European social policy which would integrate with national social policy and would be built upon basic values of solidarity and equality, precisely those of the social model which had been constructed over the previous three decades. The treaty of Amsterdam (1997) assigned new social policy powers to the Union and the Open Method of Coordination ensured that the Union had the possibility to direct national social legislation through guidelines and white papers. Significant results were soon registered in the areas of gender equality, access to social services for the most vulnerable and, most controversially, on the sustainability of national pension systems, so that the principle of solidarity between generations was maintained and the right to a dignified life in old age guaranteed.

This project has undoubtedly been downsized since Delors' presidency, largely because the so-called Maastricht parameters required that EU countries, particularly those adopting the euro, maintain strict control polices on public spending. It would seem simplistic to suggest that social policy interventions were simply a spill-over from the formation of the single market or that the ESM were only a cover to justify national welfare retrenchment policies.

Indeed, there has been a continuation of positive integration policies, with, for example, the definition of uniform social standards at European level and with the work of the Union's various central bodies leading to the creation of a core of convergent social policies in the field of employment, with the adoption of social dialogue and a method of open coordination (Cavalli and Martinelli, 2015). All this has resulted in a series of concrete achievements that have contributed to the creation of a European social space which, although it may not be perfect, has in any case had a positive impact on the lives of European citizens and which today should be defended more rigorously against those who claim that the Union has been guilty of depriving European citizens of social rights. Notable achievements include: the rulings of the Court of Justice and European governmental bodies which aim to extend the rights of European citizens, health and safety in the workplace, equal rights for men and women, the European Social Fund, the Charter of Fundamental Rights, anti-discrimination legislation, protection against dismissal, social transfers and tax benefits for non-residents, open coordination processes on employ-ment, social integration and health and pension policies.

THE EUROPEAN SOCIAL MODEL: A COMPLEX SYSTEM

While recognising that there are still great differences between European nations, it should be emphasised that in the last three decades in which the cultural and political hegemony of the neo-liberal paradigm emerged with greater force, a European approach to tackling and solving social problems has remained. This approach is not only theoretical, but rather a recognition of a number of social rights at European level. These rights include: the free movement of people and workers, the right to social security and the creation of a set of standards aimed at balancing social rights in areas such as health and safety in the workplace.

This European model is deeply rooted in the great attention that European democratic states, above all those which constitute the core of the Union, have given to maintaining social cohesion throughout the twentieth century (Servais, 2001). This has led to the creation of complex social security regimes which the state has ultimately had to deal with even though their management is entrusted to private bodies. This has enabled the state to assume the right, or even duty, to actively intervene in economic and social matters and to seek agreement with social partners in order to arrive at shared social and economic policies. Furthermore, the ESM has been able to rely upon the shared political culture of the majority of European citizens, who view social exclusion and great social inequality negatively and who, as a consequence, have given legitimacy to state intervention in order to remedy the negative effects of market functioning. This political culture is very different to that prevailing in the United States, which has historically placed a greater emphasis on the values of freedom and individual responsibility, or that of Asian countries, Japan in particular, where active state intervention has been justified above all in terms of promoting growth and economic development. Traces of this European culture can possibly be found, although in a different form, in the spread of so-called populist movements in recent years, which focus on the theme of social integration (although this is often intended in its traditional and exclusive sense) and criticism of the liberalism of markets and the subordinate role taken on by the state.

The ESM is certainly not a unitary system, but instead a set of values, achievements and social aspirations which differ from country to country, but which share some common characteristics which Giddens (2007) has summarised as follows: an interventionist state funded by high levels of taxation, a welfare system which provides effective social protection to all, particularly to those who are most needy, and the reduction of all forms of social inequality.

Ferrera (2005) has noted that over the years a European social space has formed whose role is to promote the adaptation of institutional conditions in European countries and which allows for the sharing of solutions to the political and economic challenges created by the deepening of economic ties in Europe. Indeed, the European economic area presents an increasing challenge for national welfare states. Although not perfect, some answers to this challenge have been found with a series of policy agreements and instruments that have in fact led to the creation of a social space. Agreements include those on the free movement of workers, health and safety in the workplace and gender equality. Instruments include structural funds, in particular the European Social Fund; the European Globalization Adjustment Fund; the social chapter of the Treaty of Amsterdam; the Charter of Fundamental Rights; and soft laws on issues such as employment, social inclusion, pensions and the coordination of health policies associated with the Lisbon Strategy and Europe 2020.

The construction of a European social space did not only begin with the important treaties of the late 1990s and the beginning of the new millennium. Instead, the reconstruction of the European integration process with a strong focus on social questions has led Anton Hemerijck (2013, p. 329 ss.) to state that, since the first Treaty of Rome, a long process of gradual institutional change made up of both successful and unsuccessful integration has resulted in the creation of a European social space which is relatively stable, albeit multiform. It is not a fixed area, but instead a continuous process of welfare selection which, unlike in the case of the single market and currency, has not brought about a genuine European social regime. National states continue to drive this process although their actions have been conditioned and shaped by supranational regulation, policy coordination and rulings by the European Court of Justice.

Also contributing to the establishment of this common social space are particular coordination and regulation mechanisms which Jacobsson (2004) has defined as 'discourse regulation mechanisms': mechanisms which refer to the use of language and to the production of knowledge which, as a consequence, lead to a better understanding of problems and solutions in specific policy fields.

The most important discourse mechanisms are the definition of key concepts and of common discourse, the development of common evidence bases (statistics, databases) and classification tools (indicators) and the dissemination of comparative and evaluative studies which make it possible to identify the standards which should be reached.

In the specific field of European welfare, the development of such discourse mechanisms has meant that some concepts (adaptability, employability, equal opportunities, empowerment and social investment) have become the foundation on which national social policy reform projects have been built, with reference being made to papers and guidelines employed at a European level. The creation of common European data banks and indicators has played a similar role to that performed by the birth of national statistics in the consolidation phase of nation-states, providing empirical evidence of the presence of shared problems and encouraging the formation of political thinking and common administrative procedure when this is not centralised.

However, probably the most important discourse regulation mechanism has been the production and dissemination of knowledge through the provision of analyses and evaluation at a European level. This has been greatly facilitated by the creation of transnational networks of researchers and public and political officials and by the consequent guiding role played by some political scholars and politicians. This seems to have created, through a process of socialisation and mutual learning, that which Haas (1992) called 'epistemic community' defined by: a set of shared beliefs and common values, the common identification of the causes of social problems which serve as a basis for the political action aimed at solving them, a set of shared criteria to validate knowledge in their specific domain of expertise, and a common political vision that derives from practices aimed at improving human and social well-being. Transnational epistemic communities can have an influence on states, directly influencing decision makers and, above all, shedding light on major problems and identifying solutions to solve them. It is also through these processes that a European social area has been progressively built, since alongside national areas, 'European frames of reference for social policies' have been developed, leading to a rethink of national social policies in the light of problems existing in other European countries and in Europe as a whole.

The European social area is built upon a number of pillars, first of all nation-states but also supranational elements, and can been seen also in the creation of institutionalised political networks. This is obviously an area with a largely regulatory role, with limited financial and decision-making capabilities, based on the ability to reconcile conflicting interests in the long run. It is an area where there is a continuous commitment to both the Community and to national autonomy and which includes a great variety of different welfare systems. However, as Hemerijck adds, a historic process of mutual adaptation has taken place, which has meant that the European social area has in recent years become more inclusive and coherent by better integrating its various levels.

Considering Ferrera's recent proposal (2016) it can be said that from an empirical standpoint social Europe is made up of five distinct constitutive elements and is characterised by internal issues which are, at times, conflicting:

1. The first element regards national social spaces, namely the social protection systems of each member state. These are systems which are founded upon common principles but which partly differ from each other due to their institutional and organisational profiles and their operational logic.
2. The second element is the area of social citizenship, namely the right acquired by European citizens, based on the principle of non-discrimination, to have access to the social benefits and services of the country in which they reside.

3. The third consists of sub-national social spaces: territorial or local welfare created following the processes of decentralisation. These have also been promoted and enhanced by the EU, receiving funds from the European Social Fund and subject to social policies in accordance with the principle of subsidiarity.
4. The fourth element is true European social policy, namely the set of standards common to many areas of social policy (equal opportunities, health, parental leave, workplace health and safety) and the European funds financing social, cohesion and territorial development policies.
5. The last component is the outline of a European social constitution, namely the objectives and social norms included in the treatises which, given the supremacy of European legislation, are both a guide and a constraint for national polices and for other dimensions of social Europe.

Ferrera (2016, p. 107) believes that these five components are conflicting and often contrast with each other at both a symbolic and a practical level, with resulting negative consequences on the internal cohesion of social Europe. As a result, he states that in order to overcome the imbalances present in this difficult coexistence between the five elements it is necessary to implement a political strategy which: supports modernisation and the mutual adaptation of national social areas/spaces, consolidates European social citizenship, supports local welfare with a particular focus on cross-border dynamics in order to create common social spaces in neighboring European regions, expands supranational social policies and, in line with the proposals made by former Belgian minister Frank Vandenbroucke (2013), creates a genuine European social union, building on the aims and social clauses set out in the Treaty of Lisbon.

The fact that social Europe is made up of differing elements which have to coexist together is not, however, only negative. It serves also to contribute to the originality of the ESM, which cannot be considered as perfectly defined and coherent, but rather a complex system in which the various components influence each other. Thus, national welfare systems have become European in nature since they have to interact with each other in order to make the principle of European social citizenship more concrete, receiving European funding on the basis of so-called best practices following the open coordination method, having to comply with the standards set out by European law and with the principle of vertical subsidiarity.

Hemerijck (2013) and Cavalli and Martinelli (2015) have therefore identified as many as eight policy areas in which different European states have tended to find solutions to problems in similar ways over the last thirty years, resulting in the creation of more hybrid models which are more similar to each other. These are:

1. More rigorous fiscal and monetary policies aimed at achieving macroeconomic stability, low inflation and the reduction of public debt.
2. Bargaining between social partners and the government aimed at wage adjustment.
3. Active labour market policies.
4. Flexicurity in labour market regulation in order to reconcile the flexibility required by businesses with an active reintegration of the unemployed into the job market.
5. Forms of minimum wage for those participating in vocational retraining and counselling programs.
6. The raising of the age of retirement, the change from the remuneration to the contributory system and the integration of state, corporate and individual pension schemes.
7. Greater attention given to social services dedicated to the family and to the conciliation of work and family care with the adoption of active policies such as those regarding nurseries and parental leave.
8. Changes in the funding and management of social policies with the redistribution of responsibilities and relationships between the state, the market and the community/third sector.

NEW SOCIAL RISKS, THE ECONOMIC CRISIS AND CHANGES TO THE EUROPEAN SOCIAL MODEL

Faced with the challenges of a global market, the emergence of the so-called new social risks and the long period of economic recession which began with the financial crisis of 2007–2008, European states, although still characterised by their differing historical institutional models, have been able to respond to problems following common practices and have shown how a European social model, albeit different from that developed in the previous thirty years, continues to exist.

Consequently, we can observe a convergence which has prompted national systems to become more hybrid, following certain common principles (Gilbert, 2013):

1. There has been an increasing shift towards the privatisation of welfare activities through the purchase of services provided by the private sector and the provision of cash benefits through vouchers and tax credit which give the individual the possibility to make personal choices on healthcare, education, nursing services and pensions.

2. There has been almost universal acceptance of the fact that policies which provide only passive support to the unemployed must be gradually replaced by others which promote professional training, giving individuals the skills which will enable them to participate in the job market.
3. Another element regards a more careful targeting of those eligible for benefits, with the greater use of means-testing.
4. Finally, although possibly most significantly, there has been a shift away from an emphasis on the right of citizens to receive welfare provisions to protect them from market instability and injustice. This has been replaced by an emphasis on the responsibility of welfare claimants to make an active contribution and to support themselves as quickly as possible. This emphasis on individual responsibility has been important as the state is no longer an organ which ensures and provides benefits for holders of citizenship rights, but is instead a body which gives state support to individual responsibility.

It is interesting to note how such changes, which have sometimes led to a reduction of citizens' social rights, have been registered in both northern and southern European countries, regarded as polar opposites in literature on welfare systems.

CONCLUSION

Welfare in the countries of Northern Europe, which form the nucleus of the so-called social democratic model, has latterly become more similar to that found in other European countries. One reason for this is the need to deal with the emergence of new social risks such as an increasing number of one-parent families, ethnic pluralism and the lack of employment opportunities for social groups with a low level of education (Harsløf and Ulmestig, 2013). Thus, in many areas of social policy there is a greater reliance on services outsourced to private companies. An idea which is gaining ground is that state support should be given on the condition that the receiver fulfils precise contractual commitments and that activation is the tool most able to help those who have lost out to post-industrial development. At the same time, there is stigma attached to certain types of 'unwanted' individual behaviour. For example, there is a belief that those who choose not to continue with their school education must be individually responsible for the consequences. The new system of management which rewards public and private entities based on performance (whether they be schools, hospitals or private care centres) may lead to the creaming-off of the best clients, patients and pupils. Decentralisation and regionalisation of welfare and the labour market are accentuated and, as a consequence, there is a growing risk of geographical polarisation replacing what was once universal national welfare. More generally, faced with the partial retreat of the institutions of the universal welfare state, a new social space has opened up in which groups and individuals compete to gain welfare resources and where choices are made by both individuals and by social groups on the allocation of resources and on lifestyle choices: for example, the choice of supplementary forms of social security and care or attention to nutrition and sport.

With the beginning on the new millennium the southern European nations which make up the Mediterranean welfare model (negatively considered as being most different to the northern social democratic model) have also met with new social risks which are in many ways similar to those of Northern Europe: family instability and an increasing number of one-parent families; precarious employment, above all for the low-skilled; intermittent careers; and difficulty in reconciling work and family responsibilities. Although their welfare systems are very different, the welfare reforms carried out in Mediterranean countries in recent years have in many respects followed the same path taken by northern European countries. The reason for this is that their governments were those who most carefully followed the directives and recommendations made by European institutions aimed at modernising the ESM (Marì-Klose and Moreno-Fuentes, 2013). Therefore, social insurance schemes for workers with non-standard contracts or with fragmented careers have been reformed and greater attention has been given to the conciliation of work and family life with the expansion of childcare services. However, differences between regions have been accentuated with some regional governments providing innovative answers to new social risks while others have had to face growing financial difficulties. In addition, particularly after the financial crash, the introduction of new measures of co-payment for welfare services began to spread and individuals were encouraged to take out private health insurance.

Social Europe seems therefore to be tied to a common destiny, also regarding the reduction of welfare policies and the redefining of social rights. It is clear that nowhere is perfect and that the dream that social rights might be ensured by a return to nationalism is just that, a dream.

Hemerijck (2013) has argued that the national systems of welfare which have been best able to adapt the new conditions, those set up before the process of globalisation was truly complete and before the impact of new social risks and the long economic crisis of 2007–2008, are those which have created hybrid models borrowing features belonging to the traditions of other countries. Perhaps paradoxically, the greater complexity and internal flexibility of the ESM seem to be an advantage when the rigid regulation of European social space leads to an inability to offer solutions to the prolonged economic crisis and to sovereign debts, being bound as it is to hard austerity policies and the control of public debt laid out by Europe. The social space seems however to be more resilient and able to adapt social policies to the challenges of the economic crisis, while still maintaining the ability to reconcile economic and social policies through the inclusion of national welfare policies within European governance. This may indeed be a critical factor given the profound economic and social challenges that lie ahead as a result of the Covid-19 health pandemic. It may be argued that the complexity and flexibility of the ESM will become crucial in determining the well-being of people who live and work in Europe.

REFERENCES

Alber, J. (2010), What the European and American welfare states have in common and where they differ: facts and fiction in comparison of the European Social Model and the United States, *Journal of European Social Policy*, **20** (2), 102–125.

Barbier, J.-C. (2013), To what extent can the European Union deliver 'social citizenship' to its citizens, in Evers, A., and Guillemard, A. M. (eds), *Social Policy and Citizenship*, Oxford University Press, New York, pp. 97–117.

Benassi, D., and Mingione, E. (2019), Welfare capitalism, in Orum, A. M. (ed.), *The Wiley Blackwell Encyclopedia of Urban and Regional Studies*, Wiley & Sons, Hoboken, pp. 1–7.

Cavalli, A., and Martinelli, A. (2015), *La società europea*, Il Mulino, Bologna.

Crouch, C. (1999), *Social Change in Western Europe*, Oxford University Press, New York.

Esping-Andersen, G. (1990), *The Three Worlds of Welfare Capitalism*. Polity Press, Cambridge.

EU Commission (1994), *European Social Policy: A Way Forward for the Union – A White Paper*, COM (94)333, Luxembourg.

Delanty, G., and Rumford, C. (2005), *Rethinking Europe: Social Theory and the Implications of Europeanization*, Routledge, London and New York.

European Union (2007), Treaty of Lisbon Amending the Treaty on European Union and the Treaty Establishing the European Community, 13 December 2007, 2007/C 306/01, www.refworld.org/docid/476258d32.html.

Ferrera, M. (2005), *The Boundaries of Welfare: European Integration and the New Spatial Politics of Social Protection*, Oxford University Press, Oxford.

Ferrera, M. (2016), *Rotta di collisione. Euro contro welfare?* Laterza, Rome-Bari.

Ferrera, M. (2017), Liberal neo-welfarism: New perspectives for the European social model, *Law J. Soc. & Lab. Rel.*, **3**, 72.

Giddens, A. (2007), *Europe in the Global Age*, Polity Press, Cambridge.

Gilbert, N. (2013), Citizenship in the enabling state: the changing balance of rights and obligations, in Evers, A., and Guillemard, A. M. (eds), *Social Policy and Citizenship*, Oxford University Press, New York, pp. 80–96.

Haas, P. (1992), Introduction: epistemic communities and international policy coordination, *International Organization*, **46** (1), 1–35.

Harsløf, I., and Ulmestig, R. (2013), *Changing Social Risks and Social Policy Responses in the Nordic Welfare States*, Palgrave Macmillan, New York.

Hemerijck, A. (2013), *Changing Welfare States*, Oxford University Press, Oxford.

Hermann, C. (2009), The European social models: contours of the discussion, in Frangakis, M., Hermann, C., and Hofbauer, I. (2007), The European Social Model:

between competitive modernisation and neoliberal resistance, *Capital & Class*, **93**, 125–139.

Jacobsson, K. (2004), Soft regulation and the subtle transformation of states: the case of EU employment policy, *Journal of European Social Policy*, **14** (4), 355–370.

Juhàsz, G. (2006), Exporting or pulling down? The European Social Model and eastern enlargement of the EU, *European Journal of Social Quality*, **6** (2), 82–108.

Marì-Klose, P., and Moreno-Fuentes, F. J. (2013), The southern European welfare model in the post-industrial order: still a distinctive cluster? *European Societies*, **15** (4), 475–492.

Montanari, I., Nelson, K., and Palme, J. (2008), Towards a European Social Model? Trends in social insurance among EU countries 1980–2000, *European Societies*, **10** (5), 787–810.

Moon, J. D. (2019), *Responsibility, Rights, and Welfare: The Theory of the Welfare State*, Abingdon, Routledge.

Notre Europe (2005), Presentation by Jacques Delors during his series of conferences in the United States: 'Where is the European Union heading?' 26 March to 4 April 2001, Groupement d'études et de recherches – Notre Europe, www.notre-europe.asso.fr/IMG/pdf/DiscoursIV01-en.pdf.

Pestieau, P., and Lefèbvre, M. (2018), The welfare state in Europe: economic and social perspectives, Oxford Scholarship Online, https://doi.org/10.1093/oso/9780198817055.001.0001.

Scharpf, F. W. (2002), The European Social Model: coping with the challenges of diversity, MPIfG Working Paper No. 02/8.

Servais, J.-M. (2001), Quelques Réflexions sur un modèle social européen, *Relations Industrielles/Industrial Relations*, **56** (4), 701–718.

Strauss-Kahn, D. (2004), Building a political Europe: 50 proposals for tomorrow's Europe, report by Chairperson of the Round Table 'A Sustainable Project for Tomorrow's Europe' formed on the initiative of the President of the European Commission, http://ec.europa.eu/transparency/regdoc/rep/10061/2010/EN/10061-2010-1921-EN-F1-1.pdf.

Vandenbroucke, A. (2013), A European social union: why we need it, what it means, *Rivista Italiana di Politiche Pubbliche*, **2**, 221–247.

Wilde, L. (2007), Europe and the 're-regulation of world society': a critique of Habermas, *Capital & Class*, **93**, 47–66.

4. A Europe for all with all? EU Cohesion Policy and social inclusion across EU states and regions

Marion Ellison

INTRODUCTION

The gravity of the global impact of the Covid-19 health pandemic on the well-being of human beings cannot be overstated. In light of this, the need for a unified, cooperative and progressive response to the crisis is urgent. In Europe, it may be argued that the European Social Model (ESM) offers a flexible framework for the coordinated, collaborative and unified response that will be needed if we are to face the grave and profound challenges ahead. These challenges have been articulated by a broad range of commentators (Hemerijck, 2018; Lahusen and Grasso, 2018; Nugent, 2017; Vandenbroucke, 2017; Verhofstadt, 2017; Deusdad et al., 2016; Mathers, 2016; Varoufakis, 2016; Sandermann, 2014).

Undoubtedly the gravest challenges that we all face are those emerging from the Covid-19 global health pandemic. As Patterson (2020) points out, debates about the impact and response to the pandemic have settled around a false dichotomy where the choice is between the health of individuals on one hand and the economy on the other. Critically, however, as Patterson (2020) also argues, the economy does not simply consist of profit or loss; it is fundamentally about the material conditions which people experience in society. Crucially, as a number of commentators have argued, the concept of economy itself pivots upon the interaction of work, capital, public health, poverty, formal and informal care, unemployment and social exclusion (Patterson, 2020; Bauhardt and Harcourt, 2018; Chertkovskaya et al., 2019; ILO, 2018). Exemplifying this, a renewed focus on the economy of care has illuminated the inequities faced by people delivering formal and informal care. Illustrating this, recent evidence reveals that people working within formal and informal care are often underpaid and undervalued (Cominetti et al., 2020; Gardiner, 2015). In 2018, the International Labour Organization (ILO) pointed out the profound consequences of the failure to recognise the value of formal and informal care work in the economy, arguing that decent jobs should be created for care workers for the well-being of both the care recipient and the care worker (ILO, 2018).

The lived experiences of care workers across Europe evidences the failure of the ESM to ensure observance of the European Union (EU) Charter of Fundamental Rights. Conceptually linking social and economic to civil and political rights, the Solidarity Chapter within the Charter enshrines the right to 'fair and just' employment conditions. Article 31 of the Lisbon Treaty states that every worker has the right to 'working conditions which respect his or her health, safety and dignity' and a 'limitation of maximum working hours, to daily and weekly rest periods and to an annual period of paid leave' (European Parliament, 2000, Ch. 4: Articles 27–38).

More broadly the impact of austerity policies largely justified by the financial crisis of 2007–2008 in Europe has been highly deleterious to health systems across Europe. Recent studies have evidenced the impact of reduced expenditure and reforms of health systems on people living and working in European societies (Marmot, 2020; Mossialos and Le Grand, 2019; Thomson et al., 2015). Illustrating this, Pavaloni and Guillen (2013) have argued that in recent years European health care systems have faced a 'quadrilemma' to control costs whilst guaranteeing equality of access and ensuring the responsiveness and quality of health systems. As a result, the authors argue that European countries often face a trade-off between economic efficiency, medical advances, social inequalities and patients' and workers' conditions. The imposition of harsh austerity policies and strict monetary measures across a number of European countries has reinvigorated debates concerning the future of the ESM.

For one in four people in the EU, the lived experience of multiple and complex forms of poverty and social exclusion means enduring precarious lives. Monetary poverty is the most prevalent form of poverty, pervading the lives of 17.3 per cent of the EU population in 2018. Severe material deprivation permeates the lives of 8.1 per cent of the EU population, with very low work intensity compounding the precariousness experienced by 10.6 per cent of EU citizens (Eurostat, 2018). Of critical concern, 26.3 per cent of young people aged 18 to 24 and 23.4 per cent of those aged less than 18 were at risk of poverty or social exclusion in 2018 (Eurostat, 2020). Significantly, the psychosocial impacts of poverty, social exclusion and marginalisation are becoming more evident, particularly in relation to the relationship between work, poverty and poor mental health (Marmot, 2020; Gaisbauer et al., 2019; Grimm et al., 2019; Payne, 2017; Elliott, 2016).

More broadly, the Covid-19 pandemic has exposed and amplified existing health inequalities with the lockdown having a disproportionate impact on people from socio-economically deprived backgrounds (King's Fund, 2020; ONS, 2020). Exemplifying this recent evidence from the Office for National Statistics (United Kingdom; UK) has revealed the relationship between mortality rates and socio-economic status (ONS, 2020). At the time of writing the ONS has revealed that people living in the most deprived areas in England and Wales are dying at twice the rate (55.1 deaths per 100,000) of those living in the least deprived areas of the England and Wales (25.3 deaths per 100,000) (ONS, 2020). Intersectional factors, particularly relating to ethnic background, are also critical as a disproportionately high number of people from Black and ethnic communities are key workers in the UK.

Recent evidence reveals that being in employment does not necessarily protect people from poverty and social exclusion. The share of employed persons at risk of poverty has risen in most EU member states since 2010. It may be argued that variations in labour market conditions and employment rights across European states have a considerable influence on levels of poverty and social exclusion. Significantly, 73.4 per cent of very-low-work-intensity households with dependent children and 44.8 per cent of low-work-intensity households with dependent children were at risk of poverty in the EU (Eurostat, 2020). Moreover it may be argued that recent historic shifts in the governance and provision of welfare, the imposition of austerity measures and the intensification of liberalising and de-regulating processes across European labour markets have contributed substantially to the deterioration of socio-economic conditions for many people who live and work in Europe (Liotti and Canale, 2020; Barr et al., 2015; Ellison, 2014).

More recently, the challenge of the global refugee crisis caused largely by devastating conflicts in Syria, Iraq and countries across Africa – including Liberia, Nigeria, Sierra Leone, Somalia, Togo, Burundi, Democratic Republic of the Congo and Rwanda – has led to calls for more effective integration policies in Europe, enabling a 'virtuous circle' whereby refugees and migrants are given the support they need to find jobs and pay taxes and social security contributions. It is argued that the migration debate should be constructed in terms of opportunities and human rights rather than burdens (Carrera and Vankova, 2019; Della Porta, 2018; Türk and Garlick, 2016; Long, 2013). The EU status of migrants is complex and classified into a number of distinct groups. Historically, the human rights of migrants and the recognition of their contribution to economies was recognised in the Stockholm Programme during the 1990s, the Tampere Programme (1999) and the Hague Programme (2005). More recently, migrants' contribution to the EU economy was recognised in the Europe 2020 Strategy demarcating the effective integration of migrants as a primary policy aim. The embedding of refugees and migrants into the labour market is defined as a key indicator of integration. A number of studies have questioned the adequacy of labour market conditions and access to social rights and public services (Brell et al., 2020; Oğuz, 2020; Fasani et al., 2018; Grubanov-Boskovic et al., 2017). Equally, the cumulative impact of austerity measures and welfare reforms across European settings has impeded the effective integration of refugees and migrants (Dajani, 2020; Royster, 2020; Mort, 2019; Montgomery and Baglioni, 2018). Moreover, as recent studies have revealed, the current Covid-19 public health crisis has compounded this situation, particularly with regard to the mental health of refugees and migrants (Bozorgmehr et al., 2020; Endale et al., 2020; Kapilashrami and Bhui, 2020; Kluge et al., 2020).

The multiple and intersecting economic and social challenges facing people who live and work in the EU are profound and may ultimately threaten the fundamental basis of 'solidarity' between European nations. Arguably, the recent emergence of 'populist' politics is a response to years of neo-liberalism and austerity measures across European countries. As the imminent departure of the UK from the EU powerfully illustrates, the implications for Europe as a broadly united and integrated socio-economic sphere are of growing concern. Illustrating this, across a broad range of economic and social indicators, inter-regional inequality is greater in the UK than almost all Organisation for Economic Co-operation and Development (OECD) countries, including the United States, being surpassed only by Slovakia and Ireland (McCann, 2020; OECD, 2020, 2018). For this reason, the UK is a fertile setting for the rise of populist politics characterised by simplistic solutions and a focus on blaming the 'other'.

As a manifestly counterbalancing instrument to poverty and social exclusion, the ESM can be regarded as central to attempts to secure sustainable unity of purpose across Europe. The coordinated implementation of EU funding instruments aimed at rebalancing economic and social inequalities between wealthier and poorer regions and groups within the EU is evidenced as improving living conditions in the most disadvantaged regions of Europe (Wenz-Temming and Sonnicksen, 2020; Pasimeni and Riso, 2019; Ellison, 2017). The future delivery of effective and sustainable operational programmes to mitigate socio-economic inequalities across Europe requires a continued commitment to redistributive investment strategies, coherent policy architectures and inclusive forms of governance across a range of sectors. More broadly, this chapter argues that this re-distributional capacity is critical to the future of European integration itself.

THE POLITICAL ECONOMY OF WELFARE IN EUROPE

Unified by a concern to address pressing social, economic and governance issues, recent contributions have focused on providing a vision and template for a coherent and sustainable economic and social model in Europe (Plank,

2020; Heslop et al., 2019; Barbera et al., 2018; Earle et al., 2018; Froud and Williams, 2018; Engelen et al., 2017; Rinaldi, 2016). Alternative economic models have emerged, such as the 'Foundational Economy', which proposes the provision and delivery of Universal Basic Services (UBS) as an entitlement granted to all who live and work in European societies. This model contrasts sharply with distributive approaches which focus on boosting private consumption by delivering economic growth (Plank, 2020; Heslop et al., 2019; Earle et al., 2018; Froud and Williams, 2018).

Undoubtedly, within the current neo-liberal economic context, global financial and economic pressures have exacerbated the challenges facing Europe. The global financial crisis has itself exposed interconnected vulnerabilities across fiscal, economic and social spheres in Europe. In particular, conventional welfare state frameworks have become less equipped to cope with new social vulnerabilities and risks across European societies (Ferrera, 2020; Kvist, 2017; Palier and Hay, 2017; Taylor-Gooby et al., 2017; Heidenreich and Rice, 2016; Romano and Punziano, 2016). Cognisance of this fundamental transition has led to calls for a 'Differentiated European Social Model' (Leruth, 2017) which takes account of the unique social, economic and fiscal challenges faced by distinct European settings. Certainly, recent contributions to this debate have provided a significant contribution to understandings of European welfare transformations forged within diverse political economies influenced by the global neo-liberal agenda since the financial crisis of 2007–2008 (Mathers, 2016; Varoufakis, 2016; Leschke et al., 2015). Importantly, whilst there is evidence of shared intent, the impact of different policy approaches on the lives of people living and work within distinct European societies reveals significant disparities in outcomes, particularly for vulnerable groups between European countries. As Figure 4.1 illustrates, whilst most EU countries have experienced reductions in the percentage of people who are at risk of poverty and social exclusion, between 2010 and 2018 Greece, Italy, the UK, Spain, Estonia, Luxemburg and the Netherlands all experienced increases.

The EU definition of being at 'at risk of poverty and social exclusion' (AROPE) includes people who have an income below their national poverty threshold and people who face severe material deprivation. In addition, the AROPE indicator includes people living in households with a very low work intensity, which signals a very fragile attachment to the labour market. National governments may select policy priorities relating to these vulnerabilities. Thus, whilst there is a common goal to reduce the number of people at risk of poverty and social exclusion, national governments have the scope to design multi-sectoral frameworks focusing on specific priorities. Critically, as Figure 4.2 reveals, all European member states have seen a rise in levels of people who are in work and who are also at risk of poverty and social exclusion, apart from Finland, Sweden, Ireland, Latvia, Czechia, Croatia, Lithuania, Greece,

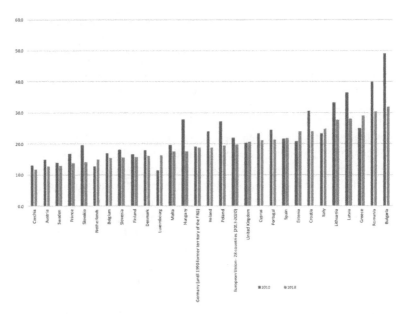

Figure 4.1   People at risk of poverty or social exclusion by broad group of country of birth (population aged 18 and over 2010 and 2018), EU Statistics on Income and Living Conditions survey (ilc_peps06)

Source: https://ec.europa.eu/knowledge4policy/dataset/ds00064_en

Denmark, Portugal and Poland. This suggests that addressing the structural problems relating to fragile, low-waged and insecure labour markets, particularly for people living in households with low work intensity, is not a policy priority in most European countries.

Evidence from a number of recent studies points to the endemic and generic insufficiencies of minimum income and social protection for households with low work intensity and households that are completely without employment across Europe (Cantillon et al., 2019; Haagh, 2019; Matilla-Santander et al., 2019; Ferreiro and Gómez, 2018; Armano et al., 2017). These findings pose fundamental structural challenges, particularly with regard to the political economy of work and welfare within European countries. Importantly, the extent and gravity of in-work poverty across Europe also impacts significantly upon the redistributive capacity of the EU. Underlining this, a recent analysis

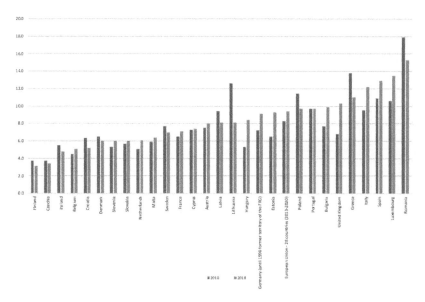

Figure 4.2   In-work at risk of poverty by broad country of birth (population aged 18 or over), EU Statistics on Income and Living Conditions survey (ilc_iw01) 2010 and 2018

Source: Eurostat, 2020. Last updated 30 July 20 (2010 data for Bulgaria, Romania and Poland unavailable)

of the allocation and operationalisation of European Social Funds across the EU clearly evidences that

> Increasing levels of in-work poverty demonstrate that while employment remains an important vehicle of social inclusion, it is not the panacea to social problems, nor it is enough to protect people from hardship. (Farrell and Brandellero, 2018, p.13)

The analysis goes on to recommend that

> Employment and training will remain a key focus for the ESF (European Social Fund). In the new period the focus must be on the quality of the employment addressing concerns about low wages, precariousness of contracts, an over-focus on activation, and the priority given to economic aims as opposed to people's needs. (p.15)

The EU's Poverty Reduction target is placed at the heart of the European Pillar of Social Rights (ESPR) implementation strategy (European Commission, 2017). As Figure 4.3 illustrates, there are considerable differences in the allocation of ESF resources to social inclusion and combating poverty between EU member states, with the Netherlands allocating 74 per cent of ESF resources to this goal and Lithuania allocating only 20 per cent of its funds to this thematic objective. Whilst most EU member states allocate between 20 and 30 per cent of their budget, eight already allocate more than 30 per cent of their allocated ESF budget to measures aimed at promoting social inclusion (the Netherlands, Latvia, Ireland, Belgium, Germany, France, Malta and Austria).

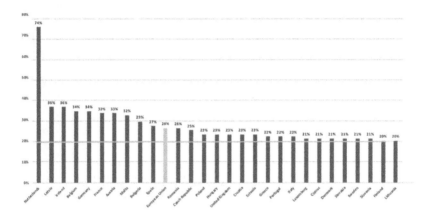

Figure 4.3   Allocation of ESF resources to social inclusion

Source: European Union (2017)

Critically, differences in the allocation of ESF budgets between member states are not only reflective of distinct socio-economic conditions and policy priorities at national level but also of the allocation of specific projects and measures at local level. A central concern of all member states is to address inter-regional inequalities. At national level a number of recent studies have pointed to the need to raise wage levels and levels of social protection by developing mechanisms which provide a minimum income for all (Hirsch, 2020; Hirsch et al., 2020; Reddy, 2020; Cantillon et al., 2019; Davis et al., 2018; Armano et al., 2017). The role of EU Cohesion Policy in facilitating locally developed, place-based approaches in addressing inter-regional ine-qualities is equally important.

Inter-regional inequality within Europe is complex and multi-dimensional. On a broad level these inequalities reflect the dichotomy between dynamic large urban centres and degenerating industrialised and remote rural regions. Recent studies have exposed how industrial degeneration and the increased isolation of peripheral regions has led to the development of fragile labour markets (Staníčková and Melecký, 2020; Sykianakis et al., 2019; Zopounidis et al., 2016). In contrast, larger urban centres have benefited from substantial investment creating proportionally greater levels of high-waged jobs (Couture et al., 2019; Lamorgese et al., 2019; Matano and Naticchioni, 2016; Sattinger, 2016; D'Costa and Overman, 2013). Critically, however, the global financial crisis of 2007–2008 had a deleterious impact on a number of large urban centres in Europe, leading to substantial levels of poverty and social exclusion within these areas (Theodore, 2020; Scheurer and Haase, 2018; Dijkstra et al., 2015).

Two key factors underpin increasing inter-regional inequality in Europe. Firstly, transformations within economic and industrial structures led to profound changes in the labour market across distinct regions of Europe (Iammarino et al., 2019; Moneta et al., 2019; Schulze, 2014). The development of technological innovation in the 1970s led to the location of high-technology and knowledge-intensive sectors in large centres in Europe drawing in highly paid, highly skilled, creative jobs (Bjørn et al., 2019). At the same time the expansion of automation within the manufacturing sector reduced factor costs, leading to the replacement of medium- and low-skilled jobs in most of the previously industrialised centres of Europe (O'Donovan, 2019; Servoz, 2019; Blit et al., 2018; Berger and Frey, 2016). As a result, manufacturing has increasingly become outsourced to countries in the developing world. The second factor emerges from longer-term regional evolutionary features, consisting of place-based forms of social, educational and economic exclusion (Kristensen et al., 2019; Storper, 2018). Recent evidence has pointed to the need for place-based policies which are relevant to growing numbers of individuals and communities within 'disconnected and disillusioned peripheries' to counter social division and political disenchantment within these peripheries (Iammarino et al., 2019; Kristensen et al., 2019; Storper, 2018).

The imminent departure of the UK from the EU highlights the urgent need to bring closer attention to pervasive economic, social, public health and political challenges which threaten the well-being of a substantial number of European citizens and European integration itself (Musat, 2020; Palomino Lozano, 2020; Soava et al., 2020; Šoltés et al., 2020; Weatherburn et al., 2020; Ellison, 2017; Feigl, 2017). This urgency is demonstrated by the situation in the UK. As evidenced earlier in this chapter, across a broad range of indicators the UK is inter-regionally more unequal than 28 other OECD countries (McCann, 2020; OECD, 2020, 2018). Mitigating this, combined EU Structural and Investment Funds and EU Investment Bank finance in the UK total approximately €10 billion per year, being largely allocated to the most underdeveloped areas of the UK (Brien, 2018; Ellison, 2017). Whilst the greatest proportion of these investments are directed at urban areas, particularly within the UK's weaker regions, funding from the Common Agricultural Policy (CAP) of approximately €3.2 billion per annum is directed at rural areas. In addition, the European Cohesion Policy currently allocates approximately €770 million to rural and maritime areas to promote economic development. This, together with €300 million of domestic UK co-financing, equates to a total funding stream of €14 billion per annum when CAP funding is included (Brien, 2018). This funding will be terminated following the UK's departure from the EU. It may be argued that inter-regional inequalities in the UK will be exacerbated by the UK's departure from the EU unless EU regional funding is replaced by UK central government funding. The continuation of sub-national governance agendas is also at risk (Billing et al., 2019). Place-based approaches are well developed in Scotland. These approaches to local governance are underpinned by a statutory requirement for community empowerment and are operational-ised within a sophisticated framework of Community Planning Partnerships across all 32 local authorities (Connolly et al., 2020; Ellison, 2020; Elliott, 2020; Revell and Dinnie, 2020; Bertin and Ellison, 2019; Elliott et al., 2019).

More broadly, recent transformations in forms of social investment and social protection across European nation states have been driven by a number of inter-related factors. These include pressures on social expenditure budgets, and policy architectures designed to re-balance the relationship between work and welfare (Ronchi, 2018; Hemerijck, 2017; Taylor-Gooby et al., 2017; Ellison and Fenger, 2013). Critically, however, it may be argued that the specificities of these arrangements are forged within the recent re-orientation of welfare policies across Europe which have coalesced around the conceptu-alisation of social investment as a productive factor rather than a cost factor (Abrahamson et al., 2019; Hemerijck, 2017; Midgley et al., 2017). Social investment is inextricably linked to economic growth and job creation (Malin, 2020; Hudson, 2019; Sabato and Verschraegen, 2019). This new social invest-ment approach focuses on human capital with concepts such as 'enabling' 'activation' and 'individual responsibility', replacing previous notions of 'compensation' and 'protection' (Wohlfarth, 2020; Saraceno, 2019; Wiggan, 2017; Ellison and Fenger, 2013). The aim is to strengthen people's capacity to fully participate in employment and social life. Essentially, to prepare them for a fast-changing society, enhance their capacity to deal with risky environments, avoid long-term dependency on assistance and minimise the intergenerational transfer of poverty and social disadvantages. In this sense the role of the welfare state is to prepare the population to face the conditions of the modern economy and to overcome the structural deficiencies of the welfare state caused by market failures and demographic transformations. Global economic pressures and the financial crisis of 2007–2008 may have led some EU countries to question the continued legitimacy of the ESM. Paradoxically the search for new solutions based upon notions of 'new welfare' and productive forms of social investment has harmonised policies and practices across a number of European countries.

Legitimated as a rational adjustment to changing global economic conditions, models of 'new welfare' have emerged across a number of European countries during the 2000s (Castrén, 2020; Wohlfarth, 2020; Taylor-Gooby et al., 2017; Ellison and Fenger, 2013). The principles underlying 'new welfare' have been the subject of debate and contention in recent years, particularly with regard to reconciling individual and societal risk (McGann et al., 2020; Dengler, 2019; Saraceno, 2019; Wiggan, 2017; Ellison, 2014). Nevertheless, it may be argued that the core function of welfare systems across most European countries continues to be the redistribution of economic, social and educational resources within societies. This redistributive function recognises the centrality of societal risks and collective responsibility. The universal right to free health care and education exemplifies the sharing of risk between individuals who are socio-economically secure and individuals who are more vulnerable and/ or living in relative or absolute poverty (Öktem, 2020; Gough, 2019; Moon, 2019). Bridging these welfare functions, the social capability approach has also been adopted, enabling individual citizens to develop collective networks. The recent re-orientation of welfare systems towards productive forms of social investment may have elevated notions of responsibilisation and individual risk; however, the notion of social capabilities has also been conceptualised in terms of the collective action through social enterprise (Sinthupundaja et al., 2020; Weaver, 2019; Zainol et al., 2019; Carlson et al., 2018).

Critiques of 'new welfare' argue that the primary focus of social policies should be to address structural inequalities across Europe by balancing the redistributive and social investment function of welfare states. Recent contributions have also evidenced the significant role that the Open Method of Coordination (OMC) has played in encouraging flexible kinds of policy-making and cooperation between EU-level, national and sub-national governments across European welfare systems (Vandenbroucke, 2017; Drachenberg and Brianson, 2016). Indeed, it may be argued that the OMC has strengthened the influence of the ESM by enabling monitoring and benchmarking of welfare policies across different welfare systems. Of equal import is the coordinated use of EU funding instruments aimed at rebalancing economic and social inequalities between wealthier and poorer regions and groups within the EU.

Crucially, these measures are supported by EU funding programmes implemented within context of a system of 'shared management'. This system is underpinned by a redistributive approach adopted within European Regional Policy. The allocation of funding to member states is based upon socio-economic conditions and is closely aligned to EU policy goals benchmarked by EU2020 targets. These targets have been adopted as part of the Europe 2020 Strategy, the EU's plan for growth and employment between

2010 and 2020. The strategy focused on smart, sustainable and inclusive growth to support a social market economy. As part of this strategy, the EU adopted targets in five key areas: employment; poverty and social exclusion; education; climate change and energy; and research and development. These targets include the reduction of people at risk of poverty by 20 million and an overall employment rate of 75 per cent across member states (population aged 20–64). Education targets include an increase in the number of people who achieve educational qualifications at tertiary level and above and a reduction in the average share of early school leavers across Europe to less than 10 per cent (European Commission, 2019). Whilst these policy goals reflect an underlying commitment to human well-being, it has also been contended that this commitment is forged within a political economy of work and welfare largely based upon a drive to achieve productive social investment economies which respond effectively to emerging economic and social challenges driven by demographic, technological and environmental transformations.

A central strand of productive social investment economies has been to link capital investment primarily to individual productive capacity. Illustrating this, the central component of inclusive growth within the EU2020 Strategy is inclusion in the labour market, achieved through investment in education and training and broader programmes to improve skills. Importantly, however, another key component of 'inclusive growth' within the EU2020 Strategy is the reduction of levels of poverty, and particularly child poverty, across Europe (European Commission, 2010). However, as the evidence above (Figure 4.2) reveals, growing levels of in-work poverty have exacerbated the lived experience of poverty and social exclusion of people living and working across a number of European countries in recent years. Thus, in many labour markets across Europe low-paid and insecure employment conditions compounded by a deterioration in employment rights and dismantling of collective bargaining processes have led to increasing levels of poverty and social exclusion.

At the same time there are some indications that social protection policies and EU social investment programmes have led to a general decrease in the numbers of children living in very-low-work-intensity households who are also experiencing severe deprivation in most countries since 2010. Critically, however, as Figure 4.4 shows, the number of children living in severe deprivation within very-low-work-intensity households has actually risen substantially in Greece, Cyprus, Lithuania and Romania. Notably also, Belgium and Greece share the second highest level of children living in severe deprivation within very-low-work-intensity households in 2018. This comparative data suggests that variations in the work-welfare policy arrangements, particularly with regard to the relationship between labour market structures and regulations, levels of and entitlement to social protection, and the governance and provision welfare services have led to very different outcomes for children who are at risk of experiencing severe deprivation across different member states in Europe.

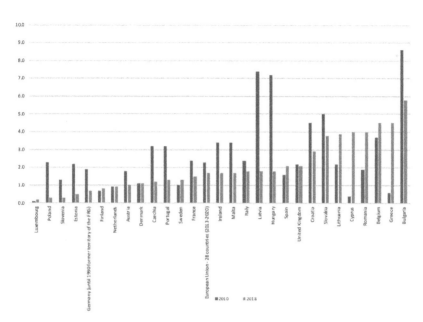

Figure 4.4   *Children and young people (aged less than 18) at risk of severe deprivation in very-low-work-intensity households in 2010 and 2018*

Source: Eurostat, https://ec.europa.eu/eurostat/databrowser/view/t2020_50/default/table?lang=en. Last updated: 8 July 2020

These variations arise within distinct national political economies of work and welfare. Whilst it is the undoubtedly the case that EU countries face unique economic, demographic and social challenges, the role and impact of EU Regional Policy is also an important factor. More broadly, the role of social investment policy strategies directed at work and welfare is a contested area, particularly within the context of neo-liberal ideology. As Malin (2020) argues,

> Moderate interpretations of neoliberalism are grounded on the assumption that the state should fight deprivation but not income inequality because the latter is understood as a precondition of economic prosperity. (p.27)

Thus, the main purpose of social investment within neo-liberal economic paradigms is to increase economic productivity by investing in human capital. 'Social investment' in neo-liberal terms is closely associated with de-regulation of the labour market and the commodification of human labour rather than the protection of employment conditions, particularly with regard to income, which forms the central core of Keynesian interpretations of social investment (Deeming and Smythe, 2015). As evidence presented earlier in this chapter (Figure 4.2) demonstrates, over the last decade income inequality and insecure employment has led to the growth of in-work poverty across most European countries, including Germany, the UK, Austria, the Netherlands, France and Belgium, clearly exposing the price paid by so many as a 'precondition of economic prosperity' during this period.

Critically, however, the European Commission has articulated 'economic growth' as being intrinsically based upon social inclusion and the realisation of human rights (European Commission, 2018a). A pivotal strand of this renewed focus on social inclusion within the operationalisation of EU Regional Policy has been the emphasis on heterogeneous bottom-up forms of network governance involving public, private and third-sector partnerships and place-based approaches. Principles of social partnership designed to increase the effectiveness of EU redistributive regional policies at local level are central to the operationalisation of EU funding instruments such as the ESF and the European Redistributive Development Fund (Bussi et al., 2019; Ellison, 2017; Schraad-Tischler, 2015; Barca, 2009). These principles have guided implementation of ESF funding across Europe since 1988 (European Commission, 2018b; Schraad-Tischler, 2015; Barca, 2009). Collaborative social partnerships between trade unions, employer organisations and other key stakeholders at local level are encouraged and indeed required by EU funding rules. Social dialogue and partnership are regarded as a central pillar of the ESM, legally embedded with the Treaty of Lisbon, Article 152 (European Union, 2007). As argued in Chapter 3 of this book, the institutionalisation of social dialogue began in the period when Jacques Delors was the president of the European Commission, bringing a clear commitment to the development of a unified European social policy integrating EU and national social policies built upon basic values of solidarity and equality. It may be argued that the emergence of a differentiated social model across European states is itself a result of local measures emerging from the Social OMC and concomitant forms of multi-level governance. The impact of distinct forms of multi-level governance, social partnership and social dialogue on the operationalisation of local welfare measures within differentiated welfare settings will now be explored.

THE ROLE OF MULTI-LEVEL GOVERNANCE AND SOCIAL DIALOGUE ON THE IMPLEMENTATION OF EU-WIDE SOCIAL POLICIES WITHIN DIFFERENTIATED WELFARE SETTINGS

The critical exploration of the impact of redistributive European funding instruments on local welfare measures requires full cognisance of the complex organisational and multi-level governing activities, policies and processes across a range of settings and governance levels within Europe. This requires the adoption of a multi-focal theoretical lens. For example, it may be argued that the analysis of the capacity of national governments to effectively implement public policies requires consideration of the complex interaction between agency, setting and power (Clarke and Newman, 2006; Peters and Pierre, 2000). The recent re-positioning of governments across Europe as 'enabling authorities' within new welfare arrangements demonstrates this. However, the dynamic interdependencies between social partners within local welfare processes may be recognised as being equally influential in determining the effectiveness and relevance of specific local welfare measures.

It may be argued that the degree to which these dynamic interdependencies between sectors, institutions and actors within economies and societies are enabled, promoted and sustained may in-itself be regarded as a pre-requisite of social welfare measures and policy changes which are capable of adapting to and even influencing European and global economic cycles. Social policies become pro-active rather than re-active. It is argued that the inclusion of dynamic interdependencies as a central concept overcomes limitations of previous theoretical approaches in this field. For example, in her work on varieties of liberalisation and new politics of social solidarity, Kathleen Thelen (2014) offers a valuable and robust theoretical basis for understanding broader processes of institutional change in three key spheres: industrial relations, vocational education and training and the labour market. Catherine Thelen identifies distinct pathways through which these processes of institutional change have occurred. These pathways are liberalisation and deregulation (declining solidarity and coordination), dualisation (a decline in solidarity but not coordination) and embedded flexibilisation (a decline in coordination but not solidarity). This analysis argues that there has been a fundamental liberalisation in industrial relations with compensatory investment in vocational education and training within national contexts in Europe. However, as Howell and Shand (2014) have noted, this framework does not take account of the influence of forms of multi-level governance across sub-national, national and European levels. It may be argued that it is important to develop a relational analysis of policy learning processes between sub-national, national and EU-level institutions, agencies and stakeholders. This approach also overcomes a central limitation relating to the specificities of socio-economic and institutional variables as understanding processes of policy-making can be regarded as a way of understanding and aligning key concepts to enable broader understandings of the dynamics of policy-change regimes and multi-level governance at EU, national and sub-national level. This may be regarded as particularly important for effective policy learning at both local and national level within differentiated welfare settings. Policy learning is enabled by relating assessments of outcomes and practice-oriented measures within processes of policy-making and social dialogue in the design implementation, and delivery of policy innovations at local level. Indicators such as 'negotiated', 'non-negotiated', 'targeted' and 'universal' are used to understand the relationship between policy innovations and measures, and the assessment of levels of inclusiveness in the policy-making processes and policy outcomes.

Previous theoretical contributions to this approach have also demonstrated its value in understanding the import of distinct forms of governance and social dialogue on policy outcomes at local level within differentiated welfare settings (del Río Villar, 2014; Hemerijck, 2012; Kvist and Saari, 2007). The analysis of influencing factors is complex as outcomes in terms of labour market resilience and social inclusion are shaped by a confluence of interacting macro-economic, demographic, fiscal, social, political and governance dimensions which may be regarded as dynamic interdependencies. Data from the INSPIRES project (2014) illustrated the impact of transnational economic factors, forms of governance and policy learning upon policy innovations within Europe. In particular, empirical data gathered by the project informs our understanding of how the financial recession of 2007–2008 impacted upon distinct socio-economic conditions and policies, labour markets, and social and employment policies and innovations. A model for understanding and investigating these processes derived from the initial analysis of innovations in INSPIRES countries between 2000 and 2016 is provided in Figure 4.5. It may be argued that forms of governance and policy learning contribute to or constrain social dialogue and new collaborative, cooperative or coordinating partnerships between public-, third- and private-sector institutions.

The integration of local policies within distinct forms of multi-level governance and social dialogue is evidenced by distinct social policy programmes within diverse welfare settings across Europe. Recent evidence has revealed that whilst clear variations between national settings are evident there are also clear commonalities, particularly with regard to the commitment to network governance and partnership (Milana et al., 2020; Daly et al., 2019; Lees, 2019; Sielker and Stead, 2019; Stead et al., 2016). Social measures and programmes such as the Jobs and Skills in the Local Economy Partnership and the BRIDGE Project in Rotterdam and Local Employment Partnerships (LEPs) in Scotland

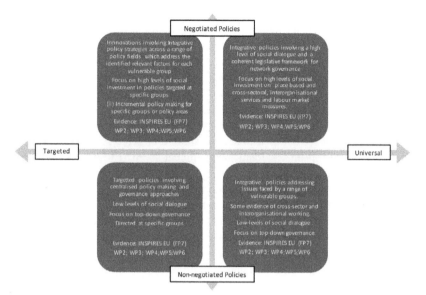

Figure 4.5   *A model for understanding the role of governance, policy learning, social dialogue and collaboration within policy innovation. Author's own model*

illustrate projects which operationalise notions of heterogenous network governance involving public-, private- and third-sector partnerships.

Whilst it is also is clear from recent empirical data that the EU2020 targets relating to poverty and social inclusion and education have not been reached there is growing evidence that the effectiveness and relevance of EU redistributive funding programmes have been strengthened by heterogeneous bottom-up forms of network governance involving public-, private- and third-sector partnerships. More broadly, partnership agreements between the EU and locally operationalised welfare programmes are viewed as promoting social cohesion and social solidarity with the EU (Telle, 2019; Ellison, 2017; Vaughan-Whitehead, 2015; Ellison, 2011). EU funding programmes are evidenced as playing a key role in supporting locally developed welfare measures and programmes. The ESF distributes €80 billion across European societies, being the central funding mechanism for local projects which focus on EU policy initiatives.

The allocation of funding to member states and regions is determined by their Gross Domestic Product per head relative to the EU average. There are three distinct funding levels for 'more developed regions', less developed regions and transition regions. Local projects are co-financed by national funding at a level between 15 per cent and 50 per cent. Projects focusing upon promoting social inclusion and combating poverty make up at least 20 per cent of European funding allocation. The ESF regulation Article 4.2 states that 'At least 20% of the total ESF resources in each Member State shall be allocated to the thematic objective "promoting social inclusion, combating poverty and any discrimination"' (European Commission, 2019, p.6).

Projects are funded under four thematic objectives (employment, education, social inclusion and public services). Projects include funding for childcare provision, support for children in social care and targeted services for Roma children. The European Regional Development Fund (ERDF), is designed to support member states by investing in regional development to reduce economic and social inequities between regions. A total of €196 billion was allocated to the ERDF for the period between 2014–2020; of this, €5.9 was allocated to educational infrastructure with €1.22 billion allocated to early years education and care infrastructure. Examples of projects include the transition of children with disabilities from large-scale institutional settings to community-based care and the Fund for European Aid to the Most Deprived (FEAD), which provides direct material support and social inclusion measures for citizens experiencing poverty, and disadvantaged households.

These projects support the most vulnerable in European societies. FEAD programmes are often used to support vulnerable children. Exemplifying this, Austria, Romania and Cyprus utilise FEAD funds to provide school supplies for children from low-income households. In Germany, FEAD funds are used to help migrant children in early years care, and in Hungary FEAD funds provide direct food aid for families with children under the age of 18. Critically, national governments are responsible for the efficient distribution of FEAD funding. The UK government failed to distribute its €3.96 million allocation of FEAD funding between 2014 and 2020 despite increasing levels of food poverty in the UK, as evidenced by the distribution of 823,145 emergency food parcels to people in crisis between April and September 2019, a 23 per cent increase on the previous year (Dempsey, 2020). According to the World Bank, nearly two million people in the UK are undernourished (World Bank, 2019). An initial programme to use FEAD funds to expand the UK's Breakfast Club provision did not meet FEAD eligibility criteria. The UK government failed to find an alternative use for the money during the whole six-year funding period and was forced to return an interim payment of €433,000 it had used on the originally planned programme. Whilst the UK government eventually agreed to use the funding for a programme which would support young refugees and potential victims of modern slavery, this agreement came too late and the funding was lost.

Commenting on the failure to direct FEAD funding to vulnerable people in the UK, Lord Jay, the Chair of the EU Home Affairs Sub-Committee, investigating the discrepancy, stated that

> The Government had an opportunity to help support the most disadvantaged people in the UK but has instead wasted over half a million pounds of its FEAD allocation through its inability to develop a suitable project. The Committee rejected the Government's explanation that the eligibility rules of the fund were too restrictive, and its administrative requirements too burdensome, noting the many and varied FEAD activities that other Member States have been able to implement. The proposed programme to support young refugees and potential victims of modern slavery is very welcome, but it is astonishing that it has taken the Government so long to come up with a possible FEAD project. With €600,000 of the UK allocation already gone, a further €600,000 is now at risk. With the prospect of a "no deal" Brexit on the horizon, the Committee has called for urgent clarity on how this would affect the UK's access to FEAD money. The clock is ticking. (House of Lords, 2019; also quoted in Peat, 2019)

Whilst it may be argued the failure of the UK government to allocate FEAD funding to vulnerable people represents a major policy failure at central government level, it is nevertheless the case that regions within the UK have benefited substantially from European funding. Exemplifying this, LEPs in Scotland are supported by the ERDF. The development and operationalisation of LEPs in Scotland is premised upon notions of heterogeneous network governance involving public-, private- and third-sector partnerships in the country (Ellison, 2020; Bertin and Ellison, 2019; McQuaid, 2012; Damgaard and Torfing, 2010).

An appreciation of the impact of LEPs requires an in-depth analysis of diverse LEPs across all 32 local authorities in Scotland. This involves the analysis of distinct network goals within each local authority and substantive network tasks. Following Considine (2013), institutional network goals are regarded as the kind of partnership within distinct LEPs; i.e. cooperative (knowledge exchange, sharing of information), coordinative (joint service plans) or collaborative (joint services, pooling of resources). Substantive tasks within each LEP describe the types of outputs or outcomes aimed for. In Scotland LEPs are embedded within multi-sectoral and multi-agency Community Planning Partnerships involving public agencies such as Health, Social Work and Housing. The way in which LEPs operationalise Scottish Government policies and the extent to which networks were actively cooperative and collaborative was found to be critical to the effectiveness of LEPs in Scotland (Ellison, 2020). These findings reflect previous findings relating to the impact of resourcing, social dialogue and collaboration on the achievement of goals, particularly with regard to the use of EU structural and social funds (Knuth, 2014; Lindsay and McQuaid, 2008; Saikku and Karjalainen, 2012).

The main substantive tasks of LEPs are to develop a local strategy and to proactively support data-sharing between partners. The aim is to provide seamless services to local people and employers. Shared data is utilised within the planning, commissioning and targeting of services to evaluate the impact of employment programmes and services on outcomes for local people and employers. In addition, LEPs are responsible for the development of robust systems and processes which develop opportunities for the co-location of services to:

1. Support individuals within the labour market.
2. Speed up an individual's entry into work.
3. Create a 'no wrong door' approach, so they are accessible via a wide range of sources.
4. Foster a partnership approach to the planning and delivery of services by developing relationships between staff in all delivery organisations operating within a local area.
5. Ensure that front-line practitioners within a local area have a clear understanding of their respective roles, enabling them to tailor services to the needs of individuals.
6. Encourage regular informal information-sharing.

The development of LEP networks in Scotland has been largely shaped by devolved institutional and socio-economic arrangements. Since the financial crisis in 2007–2008 distinctive social and employment policies and governance networks in Scotland have been framed within the broad policy architecture of 'constructive advantage', a dual-investment approach designed to build economic and labour market resilience whilst also reducing economic and social inequalities. Employability programmes designed to support vulnerable groups in the labour market are combined with significant inward investment in key economic growth sectors at local level. More broadly this approach is located within cross-cutting public-sector policies intrinsically linked to the 'Solidarity Purpose', defined as 'unlocking the economic potential of all individuals will support economic growth by increasing labour market participation and by removing the personal and social costs of poverty' (Scottish Government, 2012, p.7). Economic growth is regarded as being contingent upon reducing income inequality and the improvement of access to employment opportunities, especially for those on lower incomes. Within this context unemployment is defined as a complex, multi-dimensional problem requiring local solutions delivered collaboratively by local stakeholders including employers, public service providers and educational and training bodies. As such, local employers, particularly small and medium enterprises (SMEs), have been encouraged and incentivised to collaborate and lead on the design of local employability initiatives, and delivery at local level. SMEs make up 99.3 per cent of all private-sector enterprises in Scotland and account for 54.7 per cent of private-sector employment and 36.7 per cent of private-sector turnover (Scottish Government, 2018). The limited scope of engagement of SMEs in employer-oriented measures at local level has been a major challenge for LEPs. In terms of context, a significant variable shaping the institutional network goals and substantive tasks of LEPs are the local economic and social conditions in which they are situated. Moreover, recent data has indicated widening levels of income inequality at national level, and growing levels of relative poverty in Scotland (Scottish Government, 2018). Crucially, these projects also operate within a fragile labour market characterised by an increase in 'precarious' forms of low-paid employment, including casual, short-term and zero-hours contracts (ONS, 2020). Despite these trends, recent evaluations of ESF-funded projects have revealed LEPs as making a positive difference to outcomes for vulnerable people in Scotland. This approach is also taken in relation to key social policy programmes in the Netherlands.

The central aim of the Jobs and Skills in the Local Economy Partnership in the municipality of Rotterdam is to align young people's educational opportunities and choices with future labour market needs. These challenges are also reflected in the Urban Innovative Actions project, BRIDGE, led by the municipality of Rotterdam. This is delivered through a career and talent orientation programme that covers children from primary school age (9 years) to student entry into the labour market. Rotterdam, which is one of the coordinators of the Jobs and Skills in the Local Economy Partnership under the Urban Agenda for the EU (UAEU), ensures an integrated approach by linking its innovative solutions, 'Urban Innovative Actions' (UIAs), and its experience with the 'Integrated Territorial Investment' (ITI) to the partnership, inspiring many other cities in the Netherlands. Both in terms of UIAs and the UAEU, Rotterdam is engaged in generating plans and actions grounded in effective governance based on partnership, a central strand of the new EU Cohesion Policy for 2021–2027. At programme level, URBACT has examined the changing EU context for cities in relation to jobs and future skills as well. This work has drawn on the experiences of cities and has been informed by good practice across Europe. The URBACT programme is the European Territorial Cooperation programme which aims to encourage sustainable integrated urban development in cities across Europe and is a central instrument of European Cohesion Policy. It was cofounded by the ERDF and the 28 member states, plus Switzerland and Norway. URBACT's mission is to enable cities to work together and develop integrated solutions to common urban challenges, by networking, learning from one another's experiences, drawing lessons and identifying good practices to improve urban policies.

FUTURE SKILLS

The current Covid-19 health pandemic has exposed ways in which the EU and global socio-economic context is changing profoundly. In particular, it has revealed profound challenges emerging from inter-related inequalities across European societies. In order to address these challenges, it will be important to invest in the development of future skills programmes which support effective and sustainable relationships between public health, work and formal care within economies of well-being. An innovative approach will be needed to identify the skills that people need across post-Covid-19 European societies. It may be argued that a central strand of this approach will be to ensure that people who live in Europe have equitable access to lifelong education and training. In particular, as Ulf-Daniel Ehlers (2020) argues, it is important to identify the skills that people will need to cope with constant development and adaptation to new situations and working life. In particular, digitalisation and Artificial Intelligence (AI) have already had a significant impact on working life. When combined with the lived realities of adapting to post-Covid-19 working environments, this ability to cope with new developments will become critical. Learning designs and pedagogic approaches within lifelong education and training will also need to be relevant to current challenges and adaptable to new developments (Brewster and Holland 2020; Ehlers, 2020). Crucially, it may be argued that addressing the challenges emerging from these new technological and ecological conditions requires a renewed focus on social and economic democracy, particularly at local level. More specifically, cross-sectoral approaches centring on governance and invest-ment strategies which facilitate place-based socio-economic measures and collaborative cross-sector partnerships will support skills which are relevant to distinctive local contexts. It may also be argued that the recalibration of work and well-being in knowledge-driven, environmentally sustainable economies of well-being within these local contexts will also be necessary to meet these challenges (Hanaček et al., 2020; Hupkau and Petrongolo, 2020; Muradian and Pascual, 2020; Peters, 2020; Sulkowski, 2020).

Exemplifying this, Dubb (2016) critically analyses the capacity of local government to operationalise a more comprehensive strategy for shared well-being at local level. New organisational forms, such as Social Enterprise Ownership (SEO) at urban community level, employee stock ownership plans (ESOP), Cooperatives, Community Development Corporations (CDCs) and Community Development Financial Institutions (CDFIs), demonstrate the potential for more democratic economic planning at local level. Illustrating this, CDCs are non-profit, community-based organisations which are involved in a range of measures critical to community health, such as affordable housing, neighbourhood planning projects and lifelong education and social service provision. It may be argued that cross-sectoral, horizontal forms of democratic governance are critical in ensuring effective and sustainable relationships between public health, work, material well-being, formal care and informal social care within local economies of well-being. The actualisation of individual and collective resources at community level also relies on social investment measures which recognise the critical importance of progressive government policies such as accessible and equitable lifelong worker training and education, and investment in social care and childcare for the well-being of citizens (Kristensen, 2016).

As Kristensen (2016) argues, progressive government policies such as accessible and equitable lifelong training and education for all, and substantial investment in public social care and childcare provision, are central to the development of economically sustainable well-being economies.

A unifying theme across these socio-economic proposals is the importance of economic and social democracy. This theme is also central to economic models which focus on the green economy as a socio-ecological alternative which centres on human development and ecological regeneration (Hanaček et al., 2020; Muradian and Pascual, 2020; Spash, 2020; Tracker, 2020). Exemplifying this, Brian Milani's seminal work *Designing the Green Economy* (2000) argues that new productive forces driven by human cultural development are re-defining the nature of wealth itself from an emphasis on the quantitative accumulation of money and material wealth which is depleting the earth's natural resources, creating climate crises and inequality, to an emphasis on qualitative definitions of wealth which focus on individual and community well-being and ecological regeneration. Miliani argues that a progressive economic model requires the implementation of social and ecological alternatives which focus on human and community development and ecological regeneration.

This fundamental re-orientation of economics to a focus on human well-being has been proposed in a number of recent contributions (Allin and Hand, 2014; McGregor and Sumner, 2010; Stiglitz et al., 2009). Exemplifying this, McGregor (2007) argues for the conceptualisation of well-being as encompassing a comprehensive, hybrid conception of living well, merging notions of objective and subjective well-being. Well-being is comprised of three interacting dimensions: a material dimension, a relational dimension and a subjective dimension. Critically, McGregor argues that in order to generate well-being for people, all three of these dimensions need to be considered together as no single dimension provides sufficient insight into the well-being of an individual. The well-being of individuals in society arises from the interaction of their material well-being (what they have), their relational well-being (how they are able to use what they have) and their subjective view of their quality of their life (what they derive from what they have and can do; McGregor, 2007). Arising from this McGregor argues for economic pluralism. As people conceptualise well-being in distinct ways, so they have different views on what should be done to enable individual and community well-being to occur. Therefore, people should be encouraged to develop pluralistic ways of understanding and evaluating their local economy. This requires dialogical approaches to local economic regeneration. It is therefore crucial that an inclusive approach is taken to negotiations between all partners involved in local community regeneration strategies.

More recent transformational economic alternatives have coalesced around the concept of the Foundational Economy (Plank, 2020; Heslop et al., 2019; Barbera et al., 2018; Earle et al., 2018; Froud and Williams, 2018; Engelen et al., 2017; Bowman et al., 2014). At its core a Foundational Economy requires the operationalisation of UBS as an entitlement granted to all who live and work in European societies. This approach replaces market-based distributive approaches which focus on boosting private consumption by delivering economic growth. In essence, within a Foundational Economy, a network of provisioning systems designed to satisfy a plurality of non-substitutable needs is organised to ensure the quantity and quality of foundational services. It is argued that whilst part of this network will remain within the scope of the market, the central principles underlying UBS provide the architecture for collective provision based on access to services as a human right, citizen participation, local control and diverse models of ownership. Critically, it is argued that a Foundational Economy would offer a more equitable, efficient and sustainable distribution of services and goods required for non-substitutional needs than market transactions. The Covid-19 health pandemic has stimulated the spontaneous creation of local community and neighbourhood-based projects to distribute food and care services to meet non-substitutional needs, particularly to those people who are most vulnerable and socially isolated across European societies (ESPON, 2020). The European Commission has recently operationalised a plethora of measures to facilitate these projects. The Coronavirus Response Investment Initiative is designed to mobilise European Cohesion Policy by responding flexibly to identified needs in key sectors such as health care, labour markets and SMEs. Articulated as an initiative aimed at supporting the most affected regions in Europe and their citizens, the investment fund is consistent with the redistributive, cross-sectoral partnership principles which underpin the requirements for European social funding and European redistributive funding (ESPON, 2020). The initiative will distribute €8 billion of funding to meet immediate needs within a total public investment package of €37 billion to consolidate new initiatives at local level as part of a €2.4 trillion European recovery plan (European Commission, 2014). Importantly, the funding aims to ensure flexibility in applying EU spending rules and also extends the scope of the European Solidarity Fund (EUSF). Moreover, the Coronavirus Response Investment Initiative Plus funding initiative incorporates a number of additional measures designed to support community initiatives which have emerged spontaneously as a result of the Covid-19 crisis. A number of these community-based solutions have been facilitated by existing place-based community models of governance.

PLACE-BASED APPROACHES WITHIN COMMUNITY REGENERATION STRATEGIES

Place-making is a concept central to community planning across a growing number of national and local settings in Europe (Ellison, 2020; Bertin and Ellison, 2019). It describes a dialogical process enabling collaborative, inclusive approaches to advancing the quality of lived experiences within geographical spaces. Geographical spaces or communities are regarded as physical and socio-emotional spheres of activity (Gieryn, 2000; Hidalgo and Hernandez, 2001; Proshansky et al., 1983). Critically, the socio-emotional spheres of activity, which define place, are constructed through human interaction and experience. As Relph (1976) argues, 'While place meanings are rooted in the physical setting and its activities, they are not a property of them but a property of human interaction and experiences of those places' (p.47). Thus, it may be argued that meaningful community planning requires the collaborative and inclusive participation of members of the community as a collective process of place-making. The production of public knowledge through dialogue is central to this collective process. Importantly, place is thus socially contested involving learning, movement and fluidity. The realisation of public knowledge thus relies on partnership. As Rule (2015) argues,

> Dialogue is an unfolding process, a search or quest for knowledge and understanding usually through the medium of spoken language, but not excluding written and visual codes, involving partners who are committed to this quest. Thus, dialogue assumes relationship and is impossible without it. This is one of the differences between dialogue, on the one hand, and monologue and diatribe, on the other. (p.2)

The concept of partnership is thus central to meaningful and productive dialogical processes. As a contested concept, partnership has been theorised and evidenced as a collaborative, fluid and dynamic relationship between stakeholders within and across communities and societies (McCrea and Finnegan, 2019; Vanleene and Verschuere, 2018; Christens and Speer, 2006). A number of theorists have identified the central characteristic of partnership as being a collaborative relationship leading to innovative approaches and outcomes through unpredictable, fluid forms of decision-making (Chandler, 2019; Gilchrist, 2019; Rees et al., 2012).

A central concern of recent research has been the influence of power dynamics within collaborative partnerships within and across communities and societies (Chandler, 2019; Gilchrist, 2019; McCrea and Finnegan, 2019; Vanleene and Verschuere, 2018; Rees et al., 2012; Christens and Speer, 2006). Exemplifying the growing influence of place-based approaches within national policy frameworks, the Scottish government has undoubtedly created possibilities for publics to express their welfare needs and priorities. The adoption of innovative place-based programmes at local level is integral to the reform of public services in Scotland. Place-based approaches integrate and operationalise the key principles of public-sector reform participation, partnership, prevention and performance as outlined by the Christie Report (2011). A key recommendation of the Christie Commission, which was set up by the Scottish Government in 2010 to examine the future delivery of public services in Scotland, was to focus on place in the reform of public services as a re-orientation towards locality. This re-orientation provides a focus for local people to improve communities whilst also moving away from silo working by individual service providers. Thus, the Report argued that, 'Many effective solutions to the complex challenges we face – from tackling crime to improving public health – lie locally. The best ideas and most effective solutions will often come from those with the most direct experience of the issues at hand – that is, users of services and frontline workers' (Scottish Government, 2011, p.10). Innovative place-based approaches have been developed at neighbourhood level by most Community Planning Partnerships in response to requirements of Audit Scotland and the Community Empowerment Act (2015). These dialogical bottom-up approaches are pivotal to integrated strategic community planning across all local authorities in Scotland (Scottish Government, 2013). Local Community Partnerships involving public-, private- and third-sector stakeholders – including organisations such as WhoCaresScotland, which is run by and working for care-experienced young people – are a statutory requirement within all 32 local authorities.

Here the focus is on supporting communities to do things for themselves, ensuring that their 'voices are heard in order to bring about a real and sustainable reduction in inequalities' (Scottish Government, 2015). It may be argued that public knowledge in the form of collective intelligence is critical to this transformative agenda; it is also important to ensure that public knowledge at community level is part of broader dialogical processes across Europe.

CONCLUSION

The importance of differentiated solutions involving unique policy mixes at national level, social dialogue and multi-level governance are evidenced in this chapter as offering an effective and meaningful basis for the operationalisation of the ESM. The development of specific policy mixes and policy strategies have benefited from the further strengthening of European Cohesion Policy and European funding mechanisms. Local polices are integrated within distinct forms of multi-level governance bolstered by an emphasis on social partnership and dialogue. The evidence in this chapter has illustrated that whilst there are clear variations between European national settings, there are also unifying tendencies, including the commitment to network governance and partnership. Local social measures, such as LEPs in Scotland and the Jobs and Skills in the Local Economy Partnership and BRIDGE Project in Rotterdam, are place-based partnerships designed to encourage local collaborative work among public-, private- and third-sector organisations. It may be argued that a central function of heterogenous network governance should be to ensure that local policy approaches inform national policy and fiscal arrangements in order to address persistent structural challenges and inter-regional inequalities in Europe. Exemplifying this, a central aim of the EU is to support fair and well-functioning labour markets and social protection systems at national level with the ultimate goal of creating better-performing economies and more equitable societies in Europe. Critically, however, the realisation of this aim is mediated by the extent to which member states are committed to the maintenance of adequate systems of social protection and well-functioning labour markets. The design and implementation of national social policies and legally embedded employment rights define the degree to which each member state operationalises fair and functioning labour markets. The recent emphasis on reviving the ESM as a central plank of European integration legitimated by the ESPR is an attempt to overcome different policy approaches between member states. A fundamental part of the ESPR is to ensure that people living and working in Europe have the right to adequate minimum income benefits and welfare services to enable them to experience a life defined by dignity and the opportunity for self-actualisation. However, as a plethora of recent research has shown the lived experiences of many people who live and work in Europe do not reflect aspects of the ESPR (Cantillon et al., 2019; Goedemé et al., 2019; Sandermann, 2014).

As this chapter has shown, the operationalisation of European Cohesion Policy, guided by EU2020 targets on social inclusion, has had a positive impact on the well-being of people living and working in Europe, particularly in terms of the realisation of effective and meaningful measures at local level.

However, it may be argued that any attempt to repair the social fabric of Europe will require a re-invention of the fundamental principles underpinning the European Social and Economic Union. Recognition of the mutual inter-dependence of economy and society requires substantial public investment in innovative place-based cross-sectoral policies which promote inclusive, equitable and ecologically sustainable societies. Exemplifying this, it may be argued that alternative economic models such as the Foundational Economy involving UBS and policy ideas such as the Universal Basic Income and a recalibration of work and well-being within a digital economy (Gentilini et al., 2019; Sloman, 2019; Taylor and Bronstone, 2019) will need to be revisited to ensure resilience at times of crises (Marmot, 2020; Plank, 2020; Sułkowski, 2020; Gentilini et al., 2019; Gironde and Carbonnier, 2019; Heslop et al., 2019; Barbera et al., 2018; Froud and Williams, 2018; Engelen et al., 2017; Bowman et al., 2014). A vital lesson to us all within the current health crisis is surely that we must focus on forms of economic and social solidarity which place health equity at the heart of future social policies within well-being economies in Europe (Marmot, 2020; Trebeck and Williams, 2019). As Marmot (2020) argues, 'What the Covid crisis exposes is that we can do things differently. We must not go back to the status quo, we cannot do that' (Marmot, 2020).

The existential crisis we all face in Europe reminds us of previous periods in European history when we have had to find common purpose and common solutions for our mutual benefit. The ESM offers a flexible collaborative architecture for the operationalisation of a post-Covid-19 European well-being economy delivered within innovative economic infrastructures such as the Foundational Economy (Plank, 2020; Heslop et al., 2019; Barbera et al., 2018; Earle et al., 2018; Froud and Williams, 2018; Engelen et al., 2017; Bowman et al., 2014). Existing synergies and alignments between the architecture of the ESM, particularly with regard to place-based approaches and innovative economic infrastructures such as the Foundational Economy, will facilitate the equitable and sustainable delivery of universal services and measures vital to the health and well-being of all who live and work in Europe.

REFERENCES

Abrahamson, P., Greve, B., and Boje, T. (2019). *Welfare and Families in Europe*. London: Routledge.

Allin, P., and Hand, D. J. (2014). *The Wellbeing of Nations: Meaning, Motive and Measurement*. Edinburgh: John Wiley & Sons.

Armano, E., Bove, A., and Murgia, A. (eds) 2017. *Mapping Precariousness, Labour Insecurity and Uncertain Livelihoods: Subjectivities and Resistance*. London: Routledge.

Barbera, F., Negri, N., and Salento, A. (2018). From individual choice to collective voice: foundational economy, local commons and citizenship. *Rassegna Italiana di Sociologia*, **59** (2), 371–398.

Barca, F. (2009). *An Agenda for a Reformed Cohesion Policy: A Place-Based Approach to Meeting European Union Challenges and Expectations*. Independent report. www .dps.mef.gov.it/documentazione/comunicati/2010/report_barca_v0306.pdf.

Barr, B., Kinderman, P., and Whitehead, M. (2015). Trends in mental health inequalities in England during a period of recession, austerity and welfare reform 2004 to 2013. *Social Science & Medicine*, 147, 324–331.

Bauhardt, C., and Harcourt, W. (2018). *Feminist Political Ecology and the Economics of Care in Search of Economic Alternatives*. London: Routledge.

Berger, T., and Frey, C. B. (2016). *Structural Transformation in the OECD: Digitalisation, Deindustrialisation and the Future of Work*. Paris: OECD Publishing. https://doi.org/10.1787/5jlr068802f7-en.

Bertin, G., and Ellison, M. (2019). Social innovation and metagovernance of welfare policies. *Salute e società*, 2, 40–56.

Billing, C., McCann, P., and Ortega-Argilés, R. (2019). Interregional inequalities and UK sub-national governance responses to Brexit. *Regional Studies*, 53, 741–760.

Bjørn, A., Isaksen, A., and Trippl, M. (2019). *Regional Economic Advantage*. Cheltenham, UK, and Northampton, MA: Edward Elgar Publishing.

Blit, J., Amand, S. S., and Wajda, J. (2018). *Automation and the Future of Work: Scenarios and Policy Options*. Waterloo: Centre for International Governance Innovation. www.deslibris.ca/ID/10096711.

Bowman, A., Ertürk, I., Froud, J., Johal, S., and Law, J., 2014. *The End of the Experiment? From Competition to the Foundational Economy*. Manchester: Manchester University Press.

Bozorgmehr, K., Saint, V., Kaasch, A., Stuckler, D., and Kentikelenis, A. (2020). COVID and the convergence of three crises in Europe. *The Lancet Public Health*, **5** (5), e247–e248.

Brell, C., Dustmann, C., and Preston, I. (2020). The labor market integration of refugee migrants in high-income countries. *Journal of Economic Perspectives*, **34** (1), 94–121.

Brewster, C., and Holland, P. (2020). Work or employment in the 21st century: its impact on the employment relationship, in: Wilkinson, A., and Barry, M. (eds), *The Future of Work and Employment* (pp.19–32). Cheltenham, UK, and Northampton, MA: Edward Elgar Publishing.

Brien, P. (2018). UK funding from the EU. House of Commons Briefing Paper No. 7847, January 10. http://researchbriefings.files.parliament.uk/documents/CBP -7847/CBP-7847.pdf.

Bussi, M., Hvinden, B., and Schoyen, M. A. (2019). Has the European Social Fund been effective in supporting young people? in: Hvinden, B., Hyggen, C., Schoyen, M. A., and Sirovátka, T. (eds), *Youth Unemployment and Job Insecurity in Europe* (pp.206–229). Cheltenham, UK, and Northampton, MA: Edward Elgar Publishing.

Cantillon, B., Goedemé, T., and Hills, J. (2019). *Decent Incomes for All: Improving Policies in Europe*. New York: Oxford University Press.

Carlson, E., and Koch, J. (2018). *Building a Successful Social Venture: A Guide for Social Entrepreneurs*. San Francisco, CA: Berrett-Koehler.

Carrera, S., and Vankova, Z. (2019). Human rights aspects of immigrant and refugee integration policies: a comparative assessment in selected Council of Europe member states. Council of Europe Working Paper. https://cadmus.eui.eu/handle/1814/62307.

Castrén, M. (2020). *After Austerity: Welfare State Transformation in Europe after the Great Recession.* [Review]. *Journal of Common Market Studies,* **58** (1), 209–210.

Chandler, S. M. (2019). *Making Collaboratives Work: How Complex Organizational Partnerships Succeed.* Abingdon: Routledge.

Chertkovskaya, E., Paulsson, A., and Barca, S. (2019). *Towards a Political Economy of Degrowth.* Lanham: Rowman and Littlefield.

Christens, B., and Speer, P.W. (2006). Review essay: tyranny/transformation – power and paradox in participatory development. *Forum Qualitative Sozialforschung/Forum: Qualitative Social Research,* **7** (2). http://dx.doi.org/10.17169/fqs-7.2.91.

Clarke, J., and Newman, J. (2006). *The Managerial State: Power, Politics and Ideology in the Remaking of Social Welfare.* London: SAGE.

Cominetti, N., Gardiner, L., and Kelly, G. (2020). What happens after the clapping finishes: the pay, terms and conditions we choose for our care workers. Resolution Foundation.   www.resolutionfoundation.org/publications/what-happens-after-the-clapping-finishes/.

Connolly, J., MacGillivray, S., Munro, A., Mulhern, T., Anderson, J., Gray, N., and Toma, M. (2020). How co-production and co-creation is understood, implemented and sustained as part of improvement programme delivery within the health and social care context in Scotland. University of the West of Scotland. https://siscc.dundee.ac.uk/wp-content/uploads/2020/04/siscc-copro-redux.pdf.

Considine, M. (2013). Governance networks and the question of transformation. *Public Administration,* **91** (2), 438–447.

Couture, V., Gaubert, C., Handbury, J., and Hurst, E. (2019). *Income Growth and the Distributional Effects of Urban Spatial Sorting* (No. w26142). Stanford: National Bureau of Economic Research.

D'Costa, S., and Overman, H. (2013). The urban wage growth premium: evidence from British cities. 53rd Congress of the European Regional Science Association: 'Regional Integration: Europe, the Mediterranean and the World Economy', 27–31 August 2013, Palermo, Italy. European Regional Science Association (ERSA). http://hdl.handle.net/10419/123983.

Dajani, D. (2020). Refuge under austerity: the UK's refugee settlement schemes and the multiplying practices of bordering. *Ethnic and Racial Studies.* https://doi.org/10.1080/01419870.2020.1715453.

Daly, S., Pegan, A., and Shaw, K. (2019). Co-Production and Co-Governance, COGOV European Union Research Project. Horizon 2020 (Grant Agreement Number: 770591). Public Value and Co-Creation in the Renewal of Public Agencies across Europe. http://cogov.eu/wp-content/uploads/2019/10/COGOV-Deliverable-1.2_Aug-19_submitted.pdf.

Damgaard, B., and Torfing, J. (2010). Network governance of active employment policy: the Danish experience. *Journal of European Social Policy,* **20** (3), 248–262.

Davis, A., Hirsch, D., and Padley, M. (2018). The Minimum Income Standard as a benchmark of a 'participatory social minimum'. *Journal of Poverty and Social Justice,* **26** (1), 19–34.

Deeming, C., and Smyth, P. (2015). Social investment after neoliberalism: policy paradigms and political platforms. *Journal of Social Policy,* **44** (2), 297–318. https://doi.org/10.1017/S0047279414000828.

Del Río Villar, S. (2014). *Europe: Project and Process – Citizens, Democracy, Participation.* Brussels: PIE-Peter Lang. http://nbn-resolving.de/urn:nbn:de:101:1 -2014110416325.

Della Porta, D. (2018). Contentious moves: mobilising for refugees' rights, in: Della Porta, D. (ed.), *Solidarity Mobilizations in the 'Refugee Crisis'* (pp.1–38). Cham: Palgrave Macmillan.

Dempsey, D. (2020). Food insecurity, in-work poverty and gender: a literature review. Report No. 6. UWS-Oxfam Partnership Collaborative Research Reports Series. http:// uwsoxfampartnership.org.uk/wp-content/uploads/2020/06/Food-Insecurity-Literature -Review-Final.pdf.

Dengler, K. (2019). Effectiveness of active labour market programmes on the job quality of welfare recipients in Germany. *Journal of Social Policy*, **48** (4), 807–838.

Deusdad, B. A., Pace, C., and Anttonen, A. (2016). Facing the challenges in the development of long-term care for older people in Europe in the context of an economic crisis. *Journal of Social Service Research*, **42** (2), 144–150.

Dijkstra, L., Garcilazo, E., and McCann, P. (2015). The effects of the global financial crisis on European regions and cities. *Journal of Economic Geography*, **15** (5), 935–949.

Drachenberg, R., and Brianson, A. (2016). Policy-making in the European Union, in: Cini, M., and Pérez-Solórzano Borragán, N. (eds), *European Union Politics*, 5th ed. (pp.197–213). Oxford: Oxford University Press.

Dubb, S. (2016). Community wealth building forms: what they are and how to use them at the local level. *Academy of Management Perspectives*, **30** (2), 141–152.

Earle, J., Froud, J., Johal, S., and Williams, K. (2018). Foundational economy and foundational politics. *Welsh Economic Review*, 26, 38–45.

Ehlers, U. D. (2020). *Future Skills: The Future of Learning and Higher Education.* Norderstedt: BoD – Books on Demand. https://www.learntechlib.org/p/208249/.

Elliott, I. (2016). *Poverty and Mental Health: A Review to Inform the Joseph Rowntree Foundation's Anti-Poverty Strategy.* London: Mental Health Foundation.

Elliott, I. C. (2020). The implementation of a strategic state in a small country setting: the case of the 'Scottish Approach'. *Public Money & Management*, **40** (4), 285–293.

Elliott, I., Fejszes, V., and Tàrrega, M. (2019). The Community Empowerment Act and localism under devolution in Scotland: the perspective of multiple stakeholders in a council ward. *International Journal of Public Sector Management*, **32** (3), 302–319. https://doi.org/10.1108/IJPSM-03-2018-0080.

Ellison, M. (2020). The construction, role and influence of 'public knowledge' within Community Planning Partnerships, in: Scandrett, E. (ed.), *Public Sociology Education* (pp.199–216). Bristol: Policy Press.

Ellison, M. (2017). Through the looking glass: young people, work and the transition between education and employment in a post-Brexit UK. *Journal of Social Policy*, **46** (4), 675–698.

Ellison, M. (2014). No future to risk? The impact of economic crises and austerity on the inclusion of young people within distinct European labour market settings, in Farnsworth, K., Irving, Z., and Fenger, M. (eds), *Social Policy Review 26: Analysis and Debate in Social Policy* (pp.155–179). Bristol: Policy Press.

Ellison, M. (ed.) (2011). *Reinventing Social Solidarity across Europe.* Bristol: Policy Press.

Ellison, M., and Fenger, M. (2013). Introduction: 'new' welfare in practice – trends, challenges and dilemmas. *Social Policy and Society*, **12** (4), 547–552.

Endale, T., St. Jean, N., and Birman, D. (2020). COVID-19 and refugee and immigrant youth: a community-based mental health perspective. *Psychological Trauma: Theory, Research, Practice, and Policy*, **12** (S1), S225–S227.

Engelen, E., Froud, J., Johal, S., Salento, A., and Williams, K. (2017). The grounded city: from competitivity to the foundational economy. *Cambridge Journal of Regions, Economy and Society*, **10** (3), 407–423.

ESPON (2020). Collecting experiences and evidence on local and regional responses to COVID19. www.espon.eu/covid19.

Eurofound (2020). *COVID-19: Policy Responses across Europe*. Luxembourg: Publications Office of the European Union. www.eurofound.europa.eu/sites/default/files/ef_publication/field_ef_document/ef20064en.pdf.

European Commission (2019) European Semester Thematic Factsheet: Tertiary Education Attainment. https://ec.europa.eu/info/sites/info/files/file_import/european-semester_thematic-factsheet_tertiary-education-attainment_en.pdf.

European Commission (2018a). Analysis of ERDF support for inclusive growth in the 2014–2020 programming period. https://ec.europa.eu/regional_policy/en/information/publications/studies/2018/analysis-of-erdf-support-for-inclusive-growth-in-the-2014-2020-programming-period.

European Commission (2018b). Proposal for the Regulation of the European Parliament and of the Council on the European Social Fund Plus (ESF+). Brussels, 30.5.2018 COM (2018) 382 final 2018/0206 (COD).

European Commission (2017). Priority policy area: European Pillar of Social Rights – building a more inclusive and fairer European Union. 17 November. https://ec.europa.eu/commission/sites/beta-political/files/social-summit-european-pillar-social-rights-booklet_en.pdf.

European Commission (2014). Available budget 2014 to 2020. https://ec.europa.eu/regional_policy/en/funding/available-budget/.

European Commission (2010). *Europe 2020: A Strategy for Smart, Sustainable and Inclusive Growth*. COM (2010) 2020 final. Brussels: European Commission. http://ec.europa.eu/eu2020/pdf/COMPLET%20EN%20BARROSO%20%20%20007%20-%20Europe%202020%20-%20EN%20version.pdf.

European Parliament (2000). *Charter of Fundamental Rights of the European Union*. 18 December 2000. C 364/01. Brussels: Official Journal of the European Communities. Brussels. www.europarl.europa.eu/charter/pdf/text_en.pdf.

European Union (2017). *Report on Analysis of the Outcome of the Negotiations Concerning the Partnership Agreements and ESF Operational Programmes, for the Programming Period 2014–2020*. Luxembourg: Publications Office of the European Union. https://op.europa.eu/en/publication-detail/-/publication/b2c01d15-ffef-11e6-8a35-01aa75ed71a1.

European Union (2007). *Treaty of Lisbon Amending the Treaty on European Union and the Treaty Establishing the European Community*. 13 December 2007, 2007/C 306/01. www.refworld.org/docid/476258d32.html.

Eurostat (2020). People at risk of poverty or social exclusion. https://ec.europa.eu/eurostat/web/products-datasets/-/T2020_50.

Eurostat (2018). *Smarter, Greener, More Inclusive? Indicators to Support the Europe 2020 Strategy*. Luxembourg: Publications Office of the European Union.

Farrell, F., and Brandellero, P. (2018). Social inclusion indicators for ESF investments: areas for development in addressing the 20% social inclusion target in the ESF. European Social Fund (ESF) Thematic Network Inclusion (TNI) as part of the ESF Transnational Platform. European Association for Information on Local Development. (AEIDL). https://ec.europa.eu/esf/transnationality/content/social-inclusion-indicators-esf-investments-areas-development-addressing-20-social-inclusion.

Fasani, F., Frattini, T., and Minale, L. (2018). *(The Struggle for) Refugee Integration into the Labour Market: Evidence from Europe*. London: Centre for Economic Policy Research.

Feigl, G. (2017). From growth to well-being: a new paradigm for EU economic governance. ETUI Policy Brief No. 2. doi: 10.2139/ssrn.2921022.

Ferrera, M. (2020). More solidarity than meets the eye? Challenges and prospects for social Europe, in: Careja, R., Emmenegger, P., and Giger, N. (eds), *The European Social Model under Pressure* (pp.583–598). Wiesbaden: Springer VS.

Ferreiro, J., and Gómez, C. (2018). Employment protection and labour market performance in European Union countries during the Great Recession. Forum for Macroeconomics and Macroeconomic Policies Working Paper 31. www.econstor.eu/bitstream/10419/181489/1/fmm-imk-wp-31-2018.pdf.

Froud, J., and Williams, K. (2018). *Foundational Economy: The Infrastructure of Everyday Life*. Manchester: Manchester University Press.

Gaisbauer, H. P., Schweiger, G., and Sedmak, C. (2019). *Absolute Poverty in Europe: Interdisciplinary Perspectives on a Hidden Phenomenon*. Bristol: Policy Press.

Gardiner, L. (2015). The scale of minimum wage underpayment in social care. Resolution Foundation. www.resolutionfoundation.org/app/uploads/2015/02/NMW-social-care-note.pdf.

Gentilini, U., Grosh, M., Rigolini, J., and Yemtsov, R. (eds). (2019). *Exploring Universal Basic Income: A Guide to Navigating Concepts, Evidence, and Practices*. Washington, D.C.: World Bank.

Gieryn, T. F. (2000). A space for place in sociology. *Annual Review of Sociology*, **26** (1), 463–496.

Gilchrist, A. (2019). *The Well-Connected Community: A Networking Approach to Community Development*. Bristol: Bristol University Press.

Gironde, C., and Carbonnier, G. (2019). *The ILO @ 100: Addressing the Past and Future of Work and Social Protection*. Leiden: Brill.

Goedemé, T., Hills, J., and Cantillon, B. (2019). *Decent Incomes for All: Improving Policies in Europe*. Oxford: Oxford University Press.

Gough, I. (2019). Universal Basic Services: a theoretical and moral framework. *Political Quarterly*, **90** (3), 534–542.

Grimm, M., Ertugrul, B., and Bauer, U. (2019). *Children and Adolescents in Times of Crises in Europe*. Cham: Springer.

Grubanov-Boskovic, S., Natale, F., and Scipioni, M. (2017). Patterns of immigrants' integration in European labour markets. European Union. https://ec.europa.eu/jrc/en/publication/patterns-immigrants-integration-european-labour-markets.

Haagh, L. A. (2019). The political economy of governance capacity and institutional change: the case of basic income security reform in European welfare states. *Social Policy and Society*, **18** (2), 243–263.

Hanaček, K., Roy, B., Avila, S., and Kallis, G. (2020). Ecological economics and degrowth: proposing a future research agenda from the margins. *Ecological Economics*, **169** (C). http://dx.doi.org/10.1016/j.ecolecon.2019.106495.

Heidenreich, M., and Rice, D. (2016). *Integrating Social and Employment Policies in Europe: Active Inclusion and Challenges for Local Welfare Governance*. Cheltenham, UK, and Northampton, MA: Edward Elgar Publishing.

Hemerijck, A. (2018). Who's afraid of the European Social Union? A contribution to the ESU debate. EuVisions. www.euvisions.eu/who-afraid-of-theeuropean-social - union-hemerijck/.

Hemerijck, A. (ed.) (2017). *The Uses of Social Investment*. Oxford: Oxford University Press.

Hemerijck, A. (2012) When changing welfare states and euro crisis meet. *Sociologica*, **1**, 1–42. http://rszarf.ips.uw.edu.pl/welfare-state/hemerijck.pdf.

Heslop, J., Morgan, K., and Tomaney, J. (2019). Debating the foundational economy. *Renewal: A Journal of Labour Politics*, **27** (2), 5–12.

Hidalgo, M. C., and Hernandez, B. (2001). Place attachment: conceptual and empirical questions. *Journal of Environmental Psychology*, **21** (3), 273–281.

Hirsch, D. (2020). After a decade of austerity, does the UK have an income safety net worth its name? in: Rees, J., Pomati, M., and Heins, E. (eds), *Social Policy Review 32: Analysis and Debate in Social Policy, 2020* (pp.211–226). Bristol: Policy Press.

Hirsch, D., Padley, M., Stone, J., and Valadez-Martinez, L. (2020). The low-income gap: a new indicator based on a minimum income standard. *Social Indicators Research*, 149, 67–85.

House of Lords (2019). Home Affairs Sub-Committee, UK Government. 25 July. https://committees.parliament.uk/committee/338/eu-home-affairs.

Howell, K. E., and Shand, R. (2014). Leadership in the European Union: Europeanization crisis and austerity. *Critical Perspectives on International Public Sector Management*, **3**, 63–74.

Hudson, R. (2019). *Co-Produced Economies: Capital, Collaboration, Competition*. London: Routledge.

Hupkau, C., and Petrongolo, B. (2020). Work, care and gender during the Covid-19 crisis. LSE Centre for Economic Performance. https://cep.lse.ac.uk/pubs/download/cepcovid-19-002.pdf.

Iammarino, S., Rodríguez-Pose, A., and Storper, M. (2019). Regional inequality in Europe: evidence, theory and policy implications. *Journal of Economic Geography*, **19** (2), 273–298.

ILO (2018). Care work and care jobs for the future of decent work. Geneva: International Labour Organization. www.ilo.org/wcmsp5/groups/public/---dgreports/---dcomm/--publ/documents/publication/wcms_633135.pdf.

INSPIRES (2014). Innovative Social Policies for Inclusive and Resilient Labour Markets in Europe. EU (FP7) Project. 2013–2016. www.inspires-research.eu/home.

Kapilashrami, A., and Bhui, K. (2020). Mental health and COVID-19: is the virus racist? *British Journal of Psychiatry*, May 5, 1–3. doi: 10.1192/bjp.2020.93.

King's Fund (2020). Ethnic minority deaths and Covid-19: what are we to do? King's Fund. www.kingsfund.org.uk/blog/2020/04/ethnic-minority-deaths-covid-19.

Kluge, H. H. P., Jakab, Z., Bartovic, J., D'Anna, V., and Severoni, S. (2020). Refugee and migrant health in the COVID-19 response. *The Lancet*, **395** (10232), 1237–1239.

Knuth, M. (2014). Broken hierarchies, quasi-markets and supported networks: a governance experiment in the second tier of Germany's public employment service. *Social Policy and Administration*, **48** (2), 240–261.

Kristensen, I., Dubois, A., and Teräs, J. (2019). *Strategic Approaches to Regional Development: Smart Experimentation in Less-favoured Regions*. London: Routledge.

Kristensen, P. H. (2016). Constructing chains of enablers for alternative economic futures: Denmark as an example. *Academy of Management Perspectives*, **30** (2), 153–166.

Kvist, J. (2017). Social investment over the life course: ending European social policy as we know it? in: Kennett, P., and Lendvai-Bainton, N. (eds), *Handbook of European Social Policy*. Cheltenham, UK, and Northampton, MA: Edward Elgar Publishing.

Kvist, J., and Saari, J. (2007). *The Europeanisation of Social Protection*. Bristol: Policy Press.

Lahusen, C., and Grasso, M. T. (2018). *Solidarity in Europe: Citizens' Responses in Times of Crisis*. London: Palgrave Macmillan.

Lamorgese, A. R., Olivieri, E., and Paccagnella, M. (2019). The wage premium in Italian cities. *Italian Economic Journal*, **5** (2), 251–279.

Lees, C. (2019). *Using Social Network Analysis to Explore Patterns of Europeanisation and Multi-Level Governance in South East Europe*. London: SAGE.

Leruth, B. (2017). The Europeanization of the welfare state, in: Taylor-Gooby, P., Leruth, B., and Chung, H. (eds), *After Austerity: Welfare State Transformation in Europe after the Great Recession* (pp.180–200). Oxford: Oxford University Press.

Leschke, J., Theodoropoulou, S., and Watt, A. (2015). Towards 'Europe 2020'? Austerity and new economic governance in the EU, in: Lehndorff, S. (ed.), *Divisive Integration: The Triumph of Failed Ideas in Europe – Revisited* (pp.295–329). Brussels: European Trade Union Institute.

Lindsay, C., and McQuaid, R. (2008). Inter-agency co-operation in activation: comparing experiences in three vanguard 'active' welfare states. *Social Policy and Society*, **7** (3), 353–365.

Liotti, G., and Canale, R. R. (2020). Poverty and labour market Institutions in Europe. *Panoeconomicus*, **67** (3), 277–290.

Long, K. (2013). When refugees stopped being migrants: movement, labour and humanitarian protection. *Migration Studies*, **1** (1), 4–26. https://doi.org/10.1093/migration/mns001.

Malin, N. (2020). *De-Professionalism and Austerity: Challenges for the Public Sector*. Bristol: Policy Press.

Marmot, M. (2020). *Health Equity in England: The Marmot Review 10 Years On*. London: Institute of Health Equity. www.health.org.uk/sites/default/files/upload/publications/2020/Health%20Equity%20in%20England_The%20Marmot%20Review%2010%20Years%20On_full%20report.pdf.

Matano, A., and Naticchioni, P. (2016). What drives the urban wage premium? Evidence along the wage distribution. *Journal of Regional Science*, **56** (2), 191–209.

Mathers, A. (2016). *Struggling for a Social Europe: Neoliberal Globalization and the Birth of a European Social Movement*. London: Routledge.

Matilla-Santander, N., Lidón-Moyano, C., González-Marrón, A., Bunch, K., Martín-Sánchez, J. C., and Martínez-Sánchez, J. M. (2019). Measuring precarious employment in Europe 8 years into the global crisis. *Journal of Public Health*, **41** (2), 259–267.

McCann, P. (2020). Perceptions of regional inequality and the geography of discontent: insights from the UK. *Regional Studies*, **54** (2), 256–267. doi: 10.1080/00343404.2019.1619928.

McCrea, N., and Finnegan, F. (eds). (2019). *Funding, Power and Community Development*. Bristol: Policy Press.

McGann, M., Nguyen, P., and Considine, M. (2020). Welfare conditionality and blaming the unemployed. *Administration & Society*, **52** (3), 466–494.

McGregor, A., and Sumner, A. (2010). Beyond business as usual: what might 3-D wellbeing contribute to MDG momentum? *IDS Bulletin*, **41** (1), 104–112.

McGregor, J. A. (2007). Researching human wellbeing: from concepts to methodology, in: Gough, I., and McGregor, J. A. (eds), *Well-Being in Developing Countries: New Approaches and Research Strategies*. Cambridge: Cambridge University Press.

McQuaid, R. (2012). Regional monitoring and individual demand for skills development for low-skilled employees, in: Larsen, C., Hasberg, R., Schmid, A., Atin, E., and Brzozowski, J. (eds), Skills *Monitoring in European Regions and Localities: State of the Art and Perspectives* (pp.220–233). Munich: Rainer Hampp Verlag.

Midgley, J., Dahl, E., and Wright, A. C. (eds) (2017). *Social Investment and Social Welfare: International and Critical Perspectives*. Cheltenham, UK, and Northampton, MA: Edward Elgar Publishing.

Milana, M., Klatt, G., and Tronca, L. (2020). Towards a network governance of European lifelong learning: a structural analysis of Commission expert groups. *International Journal of Lifelong Education*, **39** (1), 31–47.

Milani, B. (2000). *Designing the Green Economy: The Post-Industrial Alternative to Corporate Globalization*. Oxford: Rowman and Littlefield.

Moneta, A., Gabellini, T., and Gasperin, S. (2019). *Economic Crisis and Economic Thought: Alternative Theoretical Perspectives on the Economic Crisis*. London: Routledge.

Montgomery, T., and Baglioni, S. (2018). Solidarity in austerity Britain: the cases of disability, unemployment and migration, in: Federico, V., and Lahusen, C. (eds), *Solidarity as a Public Virtue?* (pp.469–494). Baden-Baden: Nomos Verlagsgesellschaft.

Moon, J. D. (2019). *Responsibility, Rights, and Welfare: The Theory of the Welfare State*. London: Routledge.

Mort, L. (2019). Migration and austerity, in: Wroe, L., Larkin, R., and Maglajlic, R. A. (eds), *Social Work with Refugees, Asylum Seekers and Migrants: Theory and Skills for Practice* (pp.57–74). London: Jessica Kingsley.

Mossialos, E., and Le Grand, J. (2019). *Health Care and Cost Containment in the European Union*. Abingdon: Routledge.

Muradian, R., and Pascual, U. (2020). Ecological economics in the age of fear. *Ecological Economics*, 169. doi: 10.1016/j.ecolecon.2019.106498.

Musat, M. (2020). No poverty: the most important indicator of the development of the EU. *Global Economic Observer*, **8** (1), 72–76.

Nugent, N. (2017). *The Government and Politics of the European Union*. London: Palgrave Macmillan.

O'Donovan, N. (2019). From knowledge economy to automation anxiety: a growth regime in crisis? *New Political Economy*, **25** (2), 248–266.

OECD (2020). Regional well-being. OECD Regional Statistics (database). https://doi .org/10.1787/data-00707-en.

OECD (2018). *OECD Regions and Cities at a Glance 2018*. Paris: OECD Publishing. https://doi.org/10.1787/reg_cit_glance-2018-en.

OECD (2015). *All on Board: Making Inclusive Growth Happen*. Paris: OECD Publishing. http://dx.doi.org/10.1787/9789264218512-en.

Oğuz, G. (2020). Recent trends in labour migration in the EU, in: *Labour Migration in the European Union* (pp.79–119). Cham: Palgrave Macmillan.

Öktem, K. G. (2020). The welfare state as universal social security: a global analysis. *Social Inclusion*, **8** (1), 103–113.

ONS (2020). Deaths involving COVID-19 by local area and socioeconomic deprivation: deaths occurring between 1 March and 31 May 2020. www.ons.gov.uk/ peoplepopulationandcommunity/birthsdeathsandmarriages/deaths/bulletins/deathsinv olvingcovid19bylocalareasanddeprivation/deathsoccurringbetween1marchand17april ?hootPostID=f8f83cc51cba7b7e20edce0e1993cadf.

Palier, B., and Hay, C. (2017). The reconfiguration of the welfare state in Europe, in: King, D., and Le Galès, P. (eds), *Reconfiguring European States in Crisis* (pp.331–350). Oxford: Oxford University Press.

Palomino Lozano, R. (2020). Law, religion and states: searching for a soul for Europe, in: Hossain Bhuiyan, Md. J. and Jensen, D. (eds), *Law and Religion in the Liberal State* (pp.89–105). Oxford: Hart Publishing.

Pasimeni, P., and Riso, S. (2019). Redistribution and stabilisation through the EU budget. *Economia Politica*, **36** (1), 111–138.

Patterson, K. (2020) It's a virus, and this isn't a war. Social Europe. 28 April. www .socialeurope.eu/its-a-virus-and-this-isnt-a-war.

Pavaloni, E., and Guillen, A. M. (2013). *Health Care Systems in Europe under Austerity: Institutional Reforms and Performance*. Basingstoke: Palgrave McMillan.

Payne, S. (2017). Lone parents, poverty and mental health: results from the Poverty and Social Exclusion Survey 2012, in: Portier-Le Cocq, F. (ed.), *Fertility, Health and Lone Parenting: European Contexts* (pp.26–45). Abingdon: Routledge.

Peat, J. (2019). House of Lords committee pours scorn on government for failing to allocate EU funding to help most deprived. *London Economic*. 26 July. www.thelondoneconomic.com/politics/house-of-lords-committee-pours-scorn-on -government-for-failing-to-allocate-eu-funding-to-help-most-deprived/26/07/.

Peters, B. G., and Pierre, J. (2000). Citizens versus the new public manager: the problem of mutual empowerment. *Administration & Society*, **32** (1), 9–28.

Peters, M. A. (2020). Beyond technological unemployment: the future of work. *Educational Philosophy and Theory*, **52** (5), 485–491.

Plank, L. (2020). *Reframing Public Ownership in the Foundational Economy: (Re) Discovering a Variety of Forms*. Bristol: Bristol University Press.

Proshansky, H. M., Fabian, A. K., Kaminoff, R. (1983). Place-identity: physical world socialization of the self. *Journal of Environmental Psychology*, **3** (1), 57–83.

Reddy, S. G. (2020). Poverty: beyond obscurantism, in: Beck, V., Hahn, H., and Lepenies, R. (eds), *Dimensions of Poverty*, vol. 2 (pp.215–224). Cham: Springer.

Rees, J., Mullins, D., and Bovaird, T. (2012). *Third Sector Research Centre Research Report 88: Partnership Working*. Birmingham: TSRC Publications.

Rees, W. E. (2020). Ecological economics for humanity's plague phase. *Ecological Economics*, 169, 106519.

Relph, E. (1976). *Place and Placelessness*. London: Pion.

Revell, P., and Dinnie, E. (2020). Community resilience and narratives of community empowerment in Scotland. *Community Development Journal*, **55** (2), 218–236.

Rinaldi, D. (2016). *A New Start for Social Europe*. Notre Europe-Institut Jacques Delors. www.institutdelors.eu/wp-content/uploads/2018/01/newstartsocialeurope -rinaldi-jdi-feb16.pdf.

Romano, S., and Punziano, G. (2016). *The European Social Model Adrift: Europe, Social Cohesion and the Economic Crisis*. London: Routledge.

Ronchi, S. (2018). Which roads (if any) to social investment? The recalibration of EU welfare states at the crisis crossroads (2000–2014). *Journal of Social Policy*, **47** (3), 459–478.

Royster, J. (2020). Exploring the provision of mental health services to migrants during austerity: perspectives of third sector organisations. *The Public Sphere: Journal of Public Policy*, **8** (1).

Rule, P. N. (2015). *Dialogue and Boundary Learning*. Rotterdam: Sense Publishers.

Sabato, S., and Verschraegen, G. (2019). The multi-level governance of social inno-
    vation: how the EU supports socially innovative initiatives. *Rivista Italiana di
    Politiche Pubbliche*, 1, 35–66.
Saikku, P., and Karjalainen, V. (2012). Network governance in activation policy: health
    care as an emergent partner. *International Journal of Sociology and Social Policy*,
    32 (5–6), 299–311.
Sandermann, P. (ed.) (2014). *The End of Welfare as We Know It? Continuity and
    Change in Western Welfare State Settings and Practices*. Opladen: Verlag Barbara
    Budrich. http://site.ebrary.com/id/10842767.
Saraceno, C. (2019). Retrenching, recalibrating, pre-distributing: the welfare state
    facing old and new inequalities. *Structural Change and Economic Dynamics*, 51,
    35–41.
Sattinger, M. (2016). *Income Distribution: An Edward Elgar Research Review*.
    Cheltenham, UK, and Northampton, MA: Edward Elgar Publishing.
Scheurer, L., and Haase, A. (2018). Diversity and social cohesion in European cities:
    making sense of today's European Union–urban nexus within Cohesion Policy.
    European Urban and Regional Studies, **25** (3), 337–342.
Schraad-Tischler, D. (2015). *Social Justice in the EU 2015: Index*. Social Improvement
    Monitor.   www.social-inclusion-monitor.eu/uploads/tx_itao_download/Studie_NW
    _Social-Justice-in-the-EU-Index-Report-2015_2015_01.pdf.
Schulze, M. S. (2014). *Western Europe: Economic and Social Change since 1945*.
    Hoboken: Taylor & Francis.
Scottish Government (2018). *Monitoring the Outcomes of Planning: A Research Study*.
    Edinburgh: Scottish Government.
Scottish Government (2015). *Programme for Government*. Edinburgh: Scottish
    Government. www.gov.scot/publications/programme-government-2015-16/.
Scottish Government (2013). *Poverty and Income Inequality in Scotland*. Edinburgh:
    Scottish Government.
Scottish Government (2012). *Poverty and Social Justice*. Edinburgh: Scottish
    Government. www.gov.scot/policies/poverty-and-social-justice/.
Scottish Government (2011). *The Government Economic Strategy*. Edinburgh: Scottish
    Government. www.scotland.gov.uk/Publications/2011/09/13091128/0.
Servoz, M. (2019). *AI, the Future of Work? Work of the Future! On How Artificial
    Intelligence, Robotics and Automation Are Transforming Jobs and the Economy in
    Europe*. Luxembourg: Publications Office of the European Union. https://op.europa
    .eu/publication/manifestation_identifier/PUB_ES0119388ENN.
Sielker, F., and Stead, D. (2019). Scaling and rescaling of EU spatial governance, in:
    Abels, G., and Battke, J. (eds), *Regional Governance in the EU: Regions and the
    Future of Europe* (pp.124–139). Cheltenham, UK, and Northampton, MA: Edward
    Elgar Publishing.
Sinthupundaja, J., Kohda, Y., and Chiadamrong, N. (2020). Examining capabil-
    ities of social entrepreneurship for shared value creation. *Journal of Social
    Entrepreneurship*, **11** (1), 1–22.
Sloman, P. (2019). *Transfer State: The Idea of a Guaranteed Income and the Politics of
    Redistribution in Modern Britain*. Oxford: Oxford University Press.
Soava, G., Mehedintu, A., and Sterpu, M. (2020). Relations between income inequality,
    economic growth and poverty threshold: new evidences from EU countries panels.
    Technological and Economic Development of Economy, **26** (2), 290–310.

Šoltés, E., Vojtková, M., and Šoltésová, T. (2020). Changes in the geographical distribution of youth poverty and social exclusion in EU member countries between 2008 and 2017. *Moravian Geographical Reports*, **28** (1), 2–15.

Spash, C. L. (2020). A tale of three paradigms: realising the revolutionary potential of ecological economics. *Ecological Economics*, **169**, p.106518.

Staníčková, M., and Melecký, L. (2020). Impact of global pattern on the EU economic growth and urbanization, in: Ushakov, D. (ed.), *Migration and Urbanization: Local Solutions for Global Economic Challenges* (pp.241–264). Hershey, PA: IGI Global.

Stead, D., Sielker, F., and Chilla, T. (2016). Macro-regional strategies: agents of Europeanization and rescaling? in: Gänzle, S., and Kern, K. (eds), *A Macro-Regional Europe in the Making: Theoretical Approaches and Empirical Evidence* (pp.99–120). Basingstoke: Palgrave Macmillan.

Stiglitz, J., Sen, A., and Fitoussi, J. P. (2009). *The Measurement of Economic Performance and Social Progress Revisited: Reflections and Overview.* Paris: Commission on the Measurement of Economic Performance and Social Progress.

Storper, M. (2018). Separate worlds? Explaining the current wave of regional economic polarisation. *Journal of Economic Geography*, 18, 247–270.

Sulkowski, A. J. (2020). Covid-19: What's next? Future of work, business, and law: automation, transparency, blockchain, education, and inspiration. https://papers.ssrn .com/sol3/papers.cfm?abstract_id=3580019.

Sułkowski, Ł. (2020). Covid-19 pandemic; recession, virtual revolution leading to de-globalization? *Journal of Intercultural Management*, 12, 1–11.

Sykianakis, N., Polychronidou, P., and Karasavvoglou, A. (eds) (2019). *Economic and Financial Challenges for Eastern Europe: Proceedings of the 9th International Conference on the Economies of the Balkan and Eastern European Countries in the Changing World (EBEEC) in Athens, Greece, 2017.* Cham: Springer. https://doi.org/ 10.1007/978-3-030-12169-3.

Taylor, A., and Bronstone, A. (2019). *People, Place and Global Order: Foundations of a Networked Political Economy.* London: Routledge.

Taylor-Gooby, P., Leruth, B., and Chung, H. (eds) (2017). *After Austerity: Welfare State Transformation in Europe after the Great Recession.* Oxford: Oxford University Press.

Telle, S., Špaček, M., Crăciun, D. (2019). Divergent paths to cohesion: the (unintended) consequences of a place-based Cohesion Policy, in: Lang, T., and Görmar, F. (eds), *Regional and Local Development in Times of Polarisation.* Singapore: Palgrave Macmillan.

Thelen, K. A. (2014). *Varieties of Liberalization and the New Politics of Social Solidarity.* Cambridge: Cambridge University Press.

Theodore, N. (2020) Governing through austerity: (il)logics of neoliberal urbanism after the global financial crisis. *Journal of Urban Affairs*, **42** (1), 1–17. doi: 10.1080/07352166.2019.1623683.

Thomson, S., Figueras, J., Evetovits, T., Jowett, M., et al. (2015). *Economic Crisis, Health Systems and Health in Europe: Impact and Implications for Policy.* Copenhagen and Brussels: WHO and European Observatory on Health Systems and Policies.

Tracker, C. A. (2020). A government roadmap for addressing the climate and post COVID-19 economic crises. Climate Action Tracker. https://climateactiontracker .org/publications/addressing-the-climate-and-post-covid-19-economic-crises/.

Trebeck, K., and Williams, J. (2019). *The Economics of Arrival: Ideas for a Grown-up Economy.* Bristol: Policy Press.

Türk, V., and Garlick, M. (2016). From burdens and responsibilities to opportunities: the comprehensive refugee response framework and a global compact on refugees. *International Journal of Refugee Law*, **28** (4), 656–678.

Vandenbroucke, F. (2017). Comparative social policy analysis in the EU at the brink of a new era. *Journal of Comparative Policy Analysis: Research and Practice*, **19** (4), 390–402. doi: 10.1080/13876988.2016.1168618.

Vanleene, D., and Verschuere, B. (2018). Co-Production in community development, in: Brandsen, T., Verschuere, and Steen, T. (eds), *Co-production and Co-creation: Engaging Citizens in Public Services* (pp.198–207). Abingdon: Routledge.

Varoufakis, Y. (2016). *And the Weak Suffer What They Must? Europe, Austerity and the Threat to Global Stability*. London: Random House.

Vaughan-Whitehead, D. (ed.) (2015). *The European Social Model in Crisis: Is Europe Losing its Soul?* Cheltenham, UK, and Northampton, MA: Edward Elgar Publishing.

Verhofstadt, G. (2017). *Europe's Last Chance: Why the European States Must Form a More Perfect Union*. New York: Basic Books.

Weatherburn, A., Gutwirth, S., and De Hert, P. (2020). The fundamental rights impact of the measures taken to reduce the spread of Covid-19 on those living in poverty or in a precarious situation, in: *Societal Exit from Lockdown: Contribution of Academic Expertise* (pp.62–65). www.cartaacademica.org/post-covid.

Weaver, R. L. (2019). Social enterprise and the capability approach: exploring how social enterprises are humanizing business. *Journal of Nonprofit & Public Sector Marketing*, 1–26. doi: 10.1080/10495142.2019.1589630.

Wenz-Temming, A., and Sonnicksen, J. (2020). The double bailout: assessing new intergovernmentalism in the euro-crisis and the implications for European integration and democracy. *Journal of European Integration*, 1–17. doi: 10.1080/07036337.2020.1718672.

Wiggan, J. (2017). Contesting the austerity and 'welfare reform' narrative of the UK government. *International Journal of Sociology and Social Policy*, **37** (11/12), 639–654.

Wohlfarth, A. (2020). Renegotiating social citizenship: democracy in welfare service states. *Social Work & Society*, **18** (1: Special Issue on 'Renegotiating Social Citizenship–Democracy in Welfare Service States').

World Bank (2019). Prevalence of undernourishment in the United Kingdom. https://data.worldbank.org/indicator/SN.ITK.DEFC.ZS?locations=GB.

Zainol, N., Zainol, F., Ibrahim, Y., and Afthanorhan, A. (2019). Scaling up social innovation for sustainability: the roles of social enterprise capabilities. *Management Science Letters*, **9** (3), 457–466.

Zopounidis, C., Atsalakis, G. S., and Baourakis, G. S. (2016). The economic crisis and retardants of growth in Greece. *International Journal of Sustainable Economies Management (IJSEM)*, 5, 1–17.

5. 'Making it count': investing in a Social Europe that is meaningful for young people

Marion Ellison

INTRODUCTION

As an expanding number of economic and social policy analysts have argued, the main focus of recent macroeconomic policies in weaker European economies following the financial crisis of 2007–2008 has centred upon rapid deficit reduction, and the prioritisation of cuts to public services which penalise the poor and create new societal risks including an inadequate publicly funded education sector, weak labour markets characterised by part-time and temporary jobs and poor health and social care provision (Mori, 2020; Pape et al., 2020; Rechel, 2019; MacDonald, 2016; Ellison, 2014a; Messkoub, 2014). Recent analysis has revealed that the Covid-19 health pandemic will precipitate a severe global economic recession (IMF, 2020; Nicola et al., 2020; OBR, 2020). Young people will once again bear some of the worst dis-welfares of global recession. The European Union (EU) has recently launched a major strategy, the EU Youth Strategy 2019–2027, to respond to the profound challenges that young people transitioning into a post-Covid labour market and further and higher education system will undoubtedly face. This strategy builds on earlier strategies, such as Youth on the Move and the Youth Guarantee.

This chapter critically examines the underlying principles, forms of governance and impacts of these strategies. It also discusses the degree to which these strategies have enabled a convergence of social policies directed at the well-being of young people across European countries. Finally, the chapter examines the relevance of new alternative economic models and policies designed to support young people as they negotiate the challenges within post-Covid social and economic contexts. It draws upon an empirical analysis of recent EU policy measures directed at the complex and multi-dimensional challenges that young people face in distinct European socio-economic contexts.

THE POLITICAL ECONOMY OF YOUTH TRANSITIONS IN EUROPE

Recent research has revealed the impact of the financial crisis of 2007–2008 on the reconstruction of institutional arrangements, policy paradigms and practices central to the lived experiences of young people (Bussi et al., 2019; Schoon and Bynner, 2019; Ellison, 2017, 2014a; France, 2016). In particular, as France (2016) argues, neo-liberalism has become a growing influence across a number of European countries, transforming the meaning of youth transitions, risk and inclusion between education, training, work and welfare policy. Underlining this, differences in levels of educational inequality are demonstrated by trends in inequities in access and uptake of education within and across European societies. The most recent data relating to indicators such as early leavers from education and training (Figure 5.1) reveals stark differences in levels of educational inequality between EU member states.

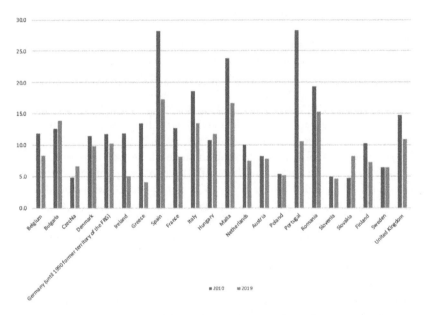

Figure 5.1   *Early leavers from education and training in 2010 and 2019 (percentage of people aged between 18 and 24)*

Source: Early leavers from education and training by sex and labour status [edat_lfse_14]. Eurostat. Extracted on 8 July 2020. https://appsso.eurostat.ec.europa.eu/nui/show.do?dataset= edat_lfse_14&lang=en.

Demonstrating this, the EU 2020 headline target is that the share of early leavers from education and training should be less than 10 per cent. However, as we can see from Figure 5.1, there are a number of member states – including Spain, 17.3 per cent; Malta, 16.7 per cent; and Romania at 15.3 per cent – where the numbers of early school leavers in 2019 are well above this percentage. In contrast, the share of early leavers from education and training in Greece is 4.1 per cent, in Slovenia 4.6 per cent and in Ireland 5.1 per cent, with Sweden at 6.5 per cent, Czechia at 6.7 per cent and Finland at 7.3 per cent in 2019. These statistics reveal significant differences in this dimension of educational inequality between member states. Only eleven member states currently meet this target (Eurostat, 2020). Differences in levels of educational inequality across Europe are also demonstrated by the numbers of young people aged between 15 and 24 who were not in employment, education or training (NEET) in 2010 and 2019 (Figure 5.2).

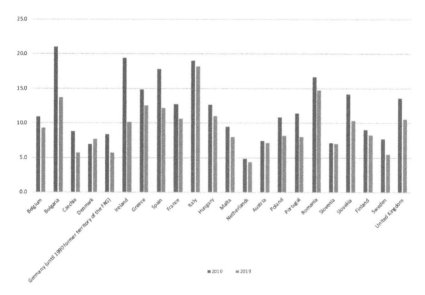

Figure 5.2   *Young people aged between 15 and 24 years who were not in employment, education or training in 2010 and 2019*

Source: Young people neither in employment nor in education and training by sex, age and degree of urbanisation (NEET rates) [edat_lfse_29] (population aged between 15 and 24 years). Eurostat. Extracted on 8 July 2020. https://appsso.eurostat.ec.europa.eu/nui/show.do/.

Underlying these differences, there is substantive evidence that many young people are disadvantaged by background, origin and income inequality

(Karlıdağ-Dennis, 2020; Schoon and Bynner, 2019; Stein, 2019; Ellison, 2017; MacDonald, 2016; Ellison, 2014a). Here it may be argued that many young people face societal risks which may lead to individual poverty and issues relating to social, psychological and emotional well-being. The impacts of these societal risks, including poverty, fragile and insecure labour markets and inadequate levels of expenditure on education, health care and formal social care, are socially stratified across all European welfare states (Stein, 2019; Ellison, 2017; MacDonald, 2016; Ellison, 2014a). The current Covid-19 pandemic has also been evidenced as being severely detrimental to the well-being and mental health of young people across societies globally (Blustein et al., 2020; González-Sanguino et al., 2020; Ivchenko et al., 2020; Lee, 2020). The well-being of young people will also be subject to substantially increased levels of societal risk as a result of the economic recession that is expected to follow the Covid-19 pandemic (Blustein et al., 2020; IMF, 2020; Karlıdağ-Dennis, 2020; OBR, 2020).

Social investment in education and training and vocational and labour market policies for young people simultaneously act to compensate for disadvantages created by inequality whilst contributing to more sustainable long-term social economies. Recent evidence has also revealed that specific interventions at local level designed to support young people when accessing and undertaking tertiary education, training and higher-level education can lead to more coherent, meaningful and positive transitions, improving educational and training outcomes and life chances for young people (Van Herpen et al., 2020; Lindsay et al., 2019; Stein, 2019; Lindsay et al., 2016). Conversely, austerity is often legitimised by the need to re-balance the economy following financial or economic crises. However, as a number of analysts have argued, the historical origins of the financial crisis of 2007–2008, and related austerity measures and welfare reforms which followed, were two-fold. Firstly, they were the direct economic consequence of the process of financialisation, or the immense manufacture of fabricated financial wealth.

Secondly, and intrinsic to this process, the financial crisis was itself a product of a global political economy which was largely forged and legitimated by neo-liberal ideology which exalted the primacy and infallibility of the market over the social (Theodore, 2020; Williams, 2020; Birch and Springer, 2019; Saad-Filho, 2019; Van Apeldoorn and Overbeek, 2012). Indeed, some recent commentators have argued that the current Covid-19 pandemic has been exacerbated by decades of minimal investment in public health care across many European countries. It is thus regarded as a crisis of neo-liberalism precipitated by an economic model which prioritises the market and argues for minimal state intervention (Nunes, 2020). As a number of studies have evidenced, European governments have exposed young people to increased levels of 'societal risk' (Stein, 2019; Ellison, 2014a; Ellison and

Fenger, 2013). Societal risk is defined as the risk that societies fail to provide adequate systems of education, health, social care, housing, labour market regulation or public infrastructure to support young people's transitions between education and employment. Recent research has illustrated the impact of societal risk on the well-being and potential of vulnerable groups in European settings (Agasisti et al., 2020; Liotti and Canale, 2020; Schweiger, 2020; Bussi et al., 2019; Ellison, 2017; Ellison, 2014a). In particular, poverty, multiple disadvantages and weak labour markets are evidenced as limiting the well-being and educational and labour market potential of young people, especially when attempting to negotiate the transition from school to employment.

More broadly, individual welfare states are defined as unique configurations of economic, social and political institutions, arrangements and processes (Buendía, 2020; Clarke, 2019; Ellison and Fenger, 2013; Schelke, 2012). These unique configurations filter the normative dimensions of the European Social Model (ESM). Importantly also, as Hay and Wincott (2012) have argued, the profound interdependence between the economic, social and political spheres serves to underline the feedback loop between socio-economic conditions of stratification and inequality and the outcomes of new policy measures directed at young people's transitions between education and employment. As a number of authors have contended, compensatory policies are usually designed to support disadvantaged young people with low levels of identity capital, including educational, social and psychological resources which are viewed as being critical, particularly during young people's transitions between education and employment. Within the context of the life-span approach, young people growing up in disadvantaged conditions require tailored support during and after their transition between education and employment (Ecchia et al., 2020; Sanders et al., 2020; Neves et al., 2019; Rinne et al., 2019; Webb et al., 2017; Riele, 2006; du Bois-Reymond et al., 2003).

The comparative analysis of policy responses designed to promote young people's transitions between education and employment in Europe thus requires a fine-grained analysis of the outcomes of innovative policy strategies designed to support young people from disadvantaged backgrounds within specific contexts. More broadly, as Schelke (2012) contends, the 'varieties of capitalism model' is limited to analysis of the functional capacities of social policies within the parameters of the operation of labour markets from the perspectives of firms. In contrast, Esping-Andersen's 'worlds of welfare' model locates policies within broader clusters of welfare regimes. However, as Antonucci et al. (2014) argue, Esping-Andersen's 'welfare regimes model' does not take account of the hybridisation or 'mix' of welfare approaches within distinct welfare states. Policy responses to diverse and complex specificities of youth poverty, deprivation and precarious labour markets have led to eclectic policy responses to the risks faced by young people within distinct European settings (Antonucci et al., 2014).

Importantly, however, it may be argued that the worlds typology developed by Esping-Andersen (1990) does provide a reference point for the analysis of recent transformations in broadly defined political and ideological parameters of European welfare states. Thus, the identification of distinct forms of de-commodification, forms of stratification and the main providers of welfare (state, family, market) within each national setting does enable the location of specific dynamics underlying youth transitions. These dynamics can then be located within broader institutional, socio-economic, political and cultural configurations. There is evidence of the adoption of policies shaped by neo-liberal ideologies characterised by individualistic principles of 'activation' and de-commodification across distinct European settings (Brown, 2020; Taylor-Gooby et al., 2019; Deeming, 2017; Taylor-Gooby et al., 2017; Ellison and Fenger, 2013). However, there is also evidence of high levels of de-commodification within redistributive fiscal regimes which are broadly defined as social democratic (Jaayfer, 2020; Kangas et al., 2017; Böger and Öktem, 2019). In particular, forms of social, economic and industrial governance underpinning the 'social democratic world' characteristically optimise investment in youth transitions through dual socialisation (the notion that the state is as responsible as the parent for the upbringing of the child) and a broader commitment to forms of government based on social dialogue. Stakeholders in this collaborative social dialogue include young people, trade unions, employers, local authorities, national government, public and social services, and educational and training providers. Moreover, within social democratic settings, higher and post-higher education are de-commodified along with a range of welfare and health services, and there is a strong commitment to collective approaches to labour market regulation and employment rights.

This encompassing form of welfare is contrasted to the welfare offered within liberal welfare states where the market is regarded as the main provider of welfare, ensuring minimal de-commodification and stigmatising stratification through means-tested benefits.

Finally, the European conservative world, characterised by diverging levels of stratification and de-commodification, may be regarded as a distinctive social investment paradigm. This distinct social investment approach is exemplified most closely by the German model of welfare and industrial relations. The weakening of collective bargaining coverage has significantly eroded the German conservative model, impacting disproportionately on young people in the German labour market and prompting the introduction of the national minimum wage in Germany in 2016 (Grabka and Schröder, 2019; Dingeldey et al., 2017; Caliendo et al., 2017). Importantly, the minimum wage in Germany does not apply to trainees, young people doing their entry-level qualifications or people in compulsory practical training as part of an apprenticeship or university-level study course. In the UK, the National Living Wage does not apply to young people under the age of 25; however, in contrast, the Living Wage Scotland Act 2013 applies to employees of all age groups (Johnson et al., 2019).

Broader socio-political and industrial relations transformations within distinct European settings are of significance in terms of how they have shaped youth transitions, particularly in terms of policy responses, levels of social investment, social security and forms of social and economic democracy. Equally significant are multi-level governance arrangements between EU, national and local economic and policy contexts in shaping innovative approaches and policies for meaningful, sustainable and coherent transitions for young people as stakeholders in both the workplace and society across Europe (Helms Jørgensen, 2019; Högberg, 2019; Parreira do Amaral and Zelinka, 2019; Cuconato, 2017; Jørgensen et al., 2017; Ellison, 2014a). Exemplifying transnational apprenticeships, programmes across Germany, Italy and Spain provide Europe-wide opportunities for young people. The multi-national company Bosch has recently launched two new educational projects in Italy and Spain. The Prepare for the Future project gives school students a first glimpse into the working world and potential career profiles. In Italy, the project reached more than 40,000 students at around 200 schools in 2015. Bosch began offering Prepare for the Future in Spain during 2016. In another project, the supplier of technology and services is adapting elements of the German dual education system to the situation in Italy (Bosch, 2016). A broad range of partners, including regional governments, non-profit organisations and companies, participate in these projects. It may be argued that the strategic alignment of policies relating to skills matching and the political economy of economic development within and between European countries is pivotal to the effectiveness of specific translations of the ESM.

Whilst the global financial crisis of 2007–2008 may have been precipitated by neo-liberal ideology, the crisis has itself led to a critical juncture which may potentially enable the emergence of more socially, economically and industrially democratic approaches to a global knowledge-based economy, particularly in light of the profound impact of the Covid-19 health pandemic on societies and economies across the world (Bailey, 2020; Nettle et al., 2020; Heslop et al., 2019; Barbera et al., 2016; Earle et al., 2018; Engelen et al., 2017). Exemplifying this, a number of recent studies have argued for innovative economic policies and measures such as Universal Basic Income (UBI) and Universal Basic Services (UBS) (Corburn, 2020; Johnson et al., 2020; Lynch, 2020; Nettle et al., 2020; Pulla, 2020; Shadmi et al., 2020). The underlying rationale for these policies is that substantial social investment in equitable and sustainable universal public services and policy measures is vital to the health and well-being of all who live and work in post-Covid European societies. These policies and measures have crystallised into calls for the 'Foundational Economy', which recommends that the provision of UBS should be regarded as an income entitlement granted to all who live and work in European societies (Moore and Collins, 2020; Heslop et al., 2019; Morgan, 2019; Barbera et al., 2016; Earle et al., 2018; Engelen et al., 2017).

Here the Foundational Economy and participative elements intrinsic to collaborative models of governance, policy-making and partnership are crucial to the sustainability of innovative social, employment and industrial policies directed at more meaningful and sustainable youth transitions within European labour markets. Indeed, as a number of analysts have argued, the repercussions of the 2007–2008 financial crisis itself stimulated fresh appeals for economic democracy and a rebalancing of the relationship between capital and labour (Cumbers et al., 2019; Harris and Scully, 2015; Sarfati, 2015; Bailey, 2014; Block, 2014). These appeals have now become demands intensified by the profound impact of the Covid-19 health crisis on the well-being of people across the world (Bedford et al., 2020; González-Sanguino et al., 2020; Marmot, 2020; ONS, 2020; WHO, 2020).

Recent analysis has also revealed that young people will be disproportionately affected by the economic impact of the Covid-19 health crisis. There are three key reasons for this. Firstly, previous research has clearly evidenced that young people are disproportionately disadvantaged by economic recessions. In particular, young people are more likely to be laid off by employers as three out of four young people work in the informal economy, carrying out non-standard work with no protection or sick pay. Secondly, in terms of the sectoral impact of the Covid-19 virus, young people are over-represented in sectors most badly hit by the economic impact of the pandemic. Young people occupy a high proportion of jobs within areas such as tourism and the service sector (Blundell et al., 2020; Blustein et al., 2020; Dias et al., 2020; ILO, 2020a). Finally, young people who do not have substantive skills in digital technology are risk of losing their jobs as a result of automation and advances in Artificial Intelligence (AI) as many entry-level jobs require competence in digital technologies. Exacerbating this, education and training are currently being disrupted by the Covid-19 health crisis (ILO, 2020a; Calvo and Coulter, 2019).

Young people facing additional barriers and challenges relating to educational inequalities will thus be at a severe disadvantage in the post-Covid-19 economy. As evidenced in Figure 5.1, in 2019 a number of European countries had a significant proportion of young people leaving school early. In particular, Spain, Malta and Romania showed the most concerning levels of early school leaving at 17.3 per cent, 16.7 per cent and 15.3 per cent. Whilst this is mainly related to regional and inter-regional economic inequalities across Europe intensified by years of austerity and related welfare reforms following the financial crisis of 2007–2008, it is also important to consider a number of cultural factors, particularly when we consider gender differences. However, these figures do clearly reveal that significant numbers of young people will face additional barriers and challenges within post-Covid-19 economies in Europe. Of central concern is the impact of decades of austerity on education infrastructures and inclusive investment in education and skills training. Importantly, distinctive national forms of governance play a key role in shaping hybrid forms of welfare that characterise distinct social models. In particular, the significance of co-decision making and co-responsibility in bolstering measures for the entry and sustainability of measures designed to ensure the full participation and inclusion of young people in the labour market (Baines et al., 2019; Ellison, 2017; Dimoulas and Papadopoulou, 2016). Taken together, the evidence relating to early school leaving and young people not in employment, education or training does reveal inadequacies in levels of invest-ment in education and training across most European states. However, there is evidence that some member states have taken a more pro-active approach, investing in appropriate and meaningful measures directed at young people, particularly at a local level. Illustrating this, recent evidence has shown that young people in the Netherlands benefit from a strong commitment to a range of innovative policies and measures which address the multi-dimensional and intersectional barriers and challenges faced by young people today (Baines et al., 2019; Van Dijk and Noorda, 2019; OECD, 2017). More broadly, in terms of public expenditure, the Netherlands also invests substantially in education and training, ensuring a high average level of skills proficiency. Eighteen per cent of all adults were high performers in literacy levels, lagging only behind Finland and Japan out of 34 OECD countries. Moreover, two out of every three young people in the Netherlands are expected to enter tertiary education at some point in their lives, indicating a commitment to encouraging and invest-ing in lifelong learning (OECD, 2017). A defining characteristic of youth policies in the Netherlands is the commitment to the promotion of a culture of lifelong learning:

> Promoting a culture of learning in the Netherlands is not only an important goal in its own right, but could also help to foster more equitable skills outcomes (priority 1) and encourage the formation of skills-intensive workplaces (priority 2). (OECD, 2017, p.2)

Critically, this approach is underpinned by a policy commitment to social inclusion:

> Skills are also critical for bolstering social participation and inclusion. Less highly skilled people have lower levels of trust, participate less actively in the democratic

process and in community life, and have poorer health. When poor outcomes are concentrated among certain population groups – such are those from low socio-economic backgrounds and immigrants – they can lead to social marginalisation and, eventually, social tension. As a consequence, having high average levels of skills is not in itself "good enough". It is essential to actively pursue greater equity in educational and skills achievement to ensure that everyone can participate fully in society. (OECD, 2017, p.3)

The diversity of approaches in relation to policies and measures directed at young people and more broadly at lifelong learning, education and skills in Europe is indicative of a central challenge facing the reinvigoration of the ESM. At the axis of these divergent approaches, distinct varieties of capitalism, ranging from Neo-liberal to Corporate and Social Investment Capitalism, forge policy responses in this area (Schröder, 2019; Ellison and Fenger, 2013). Equally, the extent of regional and inter-regional economic disparities, accentuated by the financial crisis of 2007–2008, neo-liberal policies, associated austerity measures and the current Covid-19 crisis has significantly reduced the capacity of nation-states to invest in policies and measures directed at young people. In particular, countries such as Italy, Greece, Spain, Ireland and Portugal are at a significant disadvantage given the heavy burden of the debt crisis and conditionality underlying the financial support provided by the European Commission. The central features of this conditionality were austerity and welfare reforms, severely constraining the capacity of these countries to invest in inclusive educational and skills training measures (Jones and Traianou, 2019; Capucha et al., 2016; Featherstone, 2015).

THEORETICAL CONSIDERATIONS

The global economic crisis of 2007–2008 accelerated the re-positioning of a number of European nation-states as 'enabling authorities' within new welfare and labour market arrangements that are largely premised to differing degrees on neo-liberal ideology (Ellison and Fenger, 2013). Exemplifying this, in the UK forms of labour market 'activation' introduced in 2010 for young people were largely based upon an American rather than a European policy model, being characterised by high levels of conditionality and harsh sanctions rather than a focus upon tailored support measures and strong investment in training and skills (Theodoropoulou, 2018; Crisp and Powell, 2017; Antonucci et al., 2014; Ellison, 2014a; Hamilton et al., 2014; Heyes and Lewis, 2014; Kretsos, 2014; Sloam, 2013; Chung et al., 2012). Moreover, the Welfare Reform Act 2012 introduced significant increases in levels of conditionality and the scale of sanctions (Etherington and Daguerre, 2015). Indeed, substantial evidence emerged that more vulnerable young people were being left behind by the Work Programme in the UK, particularly disabled young people or those who were socio-economically disadvantaged (Ellison, 2014a; Work and Pensions Committee, 2013). A burgeoning body of literature points to the way in which ideological preferences underpinned activation measures for young people in the UK (Ellison, 2014a; Schelke, 2012; Wiggan, 2012; Scarpetta, 2010). Thus, as Wiggan (2012) argues, the UK Coalition Government's 2010 Green Paper '21st Century Welfare' and the White Paper 'Universal Credit Welfare That Works' effectively marginalised the structural aspects of persistent unemployment, underemployment and poverty in the UK by focusing upon individual pathologies of benefit dependency and worklessness resonant with neo-liberal ideological principles of economic rationality, conditionality and competitiveness (Wiggan, 2012). The paradoxical logic underpinning the Work Programme introduced in 2011, and the Youth Obligation Support Programme introduced in April 2017 in the UK is that those most vulnerable in the labour market (the disabled and socio-economically disadvantaged or care-experienced) are evidenced as those who are given least support and investment (Atfield and Green, 2019; DWP, 2017; Work and Pensions Committee, 2013). In particular, both programmes are not tailored to the individual challenges of young people who face additional barriers during the transition between education and employment. As Atfield and Green (2019) clearly evidence in their analysis of the impact of the Youth Obligation Support Programme on disadvantaged young people in the UK,

> without an increase in flexibility and personalisation, a programme that was designed to bring young people into employment runs the risk of driving the most disadvantaged further away. The implications for these young people, their families and wider society are severe. It deprived disadvantaged young people not just of financial support, but also access to other statutory services, placed the financial burden for supporting them on families that were often already struggling to cope, and resulted in a growing subsection of society that are not only disengaged, but are unknown and unrecorded, whose re-engagement became increasingly more difficult and unlikely as time went on. (p.6)

For vulnerable young people across Europe the impact of economic crises and neo-liberal ideology has been made considerably worse by severe reductions in public investment in further and higher education and vocational training. Unemployment, underemployment, poor-quality employment and insecure youth transitions have been widely evidenced as being profound threats to the well-being of young people (Green, 2020; ILO, 2020b; Schoon and Bynner, 2019, 2017; Green and Pensiero, 2017; Berger and Frey, 2016; Furlong, 2016; MacDonald, 2016; Ellison, 2014a; ILO, 2013). Recent evidence has indicated the impact of incoherent and fragmented transitions on social isolation and 'the epidemic of loneliness' experienced by young people (Prince's Trust, 2014).

For example, in the UK recent research has revealed that young people experiencing long-term unemployment are more than twice as likely as their peers to have been prescribed anti-depressants, with one in three contemplating suicide and 40 per cent of jobless young people facing symptoms of mental illness – including suicidal thoughts and feelings of self-loathing as a direct result of unemployment (Prince's Trust, 2014, quoted in Ellison, 2014a). Extended periods of time without education or employment lead to the long-term social and political marginalisation of young people, strengthening the feeling of dependence, powerlessness and distress. Being NEET is also linked to risk behaviours, contributing to worse health conditions and further social exclusion (Eurofound 2013, p.60). For example, in the UK the cumulative impact of existing high levels of youth underemployment and the regressive impact of austerity measures on the distribution of incomes, inadequate levels of public housing and access to further and higher education and training has placed many young people into precarious and insecure conditions of living. Indeed, it may be argued that the current and future well-being of many young people already disadvantaged by situational constraints created by poverty in the UK is also limited by restricted access to further and higher education (Woodward, 2020; Donnelly and Evans, 2019; White and Lee, 2019; Détourbe and Goastellec, 2018; Adetunji and Obilanade, 2016; Iannelli et al., 2016).

The global economic crisis has also intensified the operationalisation of flexible and de-regulated labour markets which impact disproportionately on young people (ILO, 2020b; OECD, 2017; MacDonald, 2016; Ellison, 2014a). It is important to analyse the degree to which there is 'an equitable balance' between security and flexibility for young people across most European countries. The strongest imbalances are evidenced in Greece, Spain, Italy and the UK. Greece, for example, experienced a sharp transition from a distorted and unevenly protected labour market into a fully flexible one with pervasive features of labour precariousness and the threat of unemployment. More specifically, increasing levels of participation of young people in part-time and temporary work, combined with low wages, can result in young people experiencing a cycle which is locked into unemployment, temporary and low-wage work for years (Scarpetta, 2010) with psychologically 'scarring' effects for their future employment, earnings, health and well-being outcomes (Allan et al., 2020; Mousteri et al., 2020; MacDonald, 2016; Otto and Taylor-Gooby, 2014).

EUROPEAN-LEVEL POLICY RESPONSES

European-level policy responses to the territorial dimension of youth unemployment and underemployment initially crystallised around the EU 2020 Strategy Youth on the Move, which focuses upon the vulnerability of young people with low levels of education and calls for sustainable support measures to aid the transition from education to work within a global knowledge economy. The strategy argues that such measures should cover, in an integrated manner, the sequence of steps for young people in the transition from education into work, and ensure safety nets for those who risk dropping out of education and employment. Top-down initiatives such as the Youth Guarantee scheme were first introduced in the Nordic countries during the 1980s and 1990s. A central policy concern for the Commission has been the barriers and constraints faced by young people who are NEETs. Pro-active approaches to transitions between education and employment are reflected at EU, national and sub-national level. A series of measures designed to help member states tackle youth unemployment, underemployment and social exclusion was central to the Youth Employment Package launched by the European Commission in 2012. The Package contained a recommendation to launch a Youth Guarantee in every country. The European Council adopted the recommendation relating to the provision of a Youth Guarantee in April 2013. As a result, member states are required to ensure that all young people up to the age of 25 receive a quality job offer, continued education, an apprenticeship or a traineeship within four months of leaving formal education or becoming unemployed. The Commission monitors the implementation of Youth Guarantees in the European Semester exercise.

The provision of pro-active and effective policy measures directed at positive transitions between education and employment is explicitly identified as being crucial to positive transitions between education and employment (Sanderson, 2019; Ellison, 2017, 2014a, 2014b; Green and Pensiero, 2017; Kangas et al., 2017). Exemplifying this, in Scotland these policy measures were developed through Local Employment Partnerships (LEPs) as part of the Community Planning Partnerships framework in all 32 local authorities. As discussed in Chapter 4, LEPs are collaborative partnerships between employers, local authorities, public services and representatives of vulnerable groups (Ellison, 2014a). The Edinburgh Guarantee in Scotland exemplifies a locally developed innovation within an LEP which is funded largely by the European Structural Fund as a pro-active response to levels of youth unemployment and poor youth transitions in the city. In 2017/2018, 92.3 per cent of Edinburgh's school leavers entered a positive destination as a result of the Edinburgh Guarantee; this compares to 82.3 per cent of all school leavers within Edinburgh in 2011 (Edinburgh City Council, 2019). The definition of 'positive destination' includes transitions to further and higher education as well as transitions into the local labour market. It is important to note that the kinds of entry-level jobs that young people enter may not be of a high quality and may indeed include part-time or non-standard employment. At the same time, there has been a year-on-year increase in numbers of young people entering further and higher education in Scotland. A central policy of the Scottish Government is to widen access to higher education. As part of this policy young people in Scotland do not pay up-front tuition fees. Significantly, in 2017/2018 a record number of full-time first-degree students at Scottish universities were from the most deprived areas in Scotland – 15.6 per cent of students entering university were from within the 20 per cent most deprived areas. The Scottish Government's target for 2021 is 16.0 per cent (Scottish Government, 2018). In contrast, it may be argued that the high cost of tuition fees in other parts of the UK can deter students from socio-economically deprived settings from applying to university. This is a societal risk that students face in England, where high tuition fees act as a disincentive to applying to university. Universities in England have the second highest tuition fees among all OECD countries (OECD, 2019).

Critically, it may be argued that significant differences in labour market outcomes for young people and the effectiveness of specific interventions directed at young people within distinct European settings are forged within the divergent political economies of welfare. Policy frameworks and governance models, which adopt a more integrated social investment approach, particularly in reducing societal risks such as limited access to higher education and high levels of inequality and poverty, exhibit more inclusive and sustainable outcomes for young people (Leibetseder, 2018; Bouget et al., 2015; Deeming and Smyth, 2015; Ellison, 2014b; Ellison and Fenger, 2013). Moreover, the distributional aspects of economic and social well-being are also shown to have a positive impact on social cohesion and economic growth (Marmot, 2020). In particular, the impacts of austerity measures on disadvantaged and vulnerable young people are revealed as being particularly negative, with personal crises often leading to tragic consequences with growing levels of mental health problems and suicide particularly among young men across European settings with significant levels of austerity (Borrell et al., 2020; Cairns et al., 2017; Han et al., 2017; McDaid, 2017; Parmar et al., 2016; Platt, 2016).

There is also a growing evidential base re-orientating theoretical understanding of risk from the individual to the societal level (Nygren et al., 2020; Taylor-Gooby et al., 2020; Hästbacka and Nygård, 2019; Asenova et al., 2015; Woodman and Wyn, 2015; Ellison, 2014a; Ellison and Fenger, 2013). As Woodman and Wyn (2015) argue, the challenges that young people face within precarious social and economic environments necessitate a re-focusing away from previously understood notions of youth transitions to adulthood involving a linear chronological progression through school education and into full-time work (Cuervo and Chesters, 2019; Woodman and Wyn, 2015). The analysis of pro-active policy responses to the challenges faced by young people within the context of crises and austerity has also been the focus of recent contributions. A number of recent studies have adopted a holistic generational approach to youth transitions, enabling the consideration of strategies that young adults use to enter and sustain a position in European labour markets whilst also establishing their independent household with or without children. Social policies designed to support young adults in balancing work and family life are investigated (Cuervo and Chesters, 2019; Walsh et al., 2019; Dewilde et al., 2018; Roberts and Antonucci, 2018; Guerrero, 2017). Caring responsibilities are a significant constraint to young people entering and sustaining a position in European labour markets. At the same time, strategic policy innovations designed to enable a better reconciliation of work and family are also evidenced as being an effective means to support employment and the social (security) inclusion of caregivers in European countries. These policy innovations particularly focus upon the increased provision of childcare facilities in European countries. Moreover, policy innovations are of particular importance as a significant number of young people in European countries are responsible for looking after children or incapacitated adults (usually parents, grandparents or older siblings) and this severely limits their capacity to enter full-time employment. This situation is most acute in the UK, where in 2018 16.3 per cent of young people were young carers. This compares to 1.1 per cent in Spain, 1.7 per cent in Greece, 1.7 per cent in Slovenia and 4.4 per cent in Sweden (Eurostat, 2019).

Complex and inter-related factors impact upon the responsibilities of young people within distinct European countries, including distinct welfare regimes, family policies and cultural differences. In the UK recent research has revealed ways in which the disadvantages faced by young people affect their childhood, adolescent years and education. Young people caring for a family member who is disabled or physically or mentally ill are severely restricted in their capacity to enter and sustain a position in the labour market (Joseph et al., 2020; Moloney et al., 2020; Dixley et al., 2019; Aldridge, 2018; Cheesbrough et al., 2017). More broadly, young carers are also more likely to suffer issues relating to mental health as a result of the physical, psychological and emotional demands of caring (Santini et al., 2020; Gibson et al., 2019; Hawken et al., 2019; Järkestig-Berggren et al., 2019; Rahman et al., 2019; Lewis, 2018). The harmful impact of austerity-driven reductions in public expenditure funding for long-term care systems across Europe in recent decades is evidenced as being detrimental to the mental health of informal carers across Europe, including women, children and young people. It may be argued that substantive social investment in accessible long-term formal care would begin to address the mental and physical exhaustion that young carers and all informal carers face (Palmer, 2020; Barbieri and Ghibelli, 2019; Oldridge, 2019; Pickard, 2019; Schulmann et al., 2019; Murphy and Turner, 2017; Anderson, 2016).

Here the interaction between the emotional, physical and psychological burden of being simultaneously engaged in informal long-term social care of a relative or friend who is disabled or in need of support whilst also participating in the labour market underlines the significance of the relationship between public health, informal social care, formal care, work and poverty across European societies. Moreover, attempts to balance caring responsibilities with work often lead to low levels of household work intensity and the acceptance of insecure, substandard employment, including zero-hour contracts. This further exacerbates the lived experience of socio-economic deprivation (ILO, 2020b; Marmot, 2020; Patterson et al., 2020; Bauhardt and Harcourt, 2018; Vizard et al., 2019). For informal carers who struggle to cope with the demands of paid work in the formal economy, the emotional, physical and psychological burden of being an informal carer can become intolerable. Recent research has revealed that this is particularly detrimental to the health and well-being of young carers (Akkan, 2020; Moloney et al., 2020; Nap et al., 2020; Becker and Sempik, 2019; Pietikäinen, 2019). Across Europe, austerity measures have led to the retrenchment of formal personal social care services, creating a significant imbalance between levels of provision of formal care and informal care.

A plethora of recent studies have revealed the physical and emotional strain placed on people who provide informal social care with little or no support from formal care systems provided by the state (Bertogg and Strauss, 2020; Hohmeyer and Kopf, 2020; Walsh and Murphy, 2020; Kolodziej et al., 2018; van den Broek and Grundy, 2018; Verbakel et al., 2017). There is urgent need to develop policies and measures to address imbalances between formal and informal care across European settings. The creation of sustainable long-term care systems is a critical challenge for all EU countries. Recent comparative evidence clearly demonstrates that where relevant social policy frameworks and care systems are developed – as in Nordic countries, for example – informal caregiving has a less harmful direct effect on individual physical and psychological health and well-being (Chiatti et al., 2018; Sutcliffe et al., 2017; Verbakel et al., 2017; Bremer et al., 2015). More broadly, the adequacy of formal care systems and appropriate social policies has also been shown to have a direct impact on the social determinants of health, particularly with regard to poverty and participation in the labour market (Hohmeyer and Kopf, 2020; Kelle, 2020; Kolodziej et al., 2018; Schmitz and Westphal, 2017; Van Houtven et al., 2013).

The relationship between public health, work, formal care and engagement in the labour market is also illustrated by the significant barriers and challenges faced by care-experienced young people in education, training and labour markets across Europe (Boddy et al., 2020; Brady, 2020; Pinkney and Walker, 2020; Brady et al., 2019; Harrison, 2019). These vulnerabilities are particularly evident during the transition between education and employment (Brady and Gilligan, 2020; Harrison, 2019; Schoon and Bynner, 2019; Ellison, 2017). Comparative research has revealed the influence of country-specific social policies and formal care systems on differential outcomes for care-experienced young people (Boddy et al., 2020; Brady, 2020; Brady and Gilligan, 2020; Pinkney and Walker, 2020; Boddy et al., 2019).

FUTURE CHALLENGES IN A POST-COVID EUROPE

The future challenges faced by young people living and working in a post-Covid-19 Europe are considerable. As has been evidenced above, labour market conditions will change markedly as a result of the widely anticipated onset of a global economic recession. As a burgeoning body of research has shown, young people are more vulnerable to the impacts of economic recession on the labour market than any other demographic group (Blustein et al., 2020; IMF, 2020; OBR, 2020). For young people who do not have substantive skills in digital technology, the risk of losing their jobs as a result of automation and advances in AI intensifies this vulnerability. Critically also, many entry-level jobs require competence in digital technologies. Young people facing additional barriers and challenges relating to educational inequalities will thus be at a severe disadvantage in the post-Covid-19 economy. Whilst substantial top-down investment in policies and measures which focus on lifelong learning, education and skills in Europe will clearly mitigate some of the barriers faced by young people in Europe, the complexity and deep-seated nature of these multi-dimensional challenges will necessitate substantial public investment in innovative place-based cross-sectoral measures directed at the promotion of physical, psychological and emotional well-being of all young people living and working in Europe.

The most recent EU Youth Strategy 2019–2027 does provide a coherent framework for effective governance and funding of place-based measures directed at the well-being of young people in Europe (Official Journal of the European Union, 2018). Critically, however, the effectiveness of these measures is also reliant on the reduction of social, economic and health inequalities and the rejection of neo-liberal ideological generating mechanisms which have exacerbated these inequalities in recent decades. In particular, the philosophical rationale for neo-liberalism has elevated individualism and self-awareness of individual risk as a central pre-condition of success within education and the labour market.

The current Covid-19 health pandemic has simultaneously exposed the specific and complex interaction of economic, health and social inequalities whilst also revealing the kinds of societal risks that young people face within distinct European societies. These specificities have led to a hybridisation or 'mix' of welfare measures and policy responses directed at complex and intersecting issues relating to youth poverty, deprivation, poorly funded education and social care services and precarious labour markets that are faced by young people living and working in Europe. The EU Youth Strategy 2019–2027 recognises that young people are now confronted with future uncertainties relating to globalisation and climate change, technological change, demographic and socio-economic trends, populism, discrimination and social exclusion (Official Journal of the European Union, 2018). These challenges have been exacerbated by the profound social and economic implications of the Covid-19 health pandemic. As previously argued in this chapter, a focus on place-based cross-sectoral working does contribute significantly to positive outcomes for young people across Europe. In recognition of the fact that socio-economic exclusion and democratic exclusion are inextricably related, inclusive forms of governance have led to the development of more effective and sustainable place-based measures and programmes for young people within distinct European settings. The three central objectives of the EU Youth Strategy reflect these principles. The Strategy strives to:

1. Enable young people to be architects of their own lives, support their personal development and growth to autonomy, build their resilience and equip them with life skills to cope with a changing world.
2. Encourage and equip young people with the necessary resources to become active citizens, agents of solidarity and positive change inspired by EU values and a European identity.
3. Improve policy decisions with regard to their impact on young people across all sectors, notably employment, education, health and social inclusion.

Moreover, the eleven European Youth Goals which are central to the EU Youth Strategy 2019–2027 were generated through a dialogical process involving young people from across Europe. These goals identify cross-sectoral challenges, including:

1. Connecting the European Union with Youth.
2. Equality of All Genders.
3. Inclusive Societies.
4. Information & Constructive Dialogue.
5. Mental Health & Wellbeing.
6. Moving Rural Youth Forward.
7. Quality Employment for All.
8. Quality Learning.
9. Space and Participation for All.
10. Sustainable Green Europe.
11. Youth Organisations & European Programmes. (Eurodesk, n.d.)

Critically, however, it may be argued whilst that these principles and goals offer an inclusive governance approach with some emphasis on improving policies and measures directed at alleviating the challenges faced by young people, it is nevertheless clear from a growing body of evidence that these challenges have been largely generated by fundamental dis-welfares arising from the current relationship between economy and society in Europe. As has been evidenced in this chapter, these dis-welfares have arisen from socio-economic structural inequalities, particularly with regard to fundamental imbalances between public health, work, capital, formal care, informal care, inequality, poverty and the labour market (Brady, 2020; Palmer, 2020; Dixley et al., 2019; Antonucci, 2017; Elliot, 2016; Asenova et al., 2015; Ellison, 2014a). Whilst the introduction of discrete social policy measures will partially address the economic well-being of young people as they navigate the transition between education and employment, it may be argued that only the systematic reconfiguration of the relationship between economy and society in Europe will begin to address fundamental imbalances between public health, work capital, formal care, informal care, inequality, poverty and the labour market. It may be argued that a renewed focus on progressive economic alternatives aligned to the creation of a post-Covid-19 'Well-being Economy' are required to begin to address these imbalances (ILO, 2020; Marmot, 2020; Patterson et al., 2020; Bauhardt and Harcourt, 2018). For example, the operationalisation of UBS as an entitlement granted to all as a fundamental prerequisite of the Foundational Economy would address the rights of young carers and care-experienced young people by providing adequate levels of publicly funded formal care as they navigate the inter-related and complex social, economic and personal challenges during the transition between education and employment. The Covid-19 health pandemic has exacerbated these challenges, bringing a renewed urgency to the development of more equitable and ecologically sustainable economic models and social policies.

CONCLUSION

As this chapter has evidenced, the personal challenges faced by many young people living and working in Europe are forged by the lived experience of balancing complex and intersecting issues, including poverty, informal caring responsibilities, inequitable access to education, and inadequate health and social care services, with normative expectations that their well-being and future success relies on their capacity to achieve educational qualifications and skills which will enable them to 'fit' within current economic and social structures. The Covid-19 pandemic has not only revealed the extent and depth of socio-economic and health inequalities across Europe; it has also illuminated the complex relationship between public health, work, capital, formal care, informal care, inequality and poverty in Europe. Transformational economic alternatives such as the Foundational Economy, which promotes the equitable distribution of UBS as an entitlement which is granted to all, would address societal risks faced by young people across European society. In particular, young people would benefit significantly from universal entitlement to adequate health, social care, education and training services. For example, access to adequate levels of formal care would give young carers equal participation in education and the labour market.

More fundamentally, as has been argued, the transition between education and employment is often fraught with barriers and obstacles, and equitable access to adequate health and social care systems would promote the well-being of young people by providing support during challenging transitional stages in their lives. Moreover, it may be argued that the implementation of the closely related measure UBI would give young people the financial security that they need to make positive transitions between different levels of education and between education and the labour market.

The interaction between public health, work, formal care, informal care, inequality, poverty and the labour market lies at the centre of the relationship between economy and society in Europe. Calls for a new focus on a well-being economy which recognises the centrality of the economy of care have arisen (ILO, 2020a; Marmot, 2020; Patterson et al., 2020; Bauhardt and Harcourt, 2018). This focus on a well-being economy was at the forefront of the Finnish Presidency of the Council for the EU between 1 July 2019 and 31 December 2019. The central focus of the Presidency was upon building a European 'Well-being Economy' which fully supported the development of the welfare economy, contributing to a socially, economically and environmentally sustainable Europe. Fundamental to this approach was the view that the formulation of macroeconomic policy requires the comprehensive analysis of its implications upon the well-being of citizens, particularly with regard to the quality of social and health care services and the prevalence of social exclusion among vulnerable groups of people who live and work across European societies (ILO, 2020a; Marmot, 2020; Patterson, 2020; Bauhardt and Harcourt, 2018).

By recognising the collective responsibility that we all share in building economies of well-being which elevate the primacy of public health within and across European societies, it may be argued that the 'challenges' that young people face are the 'challenges' that we all face. Thus, it is time to fully address the societal risks that impede and exacerbate social, economic and health dis-welfares within European societies.

REFERENCES

Adetunji, A. T., and Obilanade, F. M. (2016). Access to higher education courses for admission into UK universities: inequality in science education in Wales. *EPH – International Journal of Business & Management Science*, **2** (7), 8–17.

Agasisti, T., Longobardi, S., Prete, V., and Russo, F. (2020). The growing incidence of educational poverty in Europe: determinants and remedies. *Journal of Policy Modeling*. www.sciencedirect.com/science/article/pii/S0161893820300879.

Akkan, B. (2020). An egalitarian politics of care: young female carers and the intersectional inequalities of gender, class and age. *Feminist Theory*, **21** (1), 47–64.

Aldridge, J. (2018). Where are we now? Twenty-five years of research, policy and practice on young carers. *Critical Social Policy*, **38** (1), 155–165.

Allan, B. A., Rolniak, J. R., and Bouchard, L. (2020). Underemployment and well-being: Exploring the dark side of meaningful work. *Journal of Career Development*, **47** (1), 111–125.

Anderson, R. (2016). Carers and employment in the EU, in: Naegele, G. (ed.), *Teilhabe im Alter gestalten* (pp.265–277). Wiesbaden: Springer VS.

Antonucci, L. (2017). *Student Lives in Crisis: Deepening Inequality in Times of Austerity*. Bristol: Policy Press.

Antonucci, L., Hamilton, M., and Roberts, S. (2014). *Young People and Social Policy in Europe*. London: Palgrave Macmillan.

Asenova, D., McKendrick, J. H., McCann, C., and Reynolds, R. (2015). *Redistribution of Social and Societal Risk: The Impact on Individuals, Communities and Their Networks in Scotland*. York: Joseph Rowntree Foundation.

Atfield, G., and Green, A. E. (2019). The impact of the youth obligation on disadvantaged young people. Warwick Institute for Employment Research/Centerpoint Publications. https://centrepoint.org.uk/media/3476/the-impact-of-the-youth-obligation.pdf.

Bailey, D. (2020). Shaping the 'new normal'. *Renewal*, **28** (2). https://renewal.org.uk/archive/vol-28-2020/shaping-the-new-normal/.

Bailey, D. J. (2014). Palliating terminal social democratic decline at the EU level? in: *European Social Democracy during the Global Economic Crisis* (pp.233–251). Manchester: Manchester University Press.

Baines, S., Bassi, A., Csoba, J., and Sipos, F. (2019). Introduction: implementing innovative social investment: strategic lessons from Europe, in: Baines, S., Bassi, A., Csoba, J., and Sipos, F. (eds), *Implementing Innovative Social Investment*. Bristol: Policy Press.

Barbera, F., Engelen, E., Salento, A., and Williams, K. (2016). Varieties of the foundational: the case of Italy. *Sociologia del Lavoro*, 143, 112–126.

Barbieri, D., and Ghibelli, P. (2019). *Formal vs Informal Long-Term Care: Economic and Social Impacts and Barriers*. Sprint European Project. https://zenodo.org/record/1410379#.X7aiM7fgqM9.

Bauhardt, C., and Harcourt, W. (eds) (2018). *Feminist Political Ecology and the Economics of Care: In Search of Economic Alternatives*. London: Routledge.

Becker, S., and Sempik, J. (2019). Young adult carers: the impact of caring on health and education. *Children & Society*, **33** (4), 377–386.

Bedford, J., Enria, D., Giesecke, J., Heymann, D. L., Ihekweazu, C., Kobinger, G., … and Ungchusak, K. (2020). COVID-19: towards controlling of a pandemic. *The Lancet*, **395** (10229), 1015–1018.

Berger, T., and Frey, C. B. (2016). *Structural Transformation in the OECD: Digitalization, Deindustrialisation and the Future of Work*. Paris: OECD Publishing.

Bertogg, A., and Strauss, S. (2020). Spousal care-giving arrangements in Europe: the role of gender, socio-economic status and the welfare state. *Ageing & Society*, **40** (4), 735–758.

Birch, K., and Springer, S. (2019). Peak neoliberalism? Revisiting and rethinking the concept of neoliberalism. *Ephemera: Theory and Politics in Organization*, **19** (3), 467–485.

Block, F. (2014). Democratizing finance. *Politics & Society*, **42** (1), 3–28.

Blundell, R., Dias, M. C., Joyce, R., and Xu, X. (2020). Covid-19 and inequalities. *Fiscal Studies*, **41** (2), 291–319.

Blustein, D. L., Duffy, R., Ferreira, J. A., Cohen-Scali, V., Cinamon, R. G., and Allan, B. A. (2020). Unemployment in the time of COVID-19: a research agenda. *Journal of Vocational Behavior*, **119** (June 2020), 103436.

Boddy, J., Bakketeig, E., and Østergaard, J. (2020). Navigating precarious times? The experience of young adults who have been in care in Norway, Denmark and England. *Journal of Youth Studies*, **23** (3), 291–306.

Boddy, J., Lausten, M., Backe-Hansen, E., and Gundersen, T. (2019). *Understanding the Lives of Care-Experienced Young People in Denmark, England and Norway: A Cross-National Documentary Review*. Bristol: Policy Press.

Böger, T., and Öktem, K. G. (2019). Levels or worlds of welfare? Assessing social rights and social stratification in Northern and Southern countries. *Social Policy & Administration*, **53** (1), 63–77.

Borrell, C., Palència, L., Marí-Dell'Olmo, M., Morrisson, J., Deboosere, P., Gotsens, M., ... and Rodríguez-Sanz, M. (2020). Socioeconomic inequalities in suicide mortality in European urban areas before and during the economic recession. *European Journal of Public Health*, **30** (1), 92–98.

Bosch (2016). Combating youth unemployment – Bosch continues Southern Europe apprenticeship initiative: additional projects in Italy and Spain. www.bosch-presse .de/pressportal/de/media/pressemappen/press_kit_45897_en.pdf.

Bouget, D., Frazer, H., Marlier, E., Sabato, S., and Vanhercke, B. (2015). Social investment in Europe: a study of national policies. European Social Policy Network (ESPN). European Commission, Brussels. doi: 10.2767/084978.

Brady, E. (2020). *A Qualitative Life Course Study of the Educational Pathways of Care-experienced Adults*. [Dissertation]. School of Social Work and Social Policy University of Dublin, Trinity College.

Brady, E., and Gilligan, R. (2020). The role of agency in shaping the educational journeys of care-experienced adults: insights from a life course study of education and care. *Children & Society*, **34** (2), 121–135.

Brady, E., Gilligan, R., and Nic Fhlannchadha, S. (2019). Care-experienced young people accessing higher education in Ireland. *Irish Journal of Applied Social Studies*, **19** (1), 5.

Bremer, P., Cabrera, E., Leino-Kilpi, H., Lethin, C., Saks, K., Sutcliffe, C., ... and Wübker, A. (2015). Informal dementia care: consequences for caregivers' health and health care use in 8 European countries. *Health Policy*, 119, 1459–1471.

Brown, P. (ed.) (2020). *Economic Restructuring and Social Exclusion: A New Europe?* Abingdon: Routledge.

Buendía, L., Serrano, P. J. G., and Molero-Simarro, R. (2020). Gone with the crisis? Welfare state change in Europe before and since the 2008 crisis. *Social Indicators Research*, **150** (1), 243–264.

Bussi, M., Schoyen, M. A., and Hvinden, B. (2019). Has the European Social Fund been effective in supporting young people? in: Hvinden, B., Hyggen, C., Schoyen, M. A., and Sirovátka, T. (eds), *Youth Unemployment and Job Insecurity in Europe* (pp.206–229). Cheltenham, UK, and Northampton, MA: Edward Elgar Publishing.

Cairns, J. M., Graham, E., and Bambra, C. (2017). Area-level socioeconomic disadvantage and suicidal behaviour in Europe: a systematic review. *Social Science & Medicine*, 192, 102–111.

Caliendo, M., Fedorets, A., Preuss, M., Schroeder, C., and Wittbrodt, L. (2017). *The Distributional Effects of the German Minimum Wage Reform*. Berlin: Mimeo Publications.

Calvo, A. G., and Coulter, S., (2019). Industrial transformation in the aftermath of the crisis: an empirical analysis of industrial policies in France, Germany, Spain and the United Kingdom. CES Open Forum Series 2018–2019. https://ces.fas.harvard.edu/publications/industrial-transformation-in-the-aftermath-of-the-crisis-an-empirical-analysis-of-industrial-policies-in-france-germany-spain-and-the-united-kingdom.

Capucha, L., Sebastião, J., da Cruz Martins, S., and Capucha, A. R. (2016). Crisis and education in Southern Europe: the effects of austerity and ideology. *Comparative Sociology*, **15** (5), 593–620.

Cheesbrough, S., Harding, C., and Webster, H. (2017). *The Lives of Young Carers in England*. Loughborough: Loughborough University Publications.

Chiatti, C., Rodríguez Gatta, D., Malmgren Fänge, A., Scandali, V. M., Masera, F., and Lethin, C. (2018). Utilization of formal and informal care by community-living people with dementia: a comparative study between Sweden and Italy. *International Journal of Environmental Research and Public Health*, **15** (12), 2679.

Chung, H., Bekker, S., and Houwing, H. (2012). Young people and the post-recession labour market in the context of Europe 2020. *Transfer: European Review of Labour and Research*, **18** (3), 301–317.

Clarke, J. (2019). Globalisation, neo-liberalism and the European Union, in: Kessl, F., Lorenz, W., Otto, H.-U., and White, S. (eds), *European Social Work: A Compendium* (pp.25–44). Leverkusen: Verlag Barbara Budrich.

Corburn, J., Vlahov, D., Mberu, B., Riley, L., Caiaffa, W. T., Rashid, S. F., Ko, A. et al. (2020). Slum health: arresting COVID-19 and improving well-being in urban informal settlements. *Journal of Urban Health*, **97** (3), 348–357.

Crisp, R., and Powell, R. (2017). Young people and UK labour market policy: a critique of 'employability' as a tool for understanding youth unemployment. *Urban Studies*, **54** (8), 1784–1807.

Cuconato, M. (2017). School to work transitions in Europe: choice and constraints. *Educational Research for Policy and Practice*, **16** (1), 43–59.

Cuervo, H., and Chesters, J. (2019). The [im] possibility of planning a future: how prolonged precarious employment during transitions affects the lives of young Australians. *Labour & Industry*, **29** (4), 295–312.

Cumbers, A., McMaster, R., Cabaço, S., and White, M. J. (2019). Reconfiguring economic democracy: generating new forms of collective agency, individual economic freedom and public participation. *Work, Employment and Society*, **34** (4). https://doi.org/10.1177/0950017019875935.

Deeming, C. (2017). The lost and the new 'liberal world' of welfare capitalism: a critical assessment of Gøsta Esping-Andersen's *The Three Worlds of Welfare Capitalism* a quarter century later. *Social Policy and Society*, **16** (3), 405–422.

Deeming, C., and Smyth, P. (2015). Social investment after neoliberalism: policy paradigms and political platforms. *Journal of Social Policy*, **44** (2), 297–318.

Détourbe, M. A., and Goastellec, G. (2018). Revisiting the issues of access to higher education and social stratification through the case of refugees: a comparative study of spaces of opportunity for refugee students in Germany and England. *Social Sciences*, **7** (10). https://doi.org/10.3390/socsci7100186.

Dewilde, C., Hubers, C., and Coulter, R. (2018). Determinants of young people's homeownership transitions before and after the financial crisis: the UK in a European context, in: Searle, B. A. (ed.), *Generational Interdependencies: The Social Implications for Welfare* (pp.51–73). Wilmington: Vernon Press.

Dias, M. C., Joyce, R., Postel-Vinay, F., and Xu, X. (2020). The challenges for labour market policy during the Covid-19 pandemic. *Fiscal Studies*, **41** (2), 371–382.

Dimoulas, C., and Papadopoulou, D. (2016). Synthetic report on the development, implementation and performance of innovations. Innovative Social Policies for Inclusive and Resilient Labour Markets in Europe (INSPIRES) European Project. www.inspires-research.eu/userfiles/Roy%20Upload/FINAL%20Synthetic %20Report%20WP4%20-%20D4.3.pdf.

Dingeldey, I., Assmann, M. L., and Steinberg, L. (2017). Strategies to improve labour market integration of young people: comparing policy coordination in nine European countries. NEGOTIATE Working Paper (No. 8.2). https://bufdir.no/Bibliotek/ Dokumentside/?docId=BUF00004232.

Dixley, A., Boughey, R., and Herrington, A. (2019). *Informal Carers and Employment: Summary Report of a Systematic Review*. London: Department for Work and Pensions.

Donnelly, M., and Evans, C. (2019). A 'home-international' comparative analysis of widening participation in UK higher education. *Higher Education*, **77** (1), 97–114.

Du Bois-Reymond, M., and López Blasco, A. (2003). Yo-yo transitions and misleading trajectories: towards integrated transition policies for young adults in Europe, in: López Blasco, A., McNeish, W., and Walther, A. (eds), *Young People and Contradictions of Inclusion: Towards Integrated Transition Policies in Europe* (pp.19–41). Bristol: Policy Press.

DWP (2017). Youth Obligation Support Programme. Department for Work and Pensions, UK Government. www.gov.uk/guidance/support-for-18-to-21-year-olds -claiming-universal-credit.

Earle, J., Froud, J., Johal, S., and Williams, K. (2018). Foundational economy and foundational politics. *Welsh Economic Review*, 26, 38–45.

Ecchia, G., Gagliardi, F., and Giannetti, C. (2020). Social investment and youth labor market participation. *Contemporary Economic Policy*, **38** (2), 343–358.

Edinburgh City Council (2019). The Edinburgh Guarantee. www.edinburghguarantee .org/.

Elliott, I. (2016). *Poverty and Mental Health: A Review to Inform the Joseph Rowntree Foundation's Anti-Poverty Strategy*. London: Mental Health Foundation.

Ellison, M. (2017). Through the looking glass: young people, work and the transition between education and employment in a post-Brexit UK. *Journal of Social Policy*, **46** (4), 675–698.

Ellison, M. (2014a). No future to risk? The impact of economic crises and austerity on young people at the margins of European employment and welfare settings, in: Farnsworth, K., Irving, Z., and Fenger, M. (eds), *Social Policy Review 26: Analysis and Debate in Social Policy* (pp.155–179). Bristol: Policy Press.

Ellison, M. (2014b). Identifying policy innovations increasing labour market resilience and inclusion of vulnerable groups. Regional report: Scotland. INSPIRES European Project. https://core.ac.uk/download/pdf/141197421.pdf.

Ellison, M., and Fenger, M. (2013). Social investment, protection and inequality within the new economy and politics of welfare in Europe. *Social Policy and Society*, **12** (4), 611–624.

Engelen, E., Froud, J., Johal, S., Salento, A., and Williams, K. (2017). The grounded city: from competitivity to the foundational economy. *Cambridge Journal of Regions, Economy and Society*, **10** (3), 407–423.

Esping-Andersen, G. (1990). *The Three Worlds of Welfare Capitalism*. Princeton: Princeton University Press.

Etherington, D., and Daguerre, A. (2015). Welfare reform, work first policies and benefit conditionality: reinforcing poverty and social exclusion. London: Centre for Enterprise and Economic Development Research, Middlesex University. www.mdx.ac.uk/__data/assets/pdf_file/0031/149827/Welfare-and-benefit-conditionality-report-January-2015.pdf.

Eurodesk (n.d.). Youth Organisations and European Programmes. www.eurodesk.org.uk/youth-organisations.

Eurofound (2013). *Study on NEETs – Young People Not in Employment, Education or Training: Characteristics, Costs and Policy Responses in Europe*. Dublin: Eurofound.

Eurostat (2019). Reconciliation of work and family life – statistics. https://ec.europa.eu/eurostat/statisticsexplained/index.php?title=Reconciliation_of_work_and_family_life_-_statistics&oldid=454330.

Eurostat (2020). Early leavers from education and training. Age: 18–24 [edat_lfse_14]. https://appsso.eurostat.ec.europa.eu/nui/show.do?dataset=edat_lfse_14&lang=en.

Featherstone, K. (2015). External conditionality and the debt crisis: the 'Troika' and public administration reform in Greece. *Journal of European Public Policy*, **22** (3), 295–314.

France, A. (2016). *Understanding Youth in the Global Economic Crisis*. Bristol: Policy Press.

Furlong, A. (2016). The changing landscape of youth and young adulthood, in: Furlong, A. (ed.), *Routledge Handbook of Youth and Young Adulthood* (pp.19–27). London: Routledge.

Gibson, J., Colton, F., and Sanderson, C. (2019). Young carers. *British Journal of General Practice*, **69** (687), 504.

González-Sanguino, C., Ausín, B., Ángel Castellanos, M., Saiz, J., López-Gómez, A., Ugidos, C., and Muñoz, M. (2020). Mental health consequences during the initial stage of the 2020 coronavirus pandemic (COVID-19) in Spain. *Brain, Behavior, and Immunity*, **2020** (87), 172–176.

Grabka, M. M., and Schröder, C. (2019). The low-wage sector in Germany is larger than previously assumed. *DIW Weekly Report*, **9** (14), 117–124.

Green, A. (2020). Unemployment and labour market policy priorities. City-REDI/WMREDI response to the BEIS inquiry on the impact of coronavirus on businesses and workers, p.71. https://blog.bham.ac.uk/cityredi/wp-content/uploads/sites/15/2020/05/Inquiry-response_v4-003.pdf.

Green, A., and Pensiero, N. (2017). *Comparative Perspectives: Education and Training System Effects on Youth Transitions and Opportunities*. Cambridge: Cambridge University Press.

Guerrero, T. J. (2017). *Youth in Transition: Housing, Employment, Social Policies and Families in France and Spain*. London: Routledge.

Hamilton, M., Antonucci, L., and Roberts, S. (2014). Introduction: young people and social policy in Europe, in: Antonucci, L., Hamilton, M., and Roberts, S. (eds), *Young People and Social Policy in Europe* (pp.1–12). Palgrave Macmillan, London.

Han, K. M., Chang, J., Won, E., Lee, M. S., and Ham, B. J. (2017). Precarious employment associated with depressive symptoms and suicidal ideation in adult wage workers. *Journal of Affective Disorders*, 218, 201–209.

Harris, K., and Scully, B. (2015). A hidden counter-movement? Precarity, politics, and social protection before and beyond the neoliberal era. *Theory and Society*, **44** (5), 415–444.

Harrison, N. (2019). Patterns of participation in higher education for care-experienced students in England: why has there not been more progress? *Studies in Higher Education*, **45** (9), 1986–2000.

Hästbacka, E., and Nygård, M. (2019). Creating capabilities for societal participation in times of welfare state change? Experiences of people with disabilities in Finland. *Alter*, **13** (1), 15–28.

Hawken, T. A., Turner-Cobb, J., and Barnett, J. (2019). An examination of hair cortisol in young caregivers: social support and resilience. 49th Annual Conference of the International Society of Psyconeuroendocrinology (ISPNE), August 2019, Milan.

Hay, C., and Wincott, D. (2012). *The Political Economy of European Welfare Capitalism*. Basingstoke: Palgrave Macmillan.

Helms Jørgensen, C., Järvinen, T., and Lundahl, L. (2019). A Nordic transition regime? Policies for school-to-work transitions in Sweden, Denmark and Finland. *European Educational Research Journal*, **18** (3), 278–297.

Heslop, J., Morgan, K., and Tomaney, J. (2019). Debating the Foundation Economy. *Renewal*, **27** (2), 5–12.

Heyes, J., and Lewis, P. (2014). Employment protection under fire: Labour market deregulation and employment in the European Union. *Economic and Industrial Democracy*, **35** (4), 587–607.

Högberg, B. (2019). Transitions from unemployment to education in Europe: the role of educational policies. *Journal of Social Policy*, **48** (4), 699–720.

Hohmeyer, K., and Kopf, E. (2020). Caught between two stools? Informal care provision and employment among welfare recipients in Germany. *Ageing & Society*, **40** (1), pp.162–187.

Iannelli, C., Smyth, E., and Klein, M. (2016). Curriculum differentiation and social inequality in higher education entry in Scotland and Ireland. *British Educational Research Journal*, **42** (4), 561–581.

ILO (2020a). ILO Monitor: COVID-19 and the world of work, 4th ed. International Labour Organization. www.ilo.org/wcmsp5/groups/public/---dgreports/---dcomm/documents/briefingnote/wcms_745963.pdf.

ILO (2020b). Global employment trends for youth 2020: technology and the future of jobs. International Labour Organization. www.ilo.org/wcmsp5/groups/public/---dgreports/---dcomm/---publ/documents/publication/wcms_737648.pdf.

ILO (2013). *The Youth Employment Crisis: A Call for Action*. Geneva: ILO.

IMF (2020). World economic outlook, April 2020. International Monetary Fund. www.imf.org/en/Publications/WEO/Issues/2020/04/14/weo-april-2020.

Ivchenko, A., Jachimowicz, J., King, G., Kraft-Todd, G., Ledda, A., MacLennan, M., Mutoi, L., Pagani, C., Reutskaja, E., Roth, C., and Slepoi, F. R. (2020). Evaluating COVID-19 public health messaging in Italy: self-reported compliance and growing mental health concerns. [Paper]. https://j.mp/39btyT2.

Jaayfer, O. (2020). *The Welfare State in the Twentieth Century: A Case Study of the Swedish Public Pension System*. Orlando: University of Central Florida.

Järkestig-Berggren, U., Bergman, A. S., Eriksson, M., and Priebe, G. (2019). Young carers in Sweden: a pilot study of care activities, view of caring, and psychological well-being. *Child & Family Social Work*, **24** (2), 292–300.

Jones, K., and Traianou, A. (2019). Austerity and the remaking of education policy in Europe since 2008, in: Traianou, A., and Jones, K. (eds), *Austerity and the Remaking of European Education* (pp.5–25). New York: Bloomsbury Academic.

Johnson, M., Johnson, E., Webber, L., and Nettle, D. (2020). Mitigating social and economic sources of trauma: the need for Universal Basic Income during the coronavirus pandemic. *Psychological Trauma: Theory, Research, Practice, and Policy*, **12** (S1), S191–S192.

Johnson, M., Koukiadaki, A., and Grimshaw, D. (2019). The Living Wage in the UK: testing the limits of soft regulation? *Transfer: European Review of Labour and Research*, **25** (3), 319–333.

Jørgensen, C. H., Järvinen, T., and Lundahl, L. (2017). Policies of school-to-work transitions and VET in Sweden, Denmark and Finland. *45th Congress of the Nordic Educational Research Association (NERA) Journal*, 10, 346–349.

Joseph, S., Sempik, J., Leu, A., and Becker, S. (2020). Young carers research, practice and policy: an overview and critical perspective on possible future directions. *Adolescent Research Review*, **5** (1), 77–89.

Kangas, O., Palme, J., and Kainu, M. (2017). The multifaceted roles of the social investment state in compensating, accumulating and multiplying endowments over the life cycle, in: Erola, J., and Kilpi-Jakonen, E. (eds), *Social Inequality Across the Generations* (pp.181–203). Cheltenham, UK, and Northampton, MA: Edward Elgar Publishing.

Karlıdağ-Dennis, E. (2020). *Higher Education, Youth and Migration in Contexts of Disadvantage: Understanding Aspirations and Capabilities* by Faith Mkwananzi. [Review]. *Journal of Human Development and Capabilities*, **21** (1), 101–103.

Kelle, N. (2020). Combining employment and care-giving: how differing care intensities influence employment patterns among middle-aged women in Germany. *Ageing & Society*, **40** (5), 925–943.

Kolodziej, I. W., Reichert, A. R., and Schmitz, H. (2018). New evidence on employment effects of informal care provision in Europe. *Health Services Research*, **53** (4), 2027–2046.

Kretsos, L. (2014). Youth policy in austerity Europe: the case of Greece. *International Journal of Adolescence and Youth*, **19** (sup1), 35–47.

Lee, J. (2020). Mental health effects of school closures during COVID-19. *The Lancet Child & Adolescent Health*. https://doi.org/10.1016/S2352-4642(20)30109-7.

Leibetseder, B. (2018). Social investment policies and the European Union: swimming against the neoliberal tide? *Comparative European Politics*, **16** (4), 581–601.

Lewis, F. M. (2018). *Who Am I? An Exploration of Identity Development of Young Adult Carers in the United Kingdom and United States*. [Dissertation]. University of Birmingham.

Lindsay, S., R. Hartman, L., and Fellin, M. (2016). A systematic review of mentorship programs to facilitate transition to post-secondary education and employment for youth and young adults with disabilities. *Disability and Rehabilitation*, **38** (14), 1329–1349.

Lindsay, S., Lamptey, D. L., Cagliostro, E., Srikanthan, D., Mortaji, N., and Karon, L. (2019). A systematic review of post-secondary transition interventions for youth with disabilities. *Disability and Rehabilitation*, **41** (21), 2492–2505.

Liotti, G., and Canale, R. R. (2020). Poverty and labour market institutions in Europe. *Panoeconomicus*, **67** (3), 277–290.

Lynch, J. (2020). Health equity, social policy, and promoting recovery from COVID-19. *Journal of Health Politics, Policy and Law.* https://doi.org/10.1215/03616878 -8641518.

MacDonald, R. (2016). Precarious work: the growing précarité of youth, in: Furlong, A. (ed.), *Routledge Handbook of Youth and Young Adulthood* (pp.156–163). London: Routledge.

Marmot, M. (2020). *Health Equity in England: The Marmot Review 10 Years On.* London: Institute of Health Equity. www.health.org.uk/sites/default/files/ upload/publications/2020/Health%20Equity%20in%20England_The%20Marmot %20Review%2010%20Years%20On_full%20report.pdf.

McDaid, D. (2017). Socioeconomic disadvantage and suicidal behaviour during times of economic recession and recovery. LSE Research Online. http://eprints .lse.ac.uk/69795/1/McDaid_Socioeconomic%20disadvantage%20and%20suicidal %20behaviour_published_2017%20LSERO%20edit.pdf.

Messkoub, M. (2014). The financial crisis and the restructuring of the EU social model, in: Dymarski, W., Frangakis, M., and Leaman, J. (eds), *The Deepening Crisis of the European Union: The Case for Radical Change* (pp.112–124). Poznan: Poznan University of Economics Press.

Moloney, B., Kroll, T., and Lafferty, A. (2020). An exploration of young carers' experiences in school and their perceptions regarding their future career: a scoping review protocol. *HRB Open Research*, **3** (41). doi: 10.12688/hrbopenres.13074.1.

Moore, H. L., and Collins, H. (2020). *Towards Prosperity: Reinvigorating Local Economies Through Universal Basic Services.* London: Institute for Global Prosperity. https://discovery.ucl.ac.uk/id/eprint/10096789/8/Moore_Towards %20Prosperity_With%20DOI.pdf.

Morgan, K. (2019). The future of place-based innovation policy (as if 'lagging regions' really mattered). *Regional Studies Policy Impact Books*, **1** (2), 79–89.

Mori, A. (2020). Public services under austerity: structure of the public sector and drivers of outsourcing, in: *Employment Relations in Outsourced Public Services* (pp.33–57). Cham: Palgrave Macmillan.

Mousteri, V., Daly, M., and Delaney, L., 2018. The scarring effect of unemployment on psychological well-being across Europe. *Social Science Research*, **72**, 146–169.

Murphy, C., and Turner, T. (2017). Formal and informal long-term care work: policy conflict in a liberal welfare state. *International Journal of Sociology and Social Policy*, **37** (3–4), 134–147.

Nap, H. H., Hoefman, R., de Jong, N., Lovink, L., Glimmerveen, L., Lewis, F., ... and Casu, G. (2020). The awareness, visibility and support for young carers across Europe: a Delphi study. BMC Health Services Research. https://reference.medscape .com/medline/abstract/33028311.

Nettle, D., Johnson, E., Johnson, M., and Saxe, R. (2020). Why has the COVID-19 pandemic increased support for Universal Basic Income? https://doi.org/10.31234/ osf.io/csr3u.

Neves, B. B., Dias de Carvalho, D., Serra, F., Torres, A., and Fraga, S. (2019). Social capital in transition(s) to early adulthood: a longitudinal and mixed-methods approach. *Journal of Adolescent Research*, **34** (1), 85–112.

Nicola, M., Alsafi, Z., Sohrabi, C., Kerwan, A., Al-Jabir, A., Iosifidis, C., ... and Agha, R. (2020). The socio-economic implications of the coronavirus and COVID-19 pandemic: a review. *International Journal of Surgery*, **2020** June (78), 185–193.

Nunes, J. (2020). The COVID-19 pandemic: securitization, neoliberal crisis, and global vulnerabilization. *Cadernos de Saúde Pública*, 36, p.e00063120.

Nygren, K. G., Olofsson, A., and Öhman, S. (2020). Risk, inequality, and (post) structure: risk as governing, in: *A Framework of Intersectional Risk Theory in the Age of Ambivalence* (pp.37–57). Cham: Palgrave Macmillan.

OBR (2020). Economic and fiscal outlook, March 2020. https://obr.uk/efo/economic-and-fiscal-outlook-march-2020/.

OECD (2019). *Education at a Glance 2019: OECD Indicators*. Paris: OECD Publishing.

OECD (2017). *OECD Skills Strategy Diagnostic Report: The Netherlands 2017*. Paris: OECD Publishing.

Official Journal of the European Union (2018). Resolution of the Council of the European Union and the representatives of the governments of the member states meeting within the Council on a framework for European cooperation in the youth field: the European Union Youth Strategy 2019-2027 (2018/C 456/01). https://eur-lex.europa.eu/legal-content/EN/TXT/PDF/?uri=OJ:C:2018:456:FULL&from=EN.

Oldridge, L. (2019). Hidden care(e)rs: supporting informal carers in the workplace, in: Nachmias, S., and Caven, V. (eds), *Inequality and Organizational Practice* (pp.105–127). Cham: Palgrave Macmillan.

ONS (2020). Deaths involving COVID-19 by local area and socioeconomic deprivation: deaths occurring between 1 March and 31 May 2020. www.ons.gov.uk/peoplepopulationandcommunity/birthsdeathsandmarriages/deaths/bulletins/deathsinvolvingcovid19bylocalareasanddeprivation/deathsoccurringbetween1marchand17april?hootPostID=f8f83cc51cba7b7e20edce0e1993cadf.

Otto, A., and Taylor-Gooby, P. (2014). National report on the labour market position of vulnerable groups in the United Kingdom. University of Kent. www.inspires-research.eu/userfiles/D3_2-Synthetic%20report-final.pdf.

Palmer, S. J. (2020). Unpaid carers and the disastrous impact of the lack of social care funding for dementia. *Nursing and Residential Care*, **22** (4), 1–3.

Pape, U., Brandsen, T., Pahl, J. B., Pieliński, B., Baturina, D., Brookes, N., Chaves-Ávila, R., et al. (2020). Changing policy environments in Europe and the resilience of the third sector. *VOLUNTAS*, **31** (1), 238–249.

Parmar, D., Stavropoulou, C., and Ioannidis, J. P. (2016). Health outcomes during the 2008 financial crisis in Europe: systematic literature review. *Bmj*, 354, i4588.

Parreira do Amaral, M., and Zelinka, J. (2019). Lifelong learning policies shaping the life courses of young adults: an interpretative analysis of orientations, objectives and solutions. *Comparative Education*, **55** (3), 404–421.

Patterson, A. S., Boadu, N. Y., Clark, M., Janes, C., Monteiro, N., Roberts, J. H., ... and Wipfli, H. (2020). Investigating global mental health: contributions from political science. *Global Public Health*, **15** (6), 805–817.

Pickard, L. (2019). Good value for money? Public investment in 'replacement care' for working carers in England. *Social Policy and Society*, **18** (3), 365–382.

Pietikäinen, S. (2019). European Parliament Informal Carers Interest Group: enabling young carers to pursue their life goals – converting research findings into policy actions. European Policy Brief. https://eurocarers.org/eurocarers-epig/.

Pinkney, S., and Walker, G. (2020). 'It was me, but it was them that helped me': exploring the issues for care-experienced young people within higher education. *Children and Youth Services Review*, 108, 104576.

Platt, S. (2016). Inequalities and suicidal behavior, in: O'Connor, R. C., and Pirkis, J. (eds), *International Handbook of Suicide Prevention* (pp.258–283). New York: John Wiley & Sons.

Prince's Trust. (2014). Prince's Trust Macquarie Youth Index 2014. www.princes-trust .org.uk/help-for-young-people/news-views/youth-index-2014.

Pulla, P. (2020). Covid-19: India imposes lockdown for 21 days and cases rise. *BMJ* 2020;368:m1251. www.bmj.com/content/368/bmj.m1251.

Rahman, N., Brown, S., Ioannou, M., Heller, D., Fertleman, C., and Datt, C. (2019). G248: the phenomenon of society's hidden young carers. BMA Journals. Archives of Disease in Childhood 2019;104:A101. https://adc.bmj.com/content/104/Suppl_2/ A101.1.

Rechel, B. (2019). Funding for public health in Europe in decline? *Health Policy*, **123** (1), 21–26.

Riele, K. T. (2006). Youth 'at risk': further marginalizing the marginalized? *Journal of Education Policy*, **21** (2), 129–145.

Rinne, R., Silvennoinen, H., Järvinen, T., and Tikkanen, J. (2019). Governing the normalisation of young adults through lifelong learning policies, in: Parreira do Amaral, M., Kovacheva, S., and Rambla, X. (eds), *Lifelong Learning Policies for Young Adults in Europe* (pp.105–126). Bristol: Policy Press.

Roberts, S., and Antonucci, L. (2018). Youth transitions, welfare policy and contemporary Europe, in: Lange, A., Steiner, C., Schutter, S., and Reiter, H. (eds), *Handbuch Kindheits- und Jugendsoziologie* (pp.281–293). Springer VS, Wiesbaden.

Saad-Filho, A. (2019). Crisis in neoliberalism or crisis of neoliberalism? in: *Value and Crisis: Essays on Labour, Money and Contemporary Capitalism* (pp.302–318). Leiden: Brill.

Sanders, J., Munford, R., Boden, J., and Johnston, W. (2020). Earning, learning, and access to support: the role of early engagement in work, employment skills development and supportive relationships in employment outcomes for vulnerable youth in New Zealand. *Children and Youth Services Review*, 110, 104753.

Sanderson, E. (2019). Youth transitions to employment: longitudinal evidence from marginalised young people in England. *Journal of Youth Studies*, 1–20. https://doi .org/10.1080/13676261.2019.1671581.

Santini, S., Socci, M., D'Amen, B., Di Rosa, M., Casu, G., Hlebec, V., Lewis, F., Leu, A., Hoefman, R., Brolin, R. and Magnusson, L. (2020). Positive and negative impacts of caring among adolescents caring for grandparents: results from an online survey in six European countries and implications for future research, policy and practice. *International Journal of Environmental Research and Public Health*, **17** (18), 6593.

Sarfati, H. (2015). *In It Together: Why Less Inequality Benefits All.* [Review]. *International Social Security Review*, **68** (4), 115–117.

Scarpetta, S. (2010). *Rising Youth Unemployment during the Crisis: How to Prevent Long-term Consequences on a Generation?* Paris: OECD.

Schelke, W. (2012). Collapsing worlds and varieties of welfare capitalism: in search of a new political economy of welfare. LSE 'Europe in Question' Discussion Paper Series, No. 54. www.lse.ac.uk/europeanInstitute/LEQS%20Discussion%20Paper %20Series/LEQSPaper54.pdf.

Schmitz, H., and Westphal, M. (2017). Informal care and long-term labor market outcomes. *Journal of Health Economics*, 56, 1–18.

Schoon, I., and Bynner, J. (2019). Young people and the Great Recession: variations in the school-to-work transition in Europe and the United States. *Longitudinal and Life Course Studies*, **10** (2), 153–173.

Schoon, I., and Bynner, J. (eds) (2017). *Young People's Development and the Great Recession: Uncertain Transitions and Precarious Futures*. Cambridge: Cambridge University Press.

Schröder, M. (2019). Varieties of capitalism and welfare regime theories: assumptions, accomplishments, and the need for different methods. *KZfSS Kölner Zeitschrift Für Soziologie Und Sozialpsychologie*, 71, 53–73.

Schulmann, K., Reichert, M., and Leichsenring, K. (2019). Social support and long-term care for older people: the potential for social innovation and active ageing, in Walker, A. (ed.), *The Future of Ageing in Europe* (pp.255–286). Singapore: Palgrave Macmillan.

Schweiger, G. (2020). Absolute poverty in European welfare states, in: Beck V., Hahn H., Lepenies, R. (eds), *Dimensions of Poverty, Philosophy and Poverty*, vol. 2 (pp.163–176). Cham: Springer.

Scottish Government (2018). *Scotland's Fiscal Outlook: The Scottish Government's Five-Year Financial Strategy*. Edinburgh: Scottish Government Publications. www.gov.scot/publications/scotlands-fiscal-outlook-scottish-governments-five -year-financial-strategy/pages/8/.

Shadmi, E., Chen, Y., Dourado, I., Faran-Perach, I., Furler, J., Hangoma, P., Hanvoravongchai, P., et al. (2020). Health equity and COVID-19: global perspectives. *International Journal for Equity in Health*, **19** (1), 1–16.

Sloam, J. (2013). The 'outraged young': how young Europeans are reshaping the political landscape. *Political Insight*, **4** (1), 4–7.

Stein, M. (2019). Supporting young people from care to adulthood: international practice. *Child & Family Social Work*, **24** (3), 400–405.

Sutcliffe, C., Giebel, C., Bleijlevens, M., Lethin, C., Stolt, M., Saks, K., Soto, M. E., et al. (2017). Caring for a person with dementia on the margins of long-term care: a perspective on burden from 8 European countries. *J. Am. Med. Dir. Assoc.*, 18, 967–973.

Taylor-Gooby, P., Heuer, J. O., Chung, H., Leruth, B., Mau, S., and Zimmermann, K. (2020). Regimes, social risks and the welfare mix: unpacking attitudes to pensions and childcare in Germany and the UK through deliberative forums. *Journal of Social Policy*, **49** (1), 61–79.

Taylor-Gooby, P., Leruth, B., and Chung, H. (2019). Identifying attitudes to welfare through deliberative forums: the emergence of reluctant individualism. *Policy & Politics*, **47** (1), 97–114.

Taylor-Gooby, P., Leruth, B., and Chung, H. (eds) (2017). *After Austerity: Welfare State Transformation in Europe after the Great Recession*. Oxford: Oxford University Press.

Theodore, N. (2020). Governing through austerity: (il) logics of neoliberal urbanism after the global financial crisis. *Journal of Urban Affairs*, **42** (1), 1–17.

Theodoropoulou, S. (ed.) (2018). *Labour Market Policies in the Era of Pervasive Austerity: A European Perspective*. Bristol: Policy Press.

Van Apeldoorn, B., and Overbeek, H. (2012). Introduction: the life course of the neoliberal project and the global crisis, in: *Neoliberalism in Crisis* (pp.1–20). London: Palgrave Macmillan.

Van den Broek, T., and Grundy, E. (2018). Does long-term care coverage shape the impact of informal care-giving on quality of life? A difference-in-difference approach. *Ageing & Society*, **40** (6), 1291–1308.

Van Dijk, A., and Noorda, J. (2019). Young leaders as a role model for youth at risk and youth policy: a study on individual effects of a pedagogical training programme in disadvantaged neighbourhoods in the Netherlands. *International Journal of Open Youth Work*, 3, 112–122.

Van Herpen, S. G., Meeuwisse, M., Hofman, W. A., and Severiens, S. E. (2020). A head start in higher education: the effect of a transition intervention on interaction, sense of belonging, and academic performance. *Studies in Higher Education*, **45** (4), 862–877.

Van Houtven, C. H., Coe, N. B., and Skira, M. M. (2013). The effect of informal care on work and wages. *Journal of Health Economics*, **32** (1), 240–252.

Verbakel, E., Tamlagsrønning, S., Winstone, L., Fjær, E. L., and Eikemo, T. A. (2017). Informal care in Europe: findings from the European Social Survey (2014) special module on the social determinants of health. *European Journal of Public Health*, **27** (Supp. 1), 90–95.

Vizard, P., Obolenskaya, P., and Burchardt, T. (2019). Child poverty amongst young carers in the UK: prevalence and trends in the wake of the financial crisis, economic downturn and onset of austerity. *Child Indicators Research*, **12** (5), 1831–1854.

Walsh, E., and Murphy, A. (2020). Examining the effects of activities of daily living on informal caregiver strain. *Journal of Health Services Research & Policy*, **25** (2), 104–114.

Walsh, L., Keary, A., and Gleeson, J. (2019). Non-linear transitions: an intergenerational longitudinal study of today's young women in education and work. *Young*, **27** (5), 468–485.

Webb, L., Cox, N., Cumbers, H., Martikke, S., Gedzielewski, E., and Duale, M. (2017). Personal resilience and identity capital among young people leaving care: enhancing identity formation and life chances through involvement in volunteering and social action. *Journal of Youth Studies*, **20** (7), 889–903.

White, P. M., and Lee, D. M. (2019). Geographic inequalities and access to higher education: is the proximity to higher education institution associated with the probability of attendance in England? *Research in Higher Education*, 61, 825–848.

WHO (2020). Mental health and psychosocial considerations during the COVID-19 outbreak? World Health Organization. www.who.int/docs/default-source/coronaviruse/mental-health-considerations.pdf.

Wiggan, J. (2012). Telling stories of 21st century welfare: the UK Coalition government and the neo-liberal discourse of worklessness and dependency. *Critical Social Policy*, **32** (3), 383–405.

Williams, A. (2020). The complex hegemony of neoliberalism, in: *Political Hegemony and Social Complexity* (pp.195–232). Cham: Palgrave Macmillan.

Woodman, D., and Wynn, J., (2015). *Youth and Generation: Rethinking Change and Inequality in the Lives of Young People*. Newbury Park: SAGE.

Woodward, P. (2020). Higher education and social inclusion: continuing inequalities in access to higher education in England, in: Papa, R. (ed.), *Handbook on Promoting Social Justice in Education* (pp.1229–1251). Cham: Springer.

Work and Pensions Committee (2013). *Public Accounts Committee: Thirty-Third Report Department for Work and Pensions – Work Programme Outcome Statistics*. London: UK Parliament. https://publications.parliament.uk/pa/cm201213/cmselect/cmpubacc/936/93602.htm.

6.   Power to the people? The European Social Model and the convergence of new social policies for empowerment

Giuseppe Moro

INTRODUCTION: THE CONSTRUCT OF EMPOWERMENT

Empowerment is a theory of individual, community and organisational change. It sees change as deriving from a process whereby people achieve control over their lives and are able to influence the factors which condition their existence in some way (Funnel and Rogers, 2011, pp. 332–334). Empowerment emphasises democratic participation, continuous improvement and self-determination and can be applied to individuals, communities and organisations (Perkins and Zimmerman, 1995).

Programmes based on empowerment theory are founded on the following assumptions:

1. Problems are more easily recognised and pinpointed by people who have experience of them.
2. People have valuable knowledge of their own needs, values and objectives.
3. People boast resources and strengths which can be recognised and on which a course for positive improvement can be built.
4. These courses should be created through independent decision-making and problem-solving processes.

According to this view, which is primarily of a functionalist type, there is a direct positive relationship between empowerment and individual and collective welfare; as a result, an individual or a social group with a high level of empowerment has no need for external support (for example, that of the state) to achieve well-being.

A slightly different concept of empowerment links it to the growth of freedom of choice, with results that do not necessarily lead to an increase in welfare. In particular, Amartya Sen (1992, 1993), proposes two theories which appear to be founded on this alternative vision of empowerment. The first is that of the capacity to acquire a set of functionings (the 'beings' and 'doings' that make up an individual's quality of life) which thus reflects the freedom of a person to lead one type of life rather than another. Sen (1992) argues that if greater freedom of choice can lead to an increase in well-being, then the capacity approach differs from the welfare and utilitarian theory since the states of being and doing can be chosen as important in their own right and not only because they produce benefits or well-being. It could be seen that it is this freedom of behaviour which produces immediate well-being, independently of whether one may have a greater number of available alternatives or alternatives which result in more benefits.

A second significant concept in a different definition of empowerment is that of agency. This can be interpreted as the freedom of individuals to achieve their own goals and values independently of whether these are necessarily linked to their well-being. This does not imply that well-being and agency are not interdependent, but rather that they can be distinguished by the fact that agency's increased freedom may also lead to lifestyle choices which can result in a decrease in well-being. One example of this could be the decision to live as a volunteer in a poor country. Thus, in line with this interpretation, empowerment can be defined as the development of skills which allow individuals to understand their own personalities, even if this is through methods which are creative or even dysfunctional according to prevalent social logic.

The concept of empowerment, above all that defined as functionalist, has been used in a number of different social disciplines such as community psychology, sociology, political theory, women's studies and education. In areas closely linked to welfare and in the field of studies on social welfare and social work it has been used to interpret conditions of poverty as a form of social, political and psychological disempowerment. It also features in the description of processes which can help the poorest and most disadvantaged social groups acquire power through the steps of mobilisation, participation and transformation of social power into political power (Friedmann, 1992).

A vital requirement for empowerment agendas is that participants share a strong interest in the programme and have an important role to play, which nurtures the desire to participate actively in the project. Moreover, empowerment derives from a feeling of belonging to a larger entity and being part of a bigger organisation and its efforts to control the environment in which the participants live.

The empowerment process develops over progressive phases. These are the recognition of existing social problems, increased awareness (Freire, 1971) in recognising their causes, mobilisation for change and fulfilment of change (Hur, 2006).

At least three different levels of empowerment can be identified. The first is intrapersonal, undertaking a personal process of transformation towards reconciliation with one's own identity and a greater control of one's own existence. The second is interpersonal, setting up a process of communication and sharing knowledge, values and, in the final analysis, power between figures in a social aid-type relationship (for example, that between a doctor and patient). The third level is that of community empowerment, which aims towards increasing community well-being through a process which starts with a better understanding of problems, opportunities and challenges. The community then compares these with the recognised abilities and resources available in order to fully exploit existing skills and develop new ones to face challenges and increase opportunities (Funnel and Rogers, 2011, pp. 370–373).

There are several key factors for individual empowerment: the necessary skills to perform a role or job, self-determination (control over one's own work) and the ability to exercise control over the organisation which one forms part of. Collective empowerment requirements include a sense of belonging within a determined group or organised context, active involvement in the life of the community, community control of the organisations present within it and the existence of a community spirit which leads people to work together to resolve problems and act for the promotion of social change (Hur, 2006). Community responses to the profound challenges we currently face as a result of the Covid-19 crisis certainly reflect this level of community spirit. As a number of commentators have argued, the recent intensification and expansion of community spirit, solidarity and development of concrete collective actions to help one another may well promote social change.

Community empowerment has also been interpreted as civil society empowerment whose objective is to support social subjects in order to make them more responsible and autonomous; this is in contrast to the systemic logic of market and state which may attempt to privatise and thus alienate these social subjects (Donati, 2015). According to this model, social policies should become 'relational guides' for a society which can regulate itself through support for social authorities. Working cooperatively, these may establish new rules to determine universally binding decisions. This vision of civil society was inspired by the Tocquevillian model in which society is composed of free and responsible people who work together in their daily lives and are able to react independently to social and personal challenges through the construction of important and ethically sound networks. The role of this so-called relational state is to encourage the empowerment of people and families and their associations so that they can develop the potential to change their lives. This means that services must supply families with frameworks which allow them to create new connections and foster change. Thus, for example, health treatment is promoted through educational methods which are designed to develop user skills.

In more general terms, the relationship between public and private sectors is governed by the principal of joint responsibility.

Empowerment strategies can support change and problem solving in a community, an organisation or society only when all steps of this process, both individual and collective, have been taken into consideration. All too often, there is a pervading interpretation of empowerment as an exclusively individual phenomenon or else its functionalist tendency is underlined rather than its social transformation approach.

Empowerment has become a reference point for a number of welfare policies that have been promoted and enacted by European countries in fields which differ greatly from one another. Examples of these include policies on employability and activation, educational system reforms with greater focus on student learning and, in broader terms, the concept of the Enabling Welfare State.

THE MODEL OF ACTIVATION AND THE ENABLING WELFARE STATE

The establishment of empowerment theory helped redesign European welfare models according to a new paradigm which was termed 'activation' (Serrano Pascual, 2007). This model redefined citizens' representation, an understanding of citizens' rights and areas of state intervention.

It is founded on three principles. Firstly, there is the individualised approach. Public policies (and in particular those concerning social areas) should no longer aim to redistribute wealth but rather change the behaviour, motivation and attitudes of individuals. Thus, strategies should focus as much as possible on customers and require the involvement of beneficiaries.

The activation model identifies the inadequacies of individuals as the cause of inequality and so legitimises measures which aim to alter individual motivation and generate a desire to work. Thus, for example, unemployment and a lack of employability are considered problems of the individual and it seems inevitable that individuals autonomously experience social hardship and learn to measure themselves against it. The role of the Welfare State is to fight against dependency (or rather, what is defined as the culture of dependency), verify that citizens share 'correct' values, and ensure that, formally, they enjoy equal opportunities. The pressure to assume individual responsibility can be applied through either incentives or coercive and punitive measures; thus, for example, a lack of motivation could be considered an illness which requires medical treatment. This strategy could trigger adverse effects when policies designed to improve work opportunities are carried out in economically underdeveloped areas and when job opportunities are limited or characterised by a high degree of insecurity.

The second principle is an emphasis on employment and on the autonomy of individuals which derives from it; the focus shifts from social and political citizenship to economic citizenship. From an emphasis on work and individual autonomy, a standard solution to social and individual problems emerges in the need for people to find a job. Therefore, the key objective of the Welfare State is no longer that of protecting citizens from the risks of the economic market so much as creating conditions whereby individuals can adapt to the needs of the market, so strengthening their human capital. In concrete terms, this means that the state promotes growth in the level of economic activity through programmes which extend working life and discourage retirement, encourage a work–life balance to increase women's employment and restrict access to monetary benefits for the unemployed and those unable to work.

The third principle is that of the contractualisation: access to citizens' rights is conditioned by a moral contract with the state, according to which individuals are obliged to change their behaviour and habits, above all in relation to work. This reciprocal regulation implies that a citizen must 'deserve' state aid. Work (and more generally activation) are considered civil obligations which form the basis of the condition of deserving support from the state. Protection, support and aid are no longer regarded as inalienable rights which are a natural consequence of social citizenship, and the social policies which are founded on these entitlements are seen as morally negative as they promote passivity in citizens. Individuals, on the other hand, have a moral obligation to be self-governed and not seek public protection.

In fact, the spread of the activation model throughout European welfare systems has seen a revision of traditional forms of welfare and the formation of new hybrid systems that combine a mixture of elements from different political cultures and social models. European institutions played a key role in promoting this process of hybridisation through the European employment strategy. This provided the cultural and ideological framework for interpreting the crisis in the European labour market as well as outlining solutions to it. Governments of countries whose political traditions were a far cry from the activation model or culture of empowerment (one can refer to so-called Mediterranean welfare countries but also to France, for example) justified their reform programmes citing demands from European supranational institutions. These conditions would have required compliance in order to avoid penalties or simply to remain credible within the European political and institutional environment. Even political and social groups in favour of welfare reform were able to use the European employment strategy as a strategic resource in promoting change. A final important factor in the hybridisation process was that of highlighting the welfare programme of some countries as 'best practice' (for example, Denmark or Holland). This had two effects: on the one hand, it spawned widespread imitation of such models. On the other, there was a freeze on these models precisely because they were considered programmes to imitate and not to modify.

In short, this new political direction represented a change from the typical guiding principles of progressive welfare policies from the second half of the twentieth century. The latter was characterised by a universalist approach, providing public benefits to protect citizens from market risks, and was based on the recognition of social rights. Now policies focused on selective support measures provided by private institutions, which aimed to promote the active participation of the workforce.

The theory at the root of this new approach can be seen as empowerment, as demonstrated by the definition of this new form of social state as the 'Enabling State' (Gilbert, 2013), driven by the principle of public support for private responsibility and in which welfare policies aimed to enable people to work and allow the private sector to widen its field of activity. Gilbert (2013, p. 90) believes that the shift from the model of Welfare State to Enabling State redefined the core aims of welfare, transforming them from protection and income support to activation and social inclusion based on an inspirational political proposal which emphasised 'activation, social inclusion, empowerment, and social responsibility'.

From a substantive point of view, the Enabling State is characterised by four underlying areas (Gilbert, 2013, pp. 85–88) which mark its most significant changes from the Welfare State model.

Firstly, there was a progressive privatisation process in services providing social welfare and monetary benefits. This is evident in the system of vouchers or tax credit which allowed individuals to make their own personal choices in matters pertaining to health, care services, education and retirement.

Secondly, there was near-universal acceptance of the principle that passive policies for unemployment income support needed to be substituted for programmes which promoted employment. This meant that from the 1990s on, reforms carried out by almost all European countries on policies for assistance, disability and unemployment were to follow a common model. This implied a restriction of access to assistance and early exit, the introduction of contractual obligations to receive assistance and the creation of incentives to impel individuals to work. Naturally, the final versions of these measures differed according to the welfare traditions of each country, but even in those welfare states strongly associated with universalism and decommodification (such as Scandinavian countries), the tendency was to comply with the general model, so resulting in a further hybridisation of European welfare systems.

The third area was in the growth of benefit targeting and the increasing use of means testing, which ended up transforming universal programmes into selective ones, such as in the cases of family allowances and various types of minimum or citizenship income.

Finally, there was a shift from the view that citizens had a social right to be beneficiaries of welfare provision to the idea that they were required to behave in a socially acceptable way, contribute to the production of their own welfare and become independent as soon as possible, so developing a sense of autonomy and control over their lives. The clearest example of this was in the various pension reforms which extended working lives, liberalised the age of retirement (more or less across the board) and increased personal contribution to pension plans. These changes were to be justified by not only the financial limits of public coffers but also the importance of encouraging an active old age.

Therefore, the framework of empowerment leads to a redefinition of the role of the state which is no longer that of compensating for risks but providing individuals with the skills to cope with them. The state has to develop the human capital of individuals and increase their power so that they can make their choices responsibly. This redefinition of the role of the state gives rise to a positive concept of beneficiaries as autonomous and responsible individuals (Evers and Guillemard, 2013). However, there is also an increased risk that the most disadvantaged individuals, deprived of welfare support, are not able to develop their autonomous skills to cope with risks and gain an advantage from investment in human capital precisely because they do not boast the same level of opportunity as other social groups.

At the centre of this concept of the role of the state and its relationship with its citizens lies the philosophical and ethical principle of the individual responsibility on which various reform strategies are founded. Programme beneficiaries must prove their willingness to act like responsible people who strive to become entrepreneurs of their own lives and to be self-sufficient (Evers and Guillemard, pp. 365–366).

The emphasis which empowerment places on beneficiaries to act in a free and responsible manner means that the guiding principle of social policy is no longer that of equality as much as that of inclusion. Social measures have to be personalised and targeted to provide individuals with the support they need to perform an active role in society. However, the risk is that targeting becomes a form of stigmatisation and that the social protection system splits into two streams whereby access to social benefits for certain groups or individuals is conditioned by their adopting responsible behaviour and showing they 'deserve' state aid, while other groups benefit from an unconditional right to assistance.

The role of the state does not only change with regard to its relationship with programme beneficiaries, but also with other forms of solidarity supported by civil society. To this end, the state performs an empowerment task for civil society, restricting the direct provision of services and acting as a proactive coordinator, both of the welfare market and of various third-sector, voluntary, community and family organisations. The aim of social policies is increasingly that of encouraging the participation of users and their associations in setting up services to meet their needs and to create synergy and complementarity between the different forms of solidarity within civil society, so creating what has been defined as an integrated multi-solidarity system (Paugam, 2007, p. 970).

EMPOWERMENT AND THE HYBRIDISATION OF EUROPEAN WELFARE SYSTEMS

The principles of empowerment and activation have been included in the political proposals of all European countries. However, it is clear that the definitive policies carried out have been the result of a hybridisation between these principles and different cultural and institutional traditions, a factor which has produced contradictory results (Evers and Guillemard, 2013).

Thus, in countries where more liberal strategies prevailed (for example, the United Kingdom), the focus was on accelerating the return of citizens to the labour market, as this was held to be the best way of rendering individuals autonomous and responsible for their own well-being, as well as that of their families (Lister and Bennett, 2010). It was thus believed that the most important role of the state was to provide public support for the private responsibility of 'active' citizens; increasingly, the offer of benefits and social services has been conditioned by the adherence of beneficiaries to this form of behaviour. The innate risk of this strategy is that the poorest are unable to exercise the responsibility required of them and do not comply with behaviour standards which are considered socially acceptable. Thus, they are considered solely responsible for their failures and deserving of any penalties incurred.

Socially democratic countries have also seen social reforms aimed at reinforcing the work ethic, and the offer of benefits deriving from social rights has been made conditional upon the efforts of individuals to return to work. However, here the emphasis has been placed more on the preventative action of the state whose priority is in offering individuals the skills necessary to deal with social risks and so ensure well-being and inclusion. Furthermore, when outlining the social obligations of beneficiaries, priority has been more on incentives rather than coercive measures. As regards governing the system, the state remains the cornerstone of new strategies and the regulator of services provided by private bodies and the third sector. It continues to carry out a 'paternalistic' role (albeit with different aims) since it encourages individuals to invest in lifelong learning and supplies them with services which help them to make the 'right' choices in investing in their future (Trägårdh and Svedberg, 2013).

Liberal and socially democratic systems have in common the fact that they operate as part of a direct interaction between state and individual and underestimate the possible role of civil and third-sector associations and community networks. However, the tendency to reinforce the autonomous role of the community and third sector is much more widespread in countries with corporate welfare models. Changes had been visible in the models of governance aiming to develop complementarity between state and civil measures, while at the same time new social policies were being enacted to promote activation and individual responsibility, and extend the choice of different options available to citizen consumers. Thus, in Germany, for example, the end of the system of full employment and of a clear identification of both universal social rights of workers and citizens' rights led to a reinforcement of individual responsibility: a number of social rights became available through market choices (Bode, 2013) rather than from traditional company social protection schemes. These included integrated pension plans, a choice of health insurance plans and their providers, and so on. A negative consequence identified by Barbier's study in France (2013) is the greater difference between those who continue to use the more generous protection schemes offered by traditional networks and those on the fringes of the labour market who are forced to revert to activation, with lower levels of protection and benefits.

As a matter of fact, the relationship between individual rights, personal activation and social rights and solidarity appears to be one of the most controversial features of empowerment policies. An emphasis on individual rights and freedom could indeed lead to a reduction in social solidarity and an individual's sense of belonging to a given community, thus actually restricting the possibility to exercise one's freedom. On the other hand, it cannot be denied that an over-rigid and state-centred concept of social protection of individuals could limit the scope for individual freedom and human rights themselves.

It is interesting to observe how these different strategic approaches tangibly influence the ways in which social services are organised and provided. The processes of alignment do not lead to a uniformity of models, but to their interpretation, which sees the co-existence of common features of innovation and conformity to the traditions of each country. Thus, for example, a comparative study was carried out on so-called one-stop shops, a new organisational model of work services which have been set up in a number of European countries and which concentrate a variety of assistance and consultancy services in one location, rather than spread throughout different organisations as before.

The research found two significant models (Minas, 2014). The first model uses an approach based on the activation and promotion of training and other initiatives aimed at developing a variety of skills, not only those abilities useful for the world of work but also social skills related to the management of everyday life. It is an approach which aims to invest in the protection and enhancement of human and social capital and which has been adopted in the one-stop shops of Finland and Norway. The other model is, however, more focused on job search and offers orientation and job start-up programmes such as intensive job search, participation in short and targeted training courses and short periods of practical work experience. This one-stop shop model is popular in countries such as the United Kingdom, Germany, Holland and Denmark.

EMPOWERMENT AND THE REFORM OF SOCIAL POLICY IN EUROPEAN COUNTRIES

The principle of empowerment would seem to be the key factor leading European countries to adopt similar policies based on activation which, in turn, have led to the creation of so-called active labour policies. Various authors have made the distinction between two types of active policy: those aimed at improving and enhancing human capital, and those that basically use incentives to move people away from state assistance to employment (Bonoli, 2012). The first type have been defined variously as offensive (Torfing, 1999), positive (Taylor-Gooby, 2004), and as a universalistic model of activation (Barbier, 2004); the second type as defensive, negative and as a liberal model of activation (Clarke, 2004). Strictly speaking, only the first type are connected to the principle of empowerment and aim to improve people's skills, while the latter rely primarily on sanctions and on the reduction of benefits for those who do not actively seek employment.

In recent years, studies on labour policies have emphasised the importance of taking responsibility for one's own employability, while the state should have the role of creating the most suitable institutional framework to support the growth of personal skills and abilities (Jacobsson, 2004). The concept of employability underlines the relationship between the workers' individual responsibility to develop their own careers and employers' need for work. It has been argued that employability is now the factor which provides job security in today's job market, rather than having one job for life. The growth of employability, therefore, gives a greater guarantee that an individual will find work, not that he or she will be always work in the same job.

This idea emphasises the importance of the individual being able to deal with the fluctuations of the market and changing organisational contexts, while also underlining the importance of the state taking responsibility for the creation of jobs. Indeed, state policies should aim to help people to develop their own employability. This means that social spending should be aimed at financing measures which promote workers' motivation (for example, encouraging entrepreneurs), the acquisition of new skills and qualifications; in particular, it emphasises the important role played by education as a tool for promoting high levels of employment and social cohesion.

The concept of employability focuses on the promotion of individual responsibility; individual human capital is the key to success in the labour market and each individual is the one most responsible for developing their own human capital, while the government is asked to provide the educational resources needed to promote such a development (Berglund and Wallinder, 2015). In particular, an institutional framework which can give people the belief that they have the necessary requirements to achieve success in the world of work must include some fundamental elements. These include work experience programmes for young people, where the acquisition of new skills will give them more confidence in themselves; and long-life-learning for adults, which will help people feel more confident in dealing with the uncertainties of employment today.

This approach based on the principles of activation and empowerment has extended from labour policies to other social policies (Lister and Bennett, 2010). The paradigm of empowerment and activation has been the basis for the reform of disability benefits aimed at reducing the number of new applicants and increasing the number of those who no longer require assistance. These reforms have also been partly the result of a political debate which has challenged the right of certain people to necessarily receive disabled benefit and which has stigmatised the so-called culture of dependence where disabled and, more generally, sick people are not actively involved in work.

Looking at the reform of incapacity benefits in the United Kingdom since the beginning of the 2000s, it has been noted that this reform is based on four key assumptions concerning the causes which lead people to claim disability benefits, negative tendencies which the reform aimed to counter (Houston and Lindsay, 2010). Firstly, dependency on the state has become more common, bringing with it the decline of the work ethic; for this reason, it is necessary to introduce measures which promote people actively seeking work. Secondly, many people who claim for disability benefits do not have a disability or illness serious enough to justify them not working. Thirdly, the reason for not working is not due to a structural lack of opportunities offered by the labour market, but is due rather to individual deficiencies; therefore, it is necessary to promote activities aimed at rehabilitation, confidence-building and retraining to get people back to work. Fourthly, the longer that someone claims state assistance, the more their employability reduces; therefore, it is necessary to get unemployed people working as quickly as possible.

The principle of empowerment has driven innovation in social services across Europe. Services are less geared to providing monetary benefits for beneficiaries, but rather to establishing relationships which reduce dependence on state assistance, offering people new opportunities and strengthening their skills (Evers and Ewert, 2015). The same cultural model can be found in various case management schemes, personal counselling and 'one-stop entry points' in that they offer support to the individual in the free choice of services and the autonomous construction of personalised support packages. Likewise, contractual workfare schemes, in which support is given on the condition that the individual commits to changing their future behaviour, may take on a particular form when access is granted on the condition that the user commits to helping others by doing voluntary work or giving support to the most vulnerable people in the community. It is presupposed in this case that the individual has the potential to put others first and the will to serve the community and that he or she simply needs to be encouraged to do so.

Other innovations which have been inspired by the principle of empowerment include the various forms of community building where families, informal networks and neighbourhoods cooperate with voluntary associations and the third sector to build services to deal with family and community problems and to assist organisations working in the community, above all in neighbourhoods experimenting with new forms of social housing. The factor influencing all of the above is the new vision of welfare that subverts the traditional one in which 'community *was* seen as a rather parochial element to be substituted stepwise by more state-public, professionalised and completely freely chosen "voluntary" elements' (Evers and Ewert, 2015, p. 34).

Empowerment of the individual and community welfare experiences can also be seen in the idea that social innovation is not necessarily the result of rational top-down planning but can derive from local experiences that are limited in time and in space, which, through a bottom-up diffusion process, are repeated over time and in other contexts, possibly after a 'developmental evaluation' (Patton, 2011). This is an evaluation which supports innovation networks and allows for a broader spread of successful local initiatives; verifying whether changes, adaptations or a modification of action strategies are necessary when new conditions emerge.

As regards policies for families in difficulty, such as single-parent families, programs have been put into place with the aim of making parents less dependent on benefits and to help them to actively seek employment.

Young people are now required to take part in education and training programmes for a longer period in order to help them to acquire further skills, and therefore provide them with more job opportunities and make them more socially responsible.

In the field of health care and social health integration, new organisational models have been developed which aim to empower the patient in the management of health and in therapeutic compliance (Barr et al., 2003; Wagner et al., 1996). Empowerment can also be accompanied by the co-production of services which provide regular, long-term relationships between professional service providers in any sector, users and other members of the community (Pestoff, 2015). Experiences of co-production in the field of health care, where patients take part in the design, delivering, evaluation and development of services, making these services both more personalised and transparent, are particularly interesting. Likewise, the co-production of pre-school services where parents are actively involved seems to lead to an improvement of these services, making them of a higher quality. Furthermore, it can be said that active participation gives participants greater power in that it increases understanding on how to improve the quality of life, with users taking on new responsibilities and benefiting from new rights deriving from their greater participation in the design and delivery of services.

Empowerment does not only refer to the users' increased ability to face social risks; it has taken on other meanings. It has been claimed that citizens' power will grow if they are given the option of choosing between different providers of services in the state, private and third sectors. In addition, the principle of universalism and the new centrality taken on by the selectivity of measures often based upon means testing have increased the discretionary power of service providers.

CRITICISM OF POLICES BASED ON EMPOWERMENT

In dealing with social problems, both centre-left and centre-right parties and coalition governments have moved away from a structural approach to one based upon individual empowerment. Therefore, it has become a commonly held opinion that poverty and social exclusion are individual rather than social problems and that the solution to these problems is to be found in individual action rather than state intervention. This approach can have positive implications if it focuses on the risk factors which can result in exclusion and poverty and, as a consequence, leads to the designing of preventative measures to work with people at risk and to reduce the likelihood that they will experience such conditions (Alcock, 2015). Moreover, it has led to the spread of the 'nudge approach' of so-called libertarian paternalism in which policies must provide individual incentives aimed at pushing people towards desired social behaviour rather than intervening through social regulation or the direct provision of services (Thaler and Sunstein, 2008).

However, the negative consequence of this individualistic approach to the problems of social exclusion and poverty is that politicians and public opinion tend more and more often to blame the victim in searching for the root of problems. As a result, those who experience poverty and social exclusion are stigmatised as being to blame for their problems and, paradoxically, find it even more difficult to find a way out.

Awareness of the perverse effects which can be brought about by the principle of empowerment has meant that it has come in for criticism from a variety of sources. Empowerment has been considered a control tool used to manipulate people's identities in order to make them fit in with social expectations (Smith, 2010). It is claimed that this gives credence to the idea that the success or failure of the individual is only down to their abilities or weaknesses, underestimating the important role played by external influences and the responsibility that the state has in creating inequality. It is argued that in the promotion of employability, the empowerment framework only focuses attention on the qualifications which each individual can offer to the market and does not consider the opportunities offered to them to make practical use of these qualifications; hence, workers are blamed for not being able to overcome the structural obstacles they encounter (McQuaid and Lindsay, 2005). It is probable that both those for and against empowerment take up a position which is too one-sided, and that a more balanced perspective can be seen in those who consider empowerment to be a concept made up of contrasting meanings which can take on either a libertarian or a repressive dimension, attempting to balance both the desire to help the poorest in society and the idea that it is imperative that the poor should help themselves (Pruijt and Yerkes, 2014).

The first antinomy is that existing between autonomy and control: the policies of empowerment promote respect for individual freedom, but this freedom is expected to be used in a 'positive' way by following normative models which are considered legitimate. Just where the balance between control and autonomy is to be found is difficult to define, since too much control would appear to contradict the concept of empowerment. However, too little control might lead to the acceptance of passive behaviour on the part of those who are to receive assistance.

A second paradox is that between the individual assumption of risk and the support needed in order to achieve goals. Empowerment polices must, on one hand, make the individual feel that he is responsible for his own success as it is the fruit of his own abilities and hard work. If the risk is too high, the challenge is almost impossible and available resources are not sufficient, a sense of helplessness might grow. On the other hand, however, if challenges are not ambitious enough and external support is too great, this may result in a lack of individual commitment.

The third contradiction regards the targeting of empowerment policies: interventions which are too focused are likely to stigmatise recipients as individuals possessing little autonomy who need to be helped. If there are too many recipients, along with creating resource-related problems, it might be difficult to provide coherent strategies. The importance of these three antinomies will depend upon how they are considered by the main social players. This will in turn determine if recipients are deserving of state help or if they are left to fend for themselves.

An over-developed vision of empowerment policies has also been questioned; policies which are the result of a positive transformation of welfare systems produced in recent years in the Nordic and Anglo-Saxon welfare models in particular. To contrast this vision, referring to labour policies, Bonoli (2012) identifies four types of active policy used to bring about the process of activation.

The first type is called 'incentive reinforcement' and includes all measures designed to give beneficiaries incentives to work and to cut passive benefits.

The second type is defined as 'employment assistance' and includes all measures which aim to eliminate the obstacles preventing participation in the labour market, through the use of placement and counselling services.

The third type is called 'occupation' and aims to offer the unemployed job opportunities, also of a temporary nature, to prevent their human capital from deteriorating; these include various kinds of socially useful work.

Finally, Bonoli identifies the fourth mechanism as 'up-skilling'; that is, the provision of vocational training for jobless people so that they might have a second chance to find employment when their skills are inadequate or obsolete. If we use this type of classification, the distinction between welfare systems and the evolutionary vision is clearly diminished. Indeed, we can see that the up-skilling of human capital is a strategy which was pursued by all European countries in the thirty years immediately after the Second World War (including countries in southern Europe such as Italy), with the great investment in vocational training to fight unemployment and to provide an adequate workforce for expanding industries.

Incentive mechanisms such as reinforcement and employment assistance have been in use since the middle of the 1990s, when in all European countries, starting with Denmark and then in countries such as the United Kingdom, Sweden and Germany, there was a reform of labour policies inspired by the principles of activism and flexicurity which aimed to make the labour market more flexible, reduce benefits for the unemployed and push individuals to make a rapid return into the labour market with the support of help services.

The greatest and most coherent effort to empower the workforce was made in the thirty glorious years after the war, and this phase could be regarded as a model to be followed today, where we see a particularly high rate of unemployment among older workers, considered obsolete, and among the young so-called NEET (Not in employment, education and training).

It is probable that the limitations displayed by empowerment-based policies are fundamentally the result of a too-individualistic and functionalist interpretation of the empowerment principle, which has resulted in interventions aimed at regulating individual behaviour and which has overshadowed the principle's creative and collective character and its ability to increase awareness and social mobility. This is a character which can be found again today in collective actions undertaken by civil society associations which offer citizens spaces to work together and help each other, promoting political campaigns in favour of structural changes, thus highlighting the transition from individual to collective and community empowerment (Alcock, 2015, p. 62). At the time of writing this chapter, the transition from individual to collective and community empowerment is clearly visible across European countries in the public response to the Covid-19 health pandemic. As a flexible framework, the European Social Model has the capacity to harness the culture and energy of innovative collective approaches developed during the current crisis to support and sustain meaningful investment within the European public sphere.

REFERENCES

Alcock, P. (2015), Reconstructing poverty and social exclusion: agency or structure? in Donati, P., and Martignani, L. (eds), *Towards a New Local Welfare: Best Practices and Networks of Social Inclusion*, Bononia University Press, Bologna, pp. 43–64.

Barbier, J.-C. (2004), *Systems of social protection in Europe: two contrasted paths to activation, and maybe a third*, in Lind, J., Knudsen, H., and Hørgensen, H. J. (eds), *Labour and Employment Regulation in Europe*, Peter Lang, Brussels, pp. 233–253.

Barbier, J.-C. (2013), Changes in social citizenship in France in a comparative perspective: 'activation strategies' and their traces, in Evers, A., and Guillemard, A. (eds), *Social Policy and Citizenship: The Changing Landscape*, Oxford University Press, New York, pp. 150–172.

Barr, V. J., Robinson, S., Marin-Link, B., Underhill, L., Dotts, A., Ravensdale, D., and Salivaras, S. (2003), The expanded Chronic Care Model: an integration of concepts and strategies from population health promotion and the Chronic Care Model, *Healthcare Quarterly*, **7** (1), 73–82.

Berglund, T., and Wallinder, Y. (2015), Perceived employability in difficult economic times: the significance of education systems and labour market policies, *European Societies*, **17** (5), 674–699.

Bode, I. (2013), A fuzzy picture: social citizenship in post-corporatist Germany, in Evers, A., and Guillemard, A. (eds), *Social Policy and Citizenship: The Changing Landscape*, Oxford University Press, New York, pp. 198–221.

Bonoli, G. (2012), Active labour market policy and social investment: a changing relationship, in Morel, N., Palier, B., and Palme, J. (eds), *Toward a Social Investment Welfare State? Ideas, Policies and Challenges*, Policy Press, Bristol, pp. 181–204.

Clarke, J. (2004), Dissolving the public realm? The logics and limits of neo-liberalism, *Journal of Social Policy*, **33** (1), 27–48.

Donati, P. (2015), Prospects: are we witnessing the emergence of a new 'relational welfare state'? in Donati, P., and Martignani, L. (eds), *Towards a New Local Welfare: Best Practices and Networks of Social Inclusion*, Bononia University Press, Bologna, pp. 207–255.

Evers, A., and Ewert, B. (2015), Social innovations on the local level: approaches, instruments and different ways of dealing with them, in Donati, P., and Martignani, L. (eds), *Towards a New Local Welfare: Best Practices and Networks of Social Inclusion*, Bononia University Press, Bologna, pp. 15–42.

Evers, A., and Guillemard, A. (2013), Reconfiguring welfare and reshaping citizenship, in Evers, A., and Guillemard, A. (eds), *Social Policy and Citizenship: The Changing Landscape*, Oxford University Press, New York, pp. 359–388.

Freire, P. (1971), *Pedagogy of the Oppressed*, Seabury Press, New York.

Friedmann, J. (1992), *Empowerment: Politics of Alternative Development*, Blackwell, Malden.

Funnel, S. C., and Rogers, P. J. (2011), *Purposeful Program Theory: Effective Use of Theories of Change and Logic Models*, Jossey-Bass, San Francisco.

Gilbert, N. (2013), Citizenship in the enabling state: the changing balance of rights and obligation, in Evers, A., and Guillemard, A. (eds), *Social Policy and Citizenship: The Changing Landscape*, Oxford University Press, New York, pp. 80–96.

Houston, D., and Lindsay, C. (2010), Introduction: fit for work? Health, employability and challenges for the UK welfare reform agenda, *Policy Studies*, **31** (2), 133–142.

Hur, M. H. (2006), Empowerment in terms of theoretical perspectives: exploring a typology of the process and components across disciplines, *Journal of Community Psychology*, **34** (5), 523–540.

Jacobsson, K. (2004), A European politics for employability: the political discourse on employability of the EU and the OECD, in Garsten, C., and Jacobsson, K. (eds), *Learning to be Employable*, Palgrave Macmillan, Basingstoke, pp. 42–62.

Lister, R., and Bennett, F. (2010), The new 'champion of progressive ideals'? Cameron's Conservative Party: poverty, family policy and welfare reform, *Renewal*, **18** (1–2), 84–109.

McQuaid, R. W., and Lindsay, C. (2005), The concept of employability, *Urban Studies*, **42** (2), 197–219.

Minas, R. (2014), One-stop shops: increasing employability and overcoming welfare state fragmentation? *International Journal of Social Welfare*, 43, 40–53.

Patton, M. Q. (2011), *Developmental Evaluation: Applying Complexity Concepts to Enhance Innovation and Use*, Guilford Press, New York.

Paugam, S. (2007), Conclusion. Vers un nouveau contrat social, in Paugam, S. (ed.), *Repenser la solidarité*, Presses Universitaires de France, Paris, pp. 948–980.

Perkins, D., and Zimmerman, M. (1995), Empowerment theory, research and application, *American Journal of Community Psychology*, **23** (5), 569–579.

Pestoff, V. A. (2015), Co-production as social innovation in public services, in P. Donati and L. Martignani (eds), *Towards a New Local Welfare: Best Practices and Networks of Social Inclusion*, Bononia University Press, Bologna, pp. 83–111.

Pruijt, H., and Yerkes, M. A. (2014), Empowerment as contested terrain: employability of the Dutch workforce, *European Societies*, **16** (1), 48–67.

Sen, A. K. (1992), *Inequality Re-Examined*, Oxford University Press, Oxford.

Sen, A. K. (1993), Capability and well-being, in Nussbaum, M. C., and Sen, A. K. (eds), *The Quality of Life*, Clarendon Press, Oxford, 30–53.

Serrano Pascual, A. (2007), Reshaping welfare states: activation regimes in Europe, in Serrano Pascual, A., and Magnusson, L. (eds), *Reshaping Welfare States and Activation Regimes in Europe*, P.I.E. – Peter Lang, Brussels, pp. 11–34.

Smith, V. (2010), Enhancing employability: human, cultural, and social capital in an era of turbulent unpredictability, *Human Relations*, **63** (2), 279–300.

Taylor-Gooby, P. (2004), New risk and social change, in Taylor-Gooby, P. (ed.), *New Risks, New Welfare?* Oxford University Press, Oxford, pp. 1–28.

Thaler, R. H., and Sunstein, C. R. (2008), *Nudge: Improving Decisions About Health, Wealth, and Happiness*, Yale University Press, New Haven.

Torfing, J. (1999), Workfare with welfare: recent reforms of the Danish welfare state, *Journal of European Social Policy*, **9** (11), 5–28.

Trägårdh, L., and Svedberg, L. (2013), The iron law of rights: citizenship and individual empowerment in modern Sweden, in Evers, A., and Guillemard, A. (eds), *Social Policy and Citizenship: The Changing Landscape*, Oxford University Press, New York, pp. 222–256.

Wagner, E. H., Austin, B. T., and Korff, M. V. (1996), Organizing care for patients with chronic illness, *Milbank Quarterly*, **74** (4), 511–544.

7. For all our futures? The European Social Model and the convergence of new social policies for older people

Giovanni Bertin

INTRODUCTION

Almost all European countries have been experiencing intense demographic change as an increase in life expectancy combined with a falling birth rate has led to a progressively ageing population. This process is forcing a number of countries to tackle the problem of the sustainability of the social protection systems put into place over the past century.

The current Covid-19 health crisis has revealed the complex and interrelated challenges that European welfare systems face across Europe. But the phenomenon of an ageing population cannot be reduced to concerns about the capacity of health and welfare systems to cope with this situation. The shift in demographic structure demands that we reflect seriously upon the organization of urban spaces, forms of urban mobility, work organization and the relationship between forms of employment and working hours and our daily lives, and on relations of solidarity within families and the community. In Western societies, ageing is a phenomenon that has taken on new forms and dimensions, but an increase in ageing rate does not automatically equate to an increase in the number of people experiencing social isolation. One of the key issues in the current debate regards the attempt to predict whether and if so to what extent ageing will be accompanied by an increase in the period of time (years of life) spent by individuals without experiencing problems linked to the loss of the capacity to live independently. An analysis of the literature (Stallard, 2016; Avolio et al., 2013; Crimmins and Beltrán-Sánchez, 2011; Fries et al., 2011; Fries, 1989) suggests that ageing might be associated with a rise in the number of people aged 65 and over in good physical and mental condition and with a good quality of life. In fact, the increased life expectancy has been transforming the categories and images traditionally associated with older people. The image of a poor, marginalized and sick older person is gradually being accompanied by the image of an older person as an active subject who is a consumer of leisure and personal care services. These polar images associated with the same concept – older people – require us to reflect further on the characteristics of the concept and on the nature of the processes accompanying ageing (Crăciun, 2019; Bugental and Hehman, 2007). Rethinking the concept of ageing also means reviewing the policies developed in recent years to free them from the stereotypes that have so often guided them, so that they can break away from the standardized image of the over-65s (Bertin, 2009; Levy and Banaji, 2002).

The complexity of this phenomenon makes it hard to approach using the concepts and operating cultures that characterized welfare systems in the latter half of the last century. Moreover, the debate has indicated a number of directions that can guide our reflections on the nature of the phenomenon and on the changes underway within today's welfare systems (Hess et al., 2017).

Burgental and Hehman (2007) propose an interpretation of the ageing process as the result of the dynamics linking the biological sphere to the social and cognitive spheres. Seen from this perspective, age is just one of the elements determining the quality of life of single individuals. The age of individuals does not automatically determine the degree of deterioration of their physical, mental and social condition. On the contrary, the condition of need associated with older people is the outcome of their life course (Dewilde, 2003; Combrinck-Graham, 1985). Their existential condition is undoubtedly linked to their age but also reflects their personal history and the social context in which they have led their life. Ultimately, old age is the result of a life course and of a personal history influenced by events originating in the following:

1. Their health history, which is determined by illnesses experienced, lifestyles, interactions with the health service, and so on.
2. Their working life, which is influenced by the type of job carried out, by working hours and workloads, but also – and above all – by stress, frustrations and gratifications, and by the fact that their job was an occasion for personal fulfilment rather than just a means for survival.
3. Their emotional life, their everyday relations and their response to the accompanying emotional dynamics.
4. Their network of relations and their continued construction and consolidation of relationships even as this network inevitably shrinks.
5. Their social life and their participation in community life and group identity, and their involvement in social and/or political voluntary activities.

All these interlinked factors mutually influence each other and can favour the development of a healthy, gratifying life or lead to the need to face and cope with situations of physical and emotional stress. During their life course, individuals will have inevitably encountered critical situations relative to each of these dimensions, and these dimensions will also have provided them with resources in dealing with difficulties. The ageing process is characterized by all of these events and will lead to very different personal histories. In other words, we could claim that old age is the result of:

1. Individual processes produced by the accumulation of experiences triggered by external changes and by the evolution of personal histories.
2. The processing of these experiences according to the individual's personal identity, beliefs and cognitive maps.
3. Encounters with the expectations connected to their role, to mechanisms of social identification and to stereotypes associated with different ages.

The organization of welfare system relies on a standardized approach to life cycles that is undermined by the complexity and differentiation of ageing processes. Moreover, the de-standardization of the ageing process leads to problems of definition. Older people should not merely be defined on the basis of age, and the entire concept needs to be revised and re-operationalized (Bertin, 2009; Levy and Banaji, 2002). The concept of older people must be linked to the increased complexity of their life course. The literature agrees that 'a life course is a multidimensional concept, an amalgam of many and interdependent trajectories of the different institutional spheres that constitute the society. These trajectories are determined by a sequence of events and state changes that are more or less improvised' (Combrinck-Graham, 1985, p. 143). In this perspective, the transition is defined as being socially determined between two positions in a particular area of life. Such events are no longer deterministically linked to age, but are regarded as transitions associated with a different stage of life.

In other words, it is necessary to understand whether an ageing population will involve dealing with an increasing number of people requiring welfare policies or whether the main effect will involve a growing number of people who find themselves coping with a transition phase and exit from the job market, but not necessarily with a simultaneous significant loss of the physical and mental capacity to lead an independent life. The hypothesis that the ageing process is accompanied by a 'compression of morbidity' was first examined in the late 1980s (Fries, 1989). According to this theory, there has been a shift in the onset of chronic infirmity and frailty of older people. This phenomenon is being confirmed in many Western countries, and experts believe that the onset of loss of self-sufficiency mainly concerns older people aged over 80 while other older people will lead independent lives characterized by personal well-being.

However, not all studies support this trend. For example, Rechel et al. (2013) describe a more complex scenario. With regard to Europe overall, increases in life expectancy do not seem to have a major impact upon the period of life without health problems (difference between age of life expectancy and age of healthy life expectancy). But a more in-depth analysis reveals very different situations within the different European contexts. These differences concern both life expectancy and increased life expectancy encountered in this century and the growth rate of the healthy life expectancy. The ageing process in Europe should therefore be seen as a heterogeneous and complex phenomenon, both in terms of geographical context but also with regard to the need to consider that the population of over-65s is distinguished by heterogeneous traits that cannot be standardized. This involves considering older people as a differentiated whole of population groups that find themselves facing a different stage of their existence. For some, their personal life course will mean facing the signs of a loss of personal independence, while for others this will involve redefining an everyday existence that is now free of work ties. Obviously, the availability of resources – economic, relationships, mental, and so on – will play a role in allowing these processes of change to be experienced in a positive manner.

To sum up, there are three macro population groups within the elderly cohort (over-65s):

1. People continuing their professional and social life course.
2. People interrupting their working life but who continue to be completely independent and are facing the need to rethink their lives as an opportunity for positive change.
3. People who have experienced a life marked by critical events and who therefore require external support to cope with a condition of need.

From this perspective, welfare policies will need to be rethought with an aim to:

1. Create conditions that will allow the older person to have a positive ageing experience delaying the onset of loss of capacity to lead an independent life.
2. Accompany the construction of processes of ageing that will help older people to take a new look at their life course and to see the third age as a series of opportunities rather than the loss of the social role that often accompanies an exit from the job market.
3. Define forms of long-term care (LTC) that will support non-self-sufficient older people during the most difficult phase of their life course.

DEMOGRAPHIC CHANGES FACING THE EUROPEAN COMMUNITY

The European Community has made dealing with demographic change one of the major issues on its agenda, drawing the attention of its member states to this theme. Given its role and the impossibility of determining the social policies of the single states, it has attempted to incentivize the development of actions that see an ageing population as a new challenge facing all countries.

Analysing documents produced by the European Union (EU) at the beginning of this century, we can identify at least two different perspectives. On the one hand, the EU has been drawing the attention of the single states to the risks connected to the economic sustainability of welfare systems consolidated during the latter half of the last century, given the simultaneous necessity to review the offer of services providing support for the lives of older people faced with a major decline in health and independence in daily life.

On the other hand, there is the proposal to consider ageing as an opportunity for development and growth throughout the European Community. This last approach derives from the tendency to consider older people as active independent subjects going through a phase of their existence where they often find themselves having more free time, energy and resources that allow them to pursue personal projects and to play an active role in their network of relationships and/or in society. The European Community refers to this prospect as the 'silver economy' (Technopolis, 2018). Moreover, viewing ageing as an opportunity for society overall or viewing it as an opportunity for the economic sustainability of welfare systems are two sides of the same coin with mutual influence. The more active a role older people are capable of playing, the longer they will live healthy lives and the later they will require care. The European Community has promoted studies into both of these aspects, bringing together experts and funding pilot projects capable of producing good practices and supporting the definition of guidelines. The analysis of these materials makes it possible to outline a series of actions that have conditioned – and continue to condition – the debate within the single states with regard to:

1. The promotion of the opportunities offered to society by the ageing population.
2. The activation of processes redefining welfare systems that will respond to the effects of the demographic changes underway.

1.   The Community Actions Tending to Support the Idea of Ageing as an Opportunity for Society

The European Community's *Population Ageing in Europe* document proposes considering demographic change and the process of ageing affecting the population as an opportunity for all of European society.

The core policy directions were identified as follows:

1. Support demographic renewal through better conditions for families and improved reconciliation of working and family life.
2. Boost employment – more jobs and longer, better-quality working lives.
3. Raise productivity and economic performance by investing in education and research.
4. Receive and integrate migrants into European society.
5. Ensure sustainable public finances to guarantee adequate pensions, health care and long-term care. (European Commission, 2006, p. 7)

In this document, the European Commission underlines the need to consider the opportunities offered by demographic change. In particular, it mentions the contribution made by older people to voluntary work and the development of economic activities meeting the demand of a new social group with specific needs as well as with resources and time available (the silver economy). Older people should no longer be seen merely as users of welfare services but also as actors within the economic dynamics and activities of solidarity supporting the social cohesion of the single countries.

In 2008, in order to support the role of older people in economic processes, the Commission drew up an Equal Treatment Directive (European Commission, 2008) intended to extend protection against discrimination at work based on age with regard to social protection, health care and other services. Beginning with the key role of the single member states in the definition of labour policies, the Commission has sought to coordinate and incentivize the development of policies that will help ensure that older workers continue to play an active role. To this end, the Commission has promoted a dialogue between the actors concerned (bodies representing employers and employees) to facilitate the construction of forms of employment and working conditions that will allow senior workers to remain active. These include:

1. Reducing incentives for early retirement in tax and benefits systems.
2. Providing financial incentives (such as reduced social contributions) to seniors who continue work or to employers who hire older workers.
3. Promoting lifelong learning and training opportunities for older workers to ensure that they remain productive.
4. Developing new roles involving intergenerational teams and mentoring or coaching roles that make effective use of the expertise of older workers.

5. Making work organization more flexible to meet the needs of seniors, including flexibility in working time, part-time work and temporary employment as well as developing opportunities to reconcile work and care responsibilities (for example, spouses and adult children caring for the elderly or grandparents caring for grandchildren). (European Commission, 2008, p. 4)

These guidelines are also intended to help reconcile working time with personal time so as to give this population group time to satisfy needs often delayed because of incompatibility with their working hours or to carry out a role as caregiver (for their children, spouse or parents who are no longer self-sufficient) that often becomes more important after the age of 60.

EU guidelines also regard opportunities for the improvement of the overall standard of living in cities in order to create conditions favouring the development of active, independent lives led by the older population (European Committee of the Regions, 2011). In 2010 the European Commission launched a pilot project (Mestheneos, 2011) involving a wide group of stakeholders representing local authorities, the world of business and the third sector in order to promote new reference standards to support the development of policies directed at ensuring accessibility in housing, transport and public sectors.

To draw further attention to the potential for positive changes resulting from an ageing population, the European Community declared 2012 the European Year for Active Ageing and Solidarity between Generations. At the end of the year, the Commission adopted a series of 'guiding principles for active ageing' (European Commission, 2014a) to be used to guide the development of policies designed to support the active lives of the over-65s. This document (European Commission, 2014b) endorses the importance of considering these key priorities in defining investments in the new social fund for 2014–20. It also promoted the construction of a synthetic indicator based on 22 simple indicators measuring the active participation of older people within social and working life. This indicator provides administrations with a useful tool in analysing and assessing its activities relative to active ageing actions as well as providing guidelines for investment actions supporting active ageing.

In this perspective, the European Community believes that local administrations should play a key role by activating policies in the following three levels:

1. Promoting the postponement of the retirement age so as to extend people's working life after the age of 60.
2. Organizing local areas and towns to ensure that they are adapted to the needs of older people, thus supporting them in leading independent lives and facilitating active ageing.
3. Promoting activities which directly aim to support active living projects for the older population.

To further this aim, in 2014 a project called 'Healthy Ageing Supported by Internet and Community' (HASIC) was launched to promote the development of healthier behaviour, improving diets, physical activity and participation in the social life of the community.

The aim of these support actions is to allow local administrations to consolidate the opportunities provided by an ageing population and to help older people live healthy active lives for longer, thus also reducing the impact of ageing on welfare systems.

2.   Community Actions Intended to Redefine Welfare Systems in Order to Make Them Sustainable and Responsive to the Care Demands of the Ageing Population

Warnings about the possible impact of an ageing population on welfare systems arise from the fact that this age range makes extensive use of welfare systems.

This impact is expected to take the shape of:

1. An increase in the demand for healthcare services. During later life people tend to make more frequent use of community and hospital-based healthcare treatment (Kreistensson et al., 2007).
2. An increase in the number of people who have left the labour market and will receive a pension. At the same time, there will be a reduction in the number of people of working age contributing to produce the resources necessary for tax-financed pension systems.
3. An increase in the number of non-self-sufficient people requiring daily care. This aspect will also be compounded by the reduction of the number of people of working age who can act as caregivers and support the system of services in providing care.

Although the European Community has no direct competences in this area, it has influenced the debate on policies within the single states.

In 2010 the European Commission drew attention to pension policies and to the need to launch revision processes capable of bringing together two aspects that risk driving reforms in different directions. The document produced points out that adequacy and sustainability are two faces of the same coin, and seeks to guide the debate within the single member states by recalling that the challenge will be to find the balance between these two needs. Thus, the central challenge faced by member states is to build the conditions that will allow older people to lead dignified lives and to take into account the resources that the single countries can earmark for these policies without clashing with the budget limits established by the European Community. These guidelines were included in the 2012 White Paper (European Commission, 2012), which not only underlines the need to find a balance between adequacy and sustainability but also recalls the importance of creating conditions favouring participation in the labour market by women and senior workers. More specifically, the White Paper recommends:

1. linking the retirement age with increases in life expectancy;
2. restricting access to early retirement schemes and other early exit pathways;
3. supporting longer working lives by providing better access to lifelong learning, adapting workplaces to a more diverse workforce, developing employment opportunities for older workers and supporting active and healthy ageing;
4. equalizing the pensionable age between men and women; and
5. supporting the development of complementary retirement savings to enhance retirement incomes. (European Commission, 2012, p. 10)

The sustainability of health services is also considered to be at risk due to the pressure exercised by the steep rise in the older population. The following two factors must be borne in mind:

1. The increased costs of the system. The Community is concerned about the potential increase in the costs of LTC. It is expected that LTC expenditure will go from 1.8 per cent of gross domestic product (GDP) in 2010 to between 3 and 5 per cent of GDP in 2060. The Community's concern also stems from the differences in LTC provision across the member states in terms of the forms of service, degree of coverage and involvement of people in contributing to costs of treatment.
2. The increasing complexity of the patients' health needs. According to Rechel et al. (2013), the epidemiological analysis reveals that an increasing number of older people are affected by comorbidity and chronic conditions. This situation makes it necessary to update health care systems originally built to respond to temporary loss of health due to specific causes.

In 2014 the European Commission published an important report intended to guide the actions of the single member states with regard to LTC policies. In this document, *Adequate Social Protection for Long-term Care Needs in an Ageing Society*, the Social Protection Committee and European Commission have summarized the results of numerous meetings between experts and stakeholders intended to draw up guidelines to support member states in coping with the demands caused by an ageing society.

The meeting between the various actors and the states adopted an approach based on the Open Method of Coordination (OMC), and resulted in three common objectives which aimed to:

1. Guarantee access for all to adequate health and long-term care and ensure that the need for care does not lead to poverty and financial dependency. Address inequities in access to care and in health outcomes.
2. Promote quality in health and long-term care and adapt care to the changing needs and preferences of society and individuals, notably by establishing quality standards reflecting best international practice and by strengthening the responsibility of health professionals and of patients and care recipients.
3. Ensure that adequate and high-quality health and long-term care remains affordable and sustainable by promoting healthy and active lifestyles, good human resources for the care sector and a rational use of resources, notably through appropriate incentives for users and providers, good governance and coordination between care systems and institutions. (European Union, 2014, p. 11).

The report defined long-term care as:

> a range of services and assistance for people who, as a result of mental and/or physical frailty and/or disability over an extended period of time, depend on help with daily living activities and/or are in need of some permanent nursing care. The daily living activities for which help is needed may be the self-care activities that a person must perform every day … or may be related to independent living. (European Union, 2014, p. 11)

According to the European Community, these guidelines must support the reform processes activated by the single member states to improve the effectiveness and efficiency of healthcare services, such as hospitals, specialist outpatient care and primary care, and pharmaceutical services in managing new demands for treatment within an ageing population. In order to support the continued independence of older people in managing their daily life, even when affected by chronic illnesses, healthcare systems will have to adopt a holistic approach integrating the actions, competences and information received by the various actors involved in care.

The cultural and organizational changes proposed are intensified by the ageing process. Demographic changes are accompanied by the risk of failing to meet the increased demand expected in the medium and long term. This risk is also increased by the reduction of the potential network of caregivers due to the projected decrease in the working-age population. Based on the current organization of informal care, this risk would mainly impact upon the female population, which would experience greater difficulties in leading a complete and fulfilling working life. In order to help prevent the onset of this scenario, interdisciplinary research (undertaken by groups of experts under the auspices of the OMC and the updating of treatment projects) financed by the European Community within the single member states identified a number of priorities for action, including the development of age-friendly and disability-friendly environments. The construction of urban environments which are designed to reduce physical and social barriers plays a vital role in reducing treatment and facilitating the independent active life of the older population. The analysis of older people's experiences in various European cities (33 cities were analysed worldwide) identified eight aspects of urban living requiring intervention:

1. outdoor spaces and buildings;
2. transport;
3. housing;
4. social participation;
5. respect and social inclusion;
6. civic participation and employment;
7. communication and information; and
8. community support and health services. (European Union, 2014, p. 49)

This checklist of features not only shows that policies for older people are capable of improving the lives of the entire population but also forces decision-makers to consider that integration of policies is one of the general principles that must guide policies at local level.

PREVENTION

Activation of policies capable of preventing the early onset of physical or mental frailty in older people is one of the aims that must guide the actions of the single member states. From this perspective, it is necessary to identify exactly which factors are the principal cause of onset of frailty and to activate targeted policies to address this. The review of these experiences has led the Community to identify the key components of prevention:

1. Identifying and targeting resources on the specific causes of dependency.
2. Adopting a "life course" approach: there is, for example, a clear link between mid-life health problems and late-life health status.
3. Identifying those within the older age group who are most at risk.
4. Drawing up "personalized action plans" in cases where risk of becoming dependent on LTC is identified so that the most effective form of prevention can be adopted in each case.
5. Implementing innovative organizational approaches and technical solutions that screen, identify and target frail older people for evidence-based interventions that achieve a more efficient use of resources.
6. Empowering LTC recipients in order to improve person-centered dimension of delivery but also self-management of people. (European Union, 2014, p. 44)

REHABILITATION AND RE-ENABLEMENT

A fall or other critical event can cause a sudden and serious loss of autonomy in an older person. In these cases, provision of rehabilitation is vital. This type of treatment, associated with the adoption of various aids, may restore the ability of older people to live independently. Another key form of response is that of re-enablement. In this case, the focus is on encouraging older people to continue carrying out daily activities even when reduced mobility, cognitive impairments and frailty make these actions more challenging. Instead of responding to the older person's progressive loss of autonomy by carrying out daily activities on their behalf ('doing for them'), it involves helping them maintain their residual capacities. The European Community's guidelines mainly involve supporting the activities of caregivers; this may include the provision of specific training. The focus here is on the importance of integrating social policies with health policies as well as informal actions embedded in professional practice within distinct health and welfare systems.

IMPROVING LTC SERVICE EFFICIENCY AND MAKING THE BEST USE OF TECHNOLOGY

The development of technologies linked to smart homes and supporting interpersonal communications provides an opportunity to support older people in living independent lives. These technologies can help them manage their daily activities as well as facilitating management of illnesses by health staff (tele-medicine). Moreover, communication technologies help older people maintain their network of relations and support caregiving by family members. These communication technologies have proven to be extremely important during the current Covid-19 health pandemic. Obviously, the use of new technologies and the speed with which they are developed raises the problem of training the various actors involved. The older people, their caregivers and health and social care professionals are all called upon to develop specific technological skills, albeit in different ways. For the European Community, this action area represents an important opportunity for economic development driven by the so-called silver economy. It also involves actions in support of research and the development of entrepreneurship for which the Community has earmarked structural funds.

INTEGRATION OF SOCIAL AND HEALTH COMPONENTS, AND OF FORMAL AND INFORMAL INTERVENTION

The complex combination of frailty and vulnerability characterizing older people requires care strategies combining health and social actions to support the daily life and network of relations of the individual concerned. Another distinctive feature, in addition to the combination of health and social care, is the formal and/or informal character of treatment. The European Community underlines that particular attention must be paid to supporting this complexity when building mechanisms to integrate these different components. Based also on the analysis of experiences within the single member states, the European Community confirms the impossibility of proposing a single form of integration, limiting itself to repeating the principles, relevance and aims of integration. It also points out that in this respect too new technologies represent an important tool that is capable of facilitating interaction, communication and information-sharing between the various actors involved in care. However, technologies can only become a resource when the underlying care culture uses a holistic approach to managing treatment, enhancing the contribution of each single actor and the operating mentality to be adopted. With regard to the latter, the European Community underlines the importance of delivering a person-centred service that will support the individual's independence and decision-making powers as well as the actions of the caregiver.

THE EXPERIENCES OF THE SINGLE MEMBER STATES

In recent years, almost all European states have modified their welfare systems in response to the gradual increase in their ageing populations (see Table 7.1). If we consider the last four years, for example, we can see that all member states have implemented policies tackling the issue of ageing, showing that this problem is on the agenda of all national governments. The welfare policies implemented are mainly intended to redefine pension systems to make them more economically sustainable and to reduce the inequalities between different categories of pensioners within the single member countries. Almost all countries (21 of 28) have activated policies to combat poverty that target the older population in particular.

A further issue tackled by the member states concerns the redefinition of LTC policies. During the period considered here (2014–17) actions of this type were implemented in 15 out of the 28 member states. While it is clear that the single member states all share concerns relating to the need for specific policies dealing with demographic change, defining their different approaches to these processes and determining the differences between the service supply systems is not so straightforward. There are only a few recent comparative studies and this, combined with differences within the single member states, makes it impossible to carry out an in-depth analysis of the overall approach being adopted by policy-makers with regard to issues linked to ageing. A number of countries have, however, introduced:

1. Policies for the reform of health and welfare systems and the provision of incentives for actions in support of informal caregiving (8 European countries).
2. Housing policies to support older people in their own system of life (7 European countries).
3. Specific policies preventing loss of autonomy in management of daily life (5 European countries).
4. Processes of redefinition with regard to the type of participation of actors in cost coverage (7 European countries).

A comparative reading of the actions of the single member states shows that they have tended to focus on three types of fundamental action to respond to an ageing population:

1. Policies in support of active ageing.
2. Policies for the organization of an LTC system.
3. Policies fighting poverty and reviewing pension systems.

ACTIVE AGEING AND PREVENTION

According to the World Health Organization (WHO):

> Active ageing is the process of optimizing opportunities for health, participation and security in order to enhance quality of life as people age. Active ageing applies to both individuals and population groups. It allows people to realize their potential for physical, social, and mental well-being throughout the life course and to participate in society according to their needs, desires and capacities, while providing them with adequate protection, security and care when they require assistance. Active ageing aims to extend healthy life expectancy and quality of life for all people as they age, including those who are frail, disabled and in need of care. (World Health Organization, 2002, p. 45)

The approach proposed by WHO shifts the aims of active ageing from a strategy oriented towards the reduction of the potential impact of ageing on welfare systems to a strategy fundamental for health and the quality of life of the older population. From this viewpoint, this body of policies not only contains pol-

Table 7.1   *Ageing policies in the single European countries in the 2014–17 period (based on data from European Union, 2015)*

	Pension reform	Elderly Poverty	Long-term care systems	Service delivery and support informal care	Housing	Preventing dependency	Financing and cost sharing
Austria	X	X		X	X	X	X
Belgium	X	X	X	X			X
Bulgaria	X	X	X		X	X	X
Croatia	X	X		X			
Cyprus	X	X	X		X		
Czech Republic	X	X	X	X			
Denmark	X	X					
Estonia	X	X	X			X	
Finland	X	X		X			
France	X						
Germany	X			X	X		X
Greece	X	X					
Hungary	X	X					X
Ireland	X	X		X		X	
Italy	X	X					
Latvia	X	X	X				
Lithuania	X	X					
Luxembourg	X	X	X		X		X
Malta	X	X					
Netherlands	X		X				
Poland	X	X	X				
Portugal	X	X			X		
Romania	X	X	X	X	X	X	X
Slovakia	X		X				
Slovenia	X		X				
Spain	X		X				
Sweden	X	X	X				

	Pension reform	Elderly Poverty	Long-term care systems	Service delivery and support informal care	Housing	Preventing dependency	Financing and cost sharing
United Kingdom	X		X				
Total	28	21	15	8	7	5	7

(The table considers reforms activated and actions oriented as key social challenges and a good social outcome.)

icies postponing people's exit from the labour market but a series of actions intended to facilitate the construction of active life courses (Foster and Walker, 2014). Participation in the social and political life of the community, caregiving within the family network, and the use of retirement to rediscover interests put aside during their working life and to explore new economic activities (Technopolis, 2018) are all possible strategies that older people can adopt in order to construct their own personal active life course. There is a focus on the construction of active ageing pathways in all European countries, although using different approaches. An interesting analysis was carried out by Walker and Zaidi (2016) using the Active Ageing Index to compare the policies implemented by the single member states (see Table 7.2). The indicator used broke down the concept of active ageing by four domains (Zaidi et al., 2017) relating to:

1. Employment (55+ employment rate).
2. Social participation (voluntary activities; informal care provision of children, grandchildren and older adults; political participation).
3. Independent healthy and secure living (physical exercise, access to health services, independent living, physical safety, lifelong learning).
4. Capacity for active ageing (remaining life expectancy at age 55, share of healthy life expectancy at age 55, mental well-being, use of information and communications technology (ICT), social connectedness, educational attainment).

The authors ranked the single member states in three groups based on their overall score. In the first group we find high-scoring countries: Sweden, Denmark, the Netherlands, the United Kingdom (UK), Finland and Ireland.

The second group includes nine countries that cluster together as the middle-scoring countries: Belgium, the Czech Republic, Germany, Estonia, France, Italy, Luxembourg, Cyprus and Austria.

Table 7.2   Active ageing index (based on data from Zaidi, 2016)

	Employment	Social participation	Independent health, secure living	Capacity for active ageing
Best performance	Sweden, Cyprus, UK, Portugal, Estonia	Ireland, Italy, Sweden, France, Netherlands	Denmark, Finland, Sweden, Netherlands, France	Sweden, Denmark, Luxembourg, UK, Netherlands
Critical performance	Hungary, Malta, Belgium, Poland, Slovakia	Poland, Bulgaria, Romania, Estonia, Germany	Latvia, Romania, Bulgaria, Greece, Croatia	Romania, Hungary, Latvia, Slovakia, Greece

The remaining 13 countries are categorized as low-scoring countries: Bulgaria, Greece, Spain, Latvia, Lithuania, Hungary, Malta, Poland, Portugal, Romania, Slovakia, Slovenia and Croatia.

Leaving aside the extent to which active ageing policies are embedded within the single countries, it may be useful to analyse the specific intervention strategies adopted.

The analysis of the Active Ageing Index reveals partial differences between the strategies in which the single countries have invested. Only Sweden has scores suggesting that this country is developing policies supporting active ageing. Portugal, Cyprus, the UK and Estonia have mainly introduced policies whose aim is to extend the working lives of older people. Ireland, Italy, France and the Netherlands have dense social networks in which older people play an important role in caregiving in extended families as well as participating in the social life of the community. Denmark, Finland, the Netherlands and France have focused on developing policies to support older people in leading independent, safe lives. Denmark, Luxembourg, the UK and the Netherlands have all introduced policies to consolidate the capacity for active ageing.

It is interesting to note that the three groups only partially reflect the type of welfare regime adopted in these countries during the last century (Esping-Andersen, 1990). In the group of countries with stronger active ageing policies we find both Sweden and Finland, which belong to the social-democratic regimes, along with Ireland and the UK, which have liberal regimes, and the Netherlands, which has the corporative system typical of central Europe. At the opposite extreme, among the countries with fewer active ageing policies we find countries that traditionally have less consolidated welfare systems like the southern European countries (Greece, Portugal, Malta and Spain) or countries belonging to the former Soviet sphere of influence (Lithuania, Bulgaria, Slovenia, Romania, Slovakia, Hungary and Poland). The group of countries with a middle score comprises those with welfare systems of very different origins. Among the countries with corporative systems we find France, Luxembourg, Germany, Austria and Belgium. Among the

Mediterranean countries we find only Italy and Cyprus. In fact, Italy is only present in this group due to the social participation produced by support activities for family networks. In this same group we can also find two countries from Eastern Europe with fairly recent welfare histories: the Czech Republic and Estonia.

A direct effect of the incentives for the development of active ageing policies was produced by the European Community through the funding of projects for cooperation using EU structural funds. In 2011, the European Committee of the Regions presented a report of projects funded to construct and diffuse best practices with regard to active ageing (European Committee of the Regions, 2011).

These projects concerned actions intended to:

1. Promote active ageing in employment. The projects provide funding support to help delay retirement by keeping older workers' skills up to date or developing services to support the employment of older workers or exchanging good practices with regard to supporting the employment of older people.
2. Promote the role of local authorities. Some of the concrete actions in this area are related to incentivizing participation in voluntary activities and in the social and political life of the local community; the construction of social networks; and support for the construction of informal networks.
3. Promote healthy ageing and independent living. In this case, actions have sought to support independent living through home-based ICT solutions, promote quality health and improve accessibility of transport and physical infrastructure.
4. Stimulate local authority actions favouring the development of intergenerational solidarity through the promotion of cross-generational educational exchanges and the facilitation of mutual understanding between generations.
5. Promote multi-thematic active ageing projects.

NATIONAL POLICIES FOR LTC

The European Community believes that active ageing policies can contribute to delaying the loss of capacity to lead an independent life by older people. However, this does not exclude the need for policies supporting older people who become non-self-sufficient. Nearly all European member states are aware of this problem (Ranci and Pavolini, 2015) and no less than 15 have introduced specific policies over the past four years. Although they share the same intentions, they differ in their approaches to service provision (Giraud et al., 2014; Damiani et al., 2011) and eligibility (Brugiavini et al., 2017). There are also key differences between European member states in relation to the level of investment in this area and forms of policy governance.

The European countries that have invested the most resources are Denmark, the Netherlands, Finland, Norway, Sweden, Belgium and Austria, the majority of which (4 out of 7) are countries with consolidated universalistic welfare systems. All these countries invest over 1.8 per cent of their GDP in LTC policies. At the other extreme, we have the countries with the lowest levels of investment, like Bulgaria, Poland, Portugal, Latvia, Romania, Hungary, Greece and Cyprus, which invest less than 0.86 per cent of their GDP. The lowest investments in LTC are in countries whose welfare systems are less consolidated and that belong to the former Soviet bloc or with 'Mediterranean-type' welfare systems. Differences in levels of investment and approaches to policy governance between member also relate to forms of LTC provision for non-self-sufficient older people (Eurostat, 2020). Research studies (Da Roit and Le Bihan, 2010; Suanet et al., 2012) reveal several main forms of LTC provision:

1. Cash. In this case, support for older people in need is funded through the payment of cash benefits, leaving the older person or caregiver free to choose how to organize care. This approach is adopted in Bulgaria, Poland, Portugal and Croatia.
2. Institutional. This approach involves residential care for older people experiencing difficulties in managing their daily lives. This form of provision is common within countries such as Latvia, Hungary, Romania and Germany.
3. Home-institutional. The provision of support for the loss of independence is based on a combination of institutional and homecare. This approach is adopted in countries like Greece, Lithuania, Luxembourg, Ireland and Slovenia.
4. Cash-institutional. This approach also adopts a differentiated approach combining institutional care with payment of cash benefits. This model of LTC organization has been adopted in countries like Cyprus, Slovak Republic and Italy.
5. Mix. The decision to build a mixed system involves LTC provision which integrates institutional care with home care and the payment of cash benefits. It is impossible to make an assessment merely on the basis of the definition of the type of care, but it is possible that this type of differentiation makes it possible to adapt the response to the particular needs of the older person. This approach is adopted in countries like the Czech Republic, Estonia, Malta, Spain, France, the UK, Finland, Norway, Austria, Belgium and Sweden.

Table 7.3   Different approaches to LTC (based on data from European Commission, 2018)

	Impact on GDP	Low >0.86	Medium low 0.86/1.34	Medium high 1.34/1.82	High >1.82
Type of policy	Cash	Bulgaria, Poland, Portugal	Croatia	-	-
	Institutional	Latvia, Hungary, Romania	Germany	-	-
	Home-institutional	Greece	Lithuania, Luxembourg, Ireland, Slovenia	-	Denmark, Netherlands
	Cash-institutional	Cyprus	Slovak Republic	Italy	-
	Mix	-	Czech Republic, Estonia, Malta, Spain	France, UK	Finland, Norway, Austria Belgium, Sweden

This overview of the differences between the national systems needs to be studied in greater depth by analysing the characteristics of LTC actually provided in local contexts. In many countries, the competences related to this type of service operate at local level.

Although it is impossible to summarize the various models due to the complexity of the situation, it is clear that the differentiation of care strategies enables a tailored response to the specific situations of older people and their caregivers (see Table 7.3).

A comparative reading of the policies which have been operationalized within distinct member states reveals three central components of policy reform in this area. The Commission states that 'The measures adopted by some Member States aim to address these challenges through structural reforms' (Social Protection Committee, 2018, p. 56). These reforms include:

1. Creating the conditions for a shift from institutional to community-based care, providing strengthened support to informal careers.
2. Improved policies for prevention, rehabilitation and independent living (Social Protection Committee, 2018), which are actions adopted by Slovenia, Finland, Bulgaria and the Czech Republic.
3. 'The development of measures designed to strengthen the coordination of Health and Social service delivery' (Social Protection Committee, 2018, p. 36). Innovative policies aimed at improving the coordination of health

and social service delivery have been enacted in Malta, Slovakia and Germany.

REFORM OF PENSION SYSTEMS AND ACTIONS TO COMBAT POVERTY

The reform of pension systems is an issue concerning all European countries (European Commission, 2018). The increase in the number of people of retirement age and improvements in life expectancy represent a serious problem for the economic sustainability of pension systems that were originally planned during the expansion phase of welfare systems in Europe. Moreover, these systems were often constructed in response to the demands of the different professional categories, and levels of protection are often imbalanced. These aspects have conditioned the reform processes that emerged at the beginning of this century, particularly in recent years. The reforms enacted in recent years have been guided by a number of strategic aims (see Table 7.4). These strategic aims include:

1. Postponing retirement. Increasing the age of retirement improves the sustainability of welfare systems in two ways. It reduces the period of time in which pensions are paid out, given the difference between the age of retirement and life expectancy, and increases the period of time in which workers pay contributions. In recent years, a number of countries have chosen this option, including Belgium, Bulgaria, Greece, Spain, France, Latvia, Malta and the Netherlands.
2. Flexible retirement pathways. This option seeks to recognize the differences in people's employment pathways and the effect that this may have had upon workers, but leaves it up to the workers to choose between various options for leaving the labour market. Two options proposed are partial exit through the reduction of working hours or complete exit. Another option included in this approach to pension reform is to provide incentives for postponing retirement. Some of the member states that have reformed their pension systems since 2014 by using this approach are Belgium, Bulgaria, Denmark, France, Croatia, Luxembourg, Austria, Portugal and Finland. In this case, workers are given the choice of continuing their working life beyond the minimum contractual threshold.
3. Rebalancing the inequalities between pension systems. One of the critical aspects of many pension systems is represented by the differences in terms of income produced and the number of years of contributions (that is, spent working) required to qualify for a pension. This strategic aim has been pursued via two approaches. The first has the direct aim of protecting low-income pensioners. In fact, reforms pursuing this type of

aim have been introduced in 18 out of the 28 states since 2014. The other strategy, which runs parallel to the first, was intended to provide protection for specific categories of workers. In this case, countries recognize that some occupations are particularly arduous and therefore hard to carry out for many years. This type of reform has been introduced by Greece, France, Italy, Lithuania, Poland, Romania and Finland. This reform is also intended to compensate for the general increase in retirement age.

4.   Supplementary pension schemes. This involves flanking state pension schemes with parallel systems constructed directly by the worker through personal, corporate or trade pension schemes. The aim of this strategy is to pre-empt the risk of a reduction in the value of pensions resulting from the reduction of the resources available overall due to the interaction between two aspects: the fall in the number of people working who are of retirement age – and therefore in the number of people paying contributions – along with the increase in the number of people of retirement age who are receiving a pension. This provides workers with the choice and indeed incentive to construct a supplementary pathway that will guarantee the expected level of pension income. In recent years the following states have passed legislation providing incentives for supplementary pension schemes: Belgium, Denmark, Germany, Estonia, Ireland, France and Slovenia.

These aims are also pursued by the reform processes launched at the beginning of this century and implemented by a number of countries prior to 2014. A final consideration with regard to this important area of reform concerns continuing differences within the single member states. The pension systems are national systems and competences are centralized, not decentralized. However, this does not equate to a homogeneous situation. In fact, there are continuing differences relative to:

1.   Categories of workers, due to their different capacities to claim.
2.   Gender due to interrupted employment (women tend to enter and leave the labour market more frequently).
3.   The single areas where corporate bargaining may have benefited from greater negotiation capacity in constructing the second pension pillar.
4.   Young people entering the labour market at a later age and with a more precarious status.

These differences represent a further challenge for national welfare systems and for the European Community's ability to influence their evolution.

Table 7.4   *Policy pension reforms (2014–17)*

	Postponing retirement	Incentive for postponing retirement	Flexible retirement pathways	Protecting low-income pensioners	Protection for specific categories of workers	Supplementary pension schemes
Austria		X	X	X		
Belgium	X	X		X		X
Bulgaria	X	X		X		
Croatia		X				
Cyprus				X		
Czech Republic	X			X		
Denmark		X				X
Estonia				X		X
Finland	X	X	X		X	
France	X	X			X	X
Germany			X			X
Greece	X				X	
Hungary						
Ireland				X		X
Italy				X	X	
Latvia	X			X		
Lithuania				X	X	
Luxembourg		X				
Malta	X			X		
Netherlands	X					
Poland				X	X	
Portugal		X		X		
Romania				X	X	
Slovakia				X		
Slovenia			X	X		X
Spain	X			X		
Sweden				X		
UK	X					

CONCLUSION

An overview of the policies that the single member states have introduced in Europe reveals a widespread attempt to tackle the risks accompanying the

demographic changes currently underway. All countries have launched policies to enhance ageing by incentivizing the construction of active ageing pathways. This approach adopts a positive vision of old age. The focus has been
on enhancing the growth potential of a market that is sensitive to the demands
of this population group and on the contribution of over-65s in constructing
networks of solidarity and in developing processes of participation in the social
and political life of the community.

The policies launched have also aimed to reduce the possibility of an over-
whelming demand occurring, which would represent a threat to the economic
sustainability of welfare systems. The member states have not only focused
on the economic dimension of welfare systems but are also looking at the
construction of offer systems that are more in line with the changing characteristics of the care demand, and at the reduction of the imbalances that arose
during the expansion phase of welfare systems. Although these actions concerned all European countries, the actual strategies implemented have very different characteristics. The reforms launched can only be partially interpreted in
the light of the type of welfare regimes consolidated in the development phase
of the national welfare systems.

The analysis of the policies introduced to respond to the demographic
changes underway confirms that a focus on solidarity is a common value characterizing all European countries. Moreover, the current Covid-19 health crisis
has elevated the need to find coordinated policy responses at European level
directed at supporting member states as they face the complex and immense
challenges that lie ahead. However, this focus is also a potential factor supporting rather than restricting the development of the single national economies.
Faced with the specificity of the European situation, we should point out that
the actual interventions and the priorities involved in launching them reveal
rather different scenarios. These differences should probably be interpreted in
the light of the single histories of the welfare systems, but also of the resources
earmarked for these policies, of the social and political cultures in the single
member states, and of the political dynamics guiding the single reform processes (Warburton and Grassman, 2011; Tepe and Vanhuysse, 2010).

A final consideration must be made with regard to the analysis of the role
that the European Community has played, and continues to play, in the development of these policies. It is extremely difficult, if not impossible on the
basis of current studies, to establish a precise causal relationship between the
actions of the Community and the choices made by the single member states.
However, we did identify a marked correspondence between the guidelines

supplied by the European Community and the actions undertaken by the single states. This correspondence is undoubtedly also due to:

1. The development of guidance documents based on the results of research undertaken under the auspices of the OMC. The European Community utilized numerous groups of experts and stakeholders from different European member states to develop welfare policies.
2. Project funding strategies that have led various countries to collaborate in redesigning their own policies while also participating in the mutual exchange of good practice with other member states.

Ultimately, the analysis of the policies launched to tackle the demographic changes underway reveals the existence of a common matrix of welfare policies taking the shape of different, specific actions linked to distinct social and political cultures and to the conditions of the specific economic systems which characterize individual EU member states. These specificities are only partially the result of the different needs presented within individual member states and risk leading to differentiated social rights among people who live and work in the European Community.

REFERENCES

Avolio, M., Montagnoli, S., Marino, M., Basso, D., Furia, G., Ricciardi, W., and de Belvis, A. G. (2013). Factors influencing quality of life for disabled and not disabled elderly population: the results of a multiple correspondence analysis, *Current Gerontology and Geriatrics Research*, Article 258274.

Bugental, D. B., and Hehman, J. A. (2007). Ageism: review of research and policy implications, *Social Issues and Policy Review*, **1** (1), 173–216.

Brugiavini, A., Carrino, L., Orso, C. E., and Pasini, G. (2017). *Vulnerability and Long-term Care in Europe*. Cham: Palgrave.

Bertin, G. (2009). *Invecchiamento e politiche per la non autosufficienza*. Trento: Erickson.

Combrinck-Graham, L. (1985). A developmental model for family systems, *Family Process*, **24** (2), 139–150.

Crăciun, I. C. (2019). Positive aging theories and views on aging, in: *Positive Aging and Precarity: International Perspectives on Aging*, vol. 21, pp. 17–34. Cham: Springer.

Crimmins, E. M., and Beltrán-Sánchez, H. (2011). Mortality and morbidity trends: is there compression of morbidity? *Journal of Gerontology Series B: Psychological Sciences and Social Sciences*, **66** (1), 75–86.

Damiani, G., Farelli, V., Anselmi, A., Sicuro, L., Solipaca, A., Burgo, A., Iezzi, D., and Ricciardi, W. (2011). Patterns of long-term care in 29 European countries: evidence from an exploratory study, *Health Services Research*, 11, Article 316, 2–9.

Da Roit, B., and Le Bihan, B. (2010). Similar and yet so different: cash-for-care in six European countries' long-term care policies, *Milbank Quarterly*, **88** (3), 286–309.

Dewilde, C. (2003). A life-course perspective on social exclusion and poverty, *British Journal of Sociology*, **54** (1), 109–128.

Esping-Andersen, G. (1990). *The Three Worlds of Welfare Capitalism*. Cambridge and Princeton, NJ: Polity and Princeton University Press.

European Commission (2006). *Population Ageing in Europe*. Brussels: European Union.

European Commission (2008). *Equal Treatment Directive*. Brussels: European Union.

European Commission (2012). *The European Approach to Demographic Change*. Brussels: European Union.

European Commission (2014a). *Adequate Social Protection for Long-term Care Needs in an Ageing Society*. Brussels: European Union.

European Commission (2014b). *Population Ageing in Europe: Facts, Implications and Policies*. Brussels: European Union.

European Commission (2018). *The 2018 Ageing Report*. Brussels: European Union.

European Committee of the Regions (2011). *How to Promote Active Ageing in Europe*. Brussels: European Union.

European Union (2015). *Review of Recent Social Policy Reforms*. Brussels: European Union.

Eurostat (2020). Government expenditure on social protection. https://ec.europa .eu/eurostat/statistics-explained/index.php/Government_expenditure_on_social _protection.

Foster, L., and Walker, A. (2014). Active and successful ageing: a European policy perspective, *The Gerontologist*, **55** (1), 83–90.

Fries, J. F. (1989). The compression of morbidity: near or far? *Milbank Quarterly*, **67** (2), 208–232.

Fries, J. F., Bruce, B. B., and Chakravarty, E. (2011). Compression of morbidity 1980–2011: a focused review of paradigms and progress, *Journal of Aging Research*. http://dx.doi.org/10.4061/2011/261702.

Giraud, O., Lucas, B., Falk, K., Kumpers, S., and Lechevalier, A. A. (2014). Innovations in local domiciliary long-term care: from libertarian criticism to normalisation, *Social Policy and Society*, **13** (3), 433–444.

Hess, M., Nauman, E., and Steinkopf, L. (2017). Population ageing, the intergenerational conflict, and active ageing policies – a multilevel study of 27 European countries, *Population Ageing*, 10, 11–23.

Kreistensson, J., Hallberg, I. R., and Jakobsson, U. (2007). Health care consumption in men and women aged 65 and above in the two years preceding decision about long-term municipal care, *Health and Social Care in the Community*, **15** (5), 474–485.

Levy, B. R., and Banaji, M. R. (2002). Implicit ageism, in: Nelson, T. D. (ed.), *Ageism: Stereotyping and Prejudice against Older People*, pp. 49–75. Cambridge, MA: MIT Press.

Mestheneos, E. (2011). Ageing in place in the European Union, *IFA Global Ageing*, **7** (2), 17–24.

Ranci, C., and Pavolini, E. (2015). Not all that glitters is gold: long-term care reforms in the last two decades in Europe, *Journal of European Social Policy*, **25** (3) 270–285.

Rechel, B., Grundy, E., Robine, J. M., Cylus, J., Mackenbach, J., Knai, C., and McKee, M. (2013). Ageing in the European Union, *The Lancet*, **381** (9874), 1312–1322.

Social Protection Committee (2014). *Review of Recent Social Policy Reforms*. Luxembourg: European Union.

Social Protection Committee (2018). *Annual Report 2018*. Luxembourg: European Union.

Stallard, E. (2016). Compression of morbidity and mortality: new perspectives, *North American Actuarial Journal*, **20** (4), 341–354. DOI:10.1080/10920277.2016 .1227269.

Suanet, B., Van Groenou, M. B., and Van Tilburg, T. (2012). Informal and formal home-care use among older adults in Europe: can cross national differences be explained by societal context and composition? *Ageing & Society*, 32, 491–515.

Technopolis (2018). *The Silver Economy*. Brussels: European Union.

Tepe, M., and Vanhuysse, P. (2010). Elderly bias, new social risks and social spending: change and timing in eight programmes across four worlds of welfare, 1980–2003, *Journal of European Social Policy*, **20** (3), 217–234.

Walker, A., and Zaidi, A. (2016). New evidence on active ageing in Europe, *Intereconomics*, 3, 139–144.

Warburton, J., and Grassman, E. J. (2011). Variations in older people's social and productive ageing activities across different social welfare regimes, *International Journal of Social Welfare*, 20, 180–191.

World Health Organization (2002). *Active Ageing: A Policy Framework*. Geneva: World Health Organization.

Zaidi, A. (2016). Active ageing index, *Studi di Sociologia*, 2, 127–137.

Zaidi, A., Gasior, K., Zolyomi, E., Schmidt, A., Rodrigues, R., and Marin, B. (2017). Measuring active and healthy ageing in Europe, *Journal of European Social Policy*, **27** (2), 138–157.

8. Fit for purpose? The architecture and processes of hybrid governance, and the overlapping of market, hierarchy and network

Giovanni Bertin

INTRODUCTION

This new century has heralded extensive overhauls to European welfare systems that were consolidated in the latter half of the previous century. All over Europe, we are seeing the emergence of a welfare mix approach in which the state is being flanked by private for-profit companies and civil society providing welfare services contributing to the social well-being of individuals. The various actors participating in welfare service provision also operate independently and do not necessarily have hierarchical relations with each other.

A second distinguishing characteristic of welfare systems in Europe today relates to the complex and multi-faceted nature of emerging social and economic risks and needs. These emerging socio-economic risks and needs have been shaped by complex and multi-causal processes necessitating the development of new policy approaches. In recognition of this complexity member states have implemented cross-sectoral policy measures directed at social protection. These new approaches recognize the complex and multi-dimensional nature of emerging social and economic risks and seek to overcome traditional divisions between different welfare policies, service provision and delivery. Illustrating this, it is no longer possible to tackle health issues without looking at working conditions, housing problems or environmental conditions. Moreover, the current Covid-19 health crisis has clearly exposed the relationship between the social determinants of health and vulnerabilities to the Covid-19 virus itself (Marmot, 2020).

The growing number of single actors from the public, private and third sectors in distinct welfare systems without any kind of hierarchical tie, together with the increased interdependence of factors generating social needs and the consequent necessity to integrate the actions of single actors, have led to the increased complexity of welfare systems and the need to rethink the dynamics governing policies. These criticalities are flanked by other factors connected to the crisis affecting the models of governance of public administrations (PAs) more generally (Bovaird et al., 2002) and the difficulties experienced by bureaucracies when tackling the dynamism of social systems.

1.   SOCIAL CHANGES AND PROCESS OF GOVERNANCE

The birth of welfare states in Europe was accompanied by the adoption of governance models typical of public planning. This approach was dictated by the aspiration to build decision-making processes based on absolute rationality and decision-implementing processes based on hierarchical links between the various actors in the system. Two factors contributed to the emergence of this approach. On the one hand, we need to remember that the birth and consolidation of welfare systems was influenced by logical positivism and the search for absolute rationality in decision-making processes; on the other, there was a gradual consolidation of the centrality of the state in the governance of welfare criteria. Moreover, the state was accompanied by the bureaucratic culture typical of the modernization that took place in European societies after the Second World War. In addition, the modern state was framed by a consistent reference to hierarchical rationales as a driver of all of its relations with internal and external actors coming into contact with it during the implementation of public policies. This tendency went into crisis due to a number of factors within and outside welfare systems that were mainly linked to:

1. The crisis of the rationalistic paradigm and the criticisms of absolute rational logic.
    Public planning experiences have shown that the absolute rational approach is incapable of providing concrete responses to the growing complexity of social systems and organizational processes. From Simon onwards (1983), the governance of social policies has had to come to grips with the characteristics of the relative rationality of decision-makers. Even studies on the analysis of bureaucracies have revealed the crisis of the Weberian model. The Weberian model refers to Max Weber's theory (1905) that the increasing complexity of the social world would lead to growing demands of citizens for government services. The need to consider the strategic behaviour of actors within bureaucracies (Crozier and Friedberg, 1980) and their links with contexts outside the organization together with the complexity of power processes, the transposition of means and goals (Merton, 1968) and formal and informal dynamics are among the main critical elements that have contributed to derailing

attempts to adopt absolute rational approaches in the management of public policies.

2.   The development of mixed welfare systems and the consequent increase in their complexity.

Central aspects of this complexity arose from the distinct forms of welfare crises that have emerged in welfare systems across Europe prompting divergent mixed economies of welfare which involve multiple social actors. Here, the public administration of welfare provision across a number of European welfare systems is flanked by for-profit and not-for-profit actors who are not necessarily linked by hierarchical dynamics of dependence. A further element of this complexity has emerged from distinct decision-making and governance processes of key actors at regional and local level. For example, if we consider PAs, we can see that in almost all European countries there is co-governance on different administrative levels. In some cases, this involves the division of policy areas, and in others relationships are based on hierarchical dependency. The presence of different actors and forms of relationships (hierarchical and non-hierarchical) results in greater complexity and destabilization, making it difficult to extrapolate the relationship between the decision-making process and the actions of the single social actors.

3.   The crisis in forms of democratic representation.

Another aspect concerns the relationship between citizens and the political forces called upon to guide the system according to the rules of democratic representation. The problem of the crisis of legitimation of the state and of its struggle to guide policies has been posed by numerous authors from the latter half of the last century onwards (Habermas, 1984; Habermas and Luhmann, 1973). Among the factors influencing these dynamics, it is worth recalling:

a.   The ineffectiveness revealed by the PA when it comes to solving overarching problems (the economic crisis, crime and security, inequalities, and so on) affecting populations in European countries.

b.   The increased capacity of the media to influence the dynamics producing consensus. The differentiation of the communication channels used by the media and the possibility of establishing bi-directional communication processes acting in real time reinforce its capacity to condition communication between citizens and maybe even policies.

c.   The crisis of representation systems, the disaffection with the leading parties born after the Second World War and the fall in voter turnout in the single countries have also influenced the complex relationships between actors within welfare systems across Europe. Moreover, these factors have opened the debate on the presence of different systems of regulations not necessarily linked by hierarchical relations. Teubner

(2015) and Sabel and Zeitling (2008) refer to polyarchy, emphasizing the need to consider that each actor acts in a complex system in which there are regulations (formal and informal) that may not necessarily be consistent with each other (Bicchieri, 2006). This joint presence leads to an increase in their discretionary powers, a weakening of hierarchical dynamics and the consequent necessity to integrate the actions of the single actors by means of processes of involvement and coordination.

4. The dynamics of post- or neo-modernity.

Another contributory element to the crisis in traditional welfare system management approaches is the impact of social changes that have emerged at the start of this new millennium. In this context, it is impossible to carry out a rigorous, comprehensive analysis of the changes that are making the governance of public policies even more complex. However, it is clear that key factors including the dynamics of globalization (Sassen, 1998), the emergence of risk societies (Beck, 1986), the speed of economic and technological change and the increased fluidity of social relations (Castells, 2004; Bauman, 2000) have contributed to the crisis in systems of welfare governance across European member states in the latter half of the last century.

2. ACTORS, THEIR IDENTITIES AND REGULATION CULTURES

The regulation of a complex system involving actors who represent different cultures and interests is inevitably fraught with issues. In particular, each actor will seek to influence the regulatory process to ensure that the regulatory environment is more consistent with their own cultural and organizational identity. Bovaird et al. (2002) suggests considering six groups of actors: single citizens, voluntary organizations, for-profit organizations, media organizations, forms of political representation operating centrally (like governments or parliaments) and local authorities. Seibel (2015) suggests using the concept of sector to represent single contexts and, referring to mixed welfare systems, lists: state, private business and civil society. These sectors are distinguished by characteristics that tend to differ in terms of the identity of actors, cultures of governance and practices.

There are two types of key actor in each sector: on the one hand, politicians whose function is to represent the population and steer the use of public resources for the production of social well-being. Their affiliation depends upon their capacity to fulfil these functions, legitimated by political consensus and on their capacity to communicate this consensus. The other state actors are PA executives and officers. Their affiliation with the system results from the recognition of their expertise (knowledge and competences) in the management of resources and processes intended to improve the quality of living of the population.

The aims of the public sector, its relations with the external environment in which actions takes place and the dynamics and rationales of affiliation are largely determined by the underlying cultural and practices of governance within the sector. The Weberian concept of bureaucracy sums up these aspects and identifies the rationale orienting management processes within these hierarchical relations. The dynamics are based on control and coercion. Links with the outside are regulated through processes of democratic representation. Citizens are called upon to guide the action of the state and to contribute to the availability of resources through taxation. The orientation of managerial activity within the public sector is based on the action of a group of executives whose actions are guided by public values. The theoretical model of bureaucracy has the following reference values: legitimation, obedience, a sense of honour and the absence of private interests or the pursuit of personal profit.

In contrast, the operations of organizations belonging to the private business sector are steered by market dynamics and the ultimate goal of their affiliation with the system is the production of economic value. Relations are determined by the dynamics of competition with money being the main medium of exchange. Their actions are guided by the ownership of enterprises and by stakeholders while the resources are produced by market rules. Even strategic actions are steered by the market and by the opportunities that arise within the commercial dynamics taking place. Management is consumer-oriented and designed to create economic values; that is, entrepreneurship, innovation, the capacity to face risks, compliance with contracts and investments intended for basic needs and development.

Within the sector of civil society, we can find different forms of organization all motivated by the wish to work for the good of the community using an approach based on spontaneous solidarity. Here, social action involves the collective endeavours of individuals motivated by solidarity to provide an informal response to requests for help from the community. Within this sector relationships are based on trust and resources come from the direct work of members of third-sector organizations (TSOs) and from donations collected by appealing to a sense of belonging and to the ties of trust that have been built up within society. These values are community oriented and are based on altruistic actions. Solidarity, trust, responsibility, dignity and social justice form the fundamental value system for third-sector activity. Finally, these organizations are collaborative rather than competitive and the main resource for their actions is their social capital. Cooperatives also belong to the civil society sector. The actions of people involved in this sector revolve around solidaristic value systems. The analysis of TSOs is particularly interesting because it draws attention to the hybrid nature of their organizations. Hustinx et al. (2014) claim that TSOs can be considered hybrid because they have the following characteristics:

1. They receive funding from public actors and, at the same time, from private subjects such as individual citizens or charitable foundations.
2. They employ paid staff as well as unpaid volunteers.
3. They supply services as well as advocacy.
4. They are partially independent of government entities and define action strategies oriented by their internal dynamics and by negotiation with the government actor.
5. They are oriented towards the realization of a body of values mixing values typical of voluntary organizations with those typical of government organizations.

Moreover, there are different forms of hybridization (Hustinx et al., 2014), and here we can even refer to:

1. Corporatist hybrid TSOs. Corporatist hybrid TSOs still have strong roots in the public sector. Funding is exclusively public, and this leads to the assumption of the values of public organizations and a narrow margin for autonomy. Ultimately, the main function of these TSOs is to supply services on behalf of public bodies.
2. Post-corporatist hybrid TSOs. Given that the post-corporatist hybrid TSOs benefit from both public and private funding, the value base originates in both public and private spheres. Decisions are the result of interaction processes between government bodies and TSOs. The role they actually play changes, and they provide advocacy as well as services.
3. Grassroots TSOs. The private dimension of grassroots TSOs often becomes dominant and flanks the voluntary dimension. The main function is advocacy. This type of organization is directly autonomous and defines its mission and operating strategies independently, in a manner consistent with its grassroots reference values (Hustinx et al., 2014).

The highly interactive relations between the various actors in welfare systems tend to give rise to processes in which they mutually influence each other. Seibel (2015) points out that the need to interact leads single actors to experience transformation processes that influence the characteristics of the organizations in which they work. These organizational characteristics and mechanisms then become institutionalized as ideal organizational types with specific sectors. Exemplifying this, foundations are a typical example of an organizational type which hybridizes the attributes of private businesses with those of civil society. Another interesting example is represented by cooperatives operating on behalf of public bodies. These organizations bring together the dynamics of civil society, which defines their affiliation, with those of the state that is both the buyer and main stakeholder, and of private business because they are competing with other for-profit and non-profit actors.

3.   COMPLEXITY OF REGULATION PROCESSES AND HYBRID GOVERNANCE

The interaction between different actors and their internal hybridization process inevitably impacts upon the dynamics of regulation processes. In this regard, Aliu et al. (2015) have put forward a preliminary classification of regulation systems, built up from three variables: the identity of the actor carrying out the key functions within the organizational process, the dominant orientation of governance and the procedural models that develop within specific regulation systems. Based on these variables, they suggest four types of approach to regulation defined respectively as:

1. Statism. The state plays a dominant role in statism approaches to regulation. It achieves this dominance by exercising its authority through public planning which is steered by coercive criteria and close monitoring activity. Here decisions are driven by national interests.
2. Pluralism. In pluralist approaches to regulation, the state plays a key role, by involving interested parties and other stakeholders. Relationship dynamics between stakeholders and other parties are guided by competitive criteria and by the construction of successful coalitions. Actors are all oriented towards their own system of preferences but also act according to the relationship dynamics intended to build a coalition. The aims pursued within pluralistic approaches are forged by relationship dynamics within and outside of the dominant coalition.
3. Corporatism. In corporatist approaches the influence of the state is pursued through the adoption of close corporate relationships with key organizations. The construction of consensus between influential actors within these organizations is central to this process. Mediation between groups representing specific stakeholder interests is critical to the construction of consensus within corporate relationships.
4. Network. In network approaches the centrality of public actors is derived from the dynamic processes which promote stakeholder involvement. The dynamics of multilateral negotiation and the coordination of the interests of individual actors assume undeniable relevance. The role of the public within network approaches involves the activation of single actors in the network.

The first three perspectives considered all place the role of the state and its capacity to steer the behaviour of the other actors at the centre of the regulatory process. The pluralist corporatist approach focuses on the presence of political dynamics and on the relevance of consensus construction. Consensus is considered central to the achievement of strategic decisions. In addition, the effectiveness of strategic decision-making processes intrinsically relies on the state establishing consistent forms of decision-making behaviour while ensuring that single actors fully enact the decisions that are taken. In this case, participation in the decision-making process by individual actors is regarded as an inevitable process and ensures that actors adhere to decisions taken at a strategic level. The regulation network is the only approach to challenge the centrality of the hierarchical rationale and to fully recognize the autonomy of the single actors. Consistency between decisions and actions is built up by means of a process involving actors and the construction of meaning. These forms of regulation cannot be analyzed from the perspective of the state but should rather be viewed as the combined effect of the interaction between the actors involved in developing welfare policies. It is the system of concrete actions (Crozier and Friedberg, 1980) that defines the complexity of the dynamics influencing the construction of regulation practices. At least two factors of complexity must be considered in this regard.

Firstly, according to Jochim and May (2010), an initial element of complexity derives from the interdependence of public policies. They refer to the concept of the 'boundary-spanning policy regime'. In fact, it would be hard to tackle the issues encountered using an approach based on subsystems seen as autonomous parts of a system. The relevance of the 'boundary-spanning policy regime' becomes apparent once we consider key issues underlying the development and operationalization of welfare policies. For example, the health of a population depends only in part on health service management processes. In fact, health is the result of life choices made by individuals and depends on their economic and work histories, their education and cultural background and on the networks of relations that they have built up. Critically, the health of a population also depends upon the characteristics of the environment in which they live and on the quality of welfare policies in their local area. The debate on the social determinants of health has long since revealed the complexity of the processes leading to health and ill health (Marmot, 2020; Alderwick and Gottlieb, 2019; Artiga and Hinton, 2019; Gottlieb et. al., 2019; Jochim and May, 2010; WHO Commission on Social Determinants of Health, 2008; Howlett and Rayner, 2007). A unifying theme across debates relating to the processes leading to health and ill health is that new governance criteria must take the interdependency of policies into account. The concurrence of policies belonging to systems with few formal links between health and welfare services and to independent organizations mitigates against holistic approaches to heath which consider the broad range of interacting components which make up the social determinants of health within society.

A second element of complexity refers to differentiation and interaction between actors within distinct organizational cultures. The presence of actors from different sectors not only activates internal hybridization processes with regard to the actions of single actors but also destabilizes the hierarchical regulation criteria typical of traditional welfare state systems.

These two processes highlight the complexity of the regulation dynamics that engage/clash with policies and organizations seeking to build ties based on different organizational cultures. Joint participation in developing policies and managing services has activated regulation processes which follow different paths and are characterized by distinct dynamics. One dynamic concerns the attempt to utilize governance practices which integrate the characteristics of different forms of regulation. In this context we can refer to hybridization: the 'hybrid model is typically related to governance involving governments because public actors, private actors and civil society actors share common interests and these interests are quite important in terms of reciprocal understanding' (Aliu et al., 2015, p. 1753).

Alongside these attempts, however, we continue to find resistance to regulatory changes. Here, each actor will seek to ensure that broad regulatory models align closely with regulatory models which characterize their own sector and their own organizational culture. According to Aliu et al. (2015), however, actors from the public sector will seek to consolidate their own central role and authority particularly with regard to the way in which public resources are used to guide the action of actors from the private and third sectors. At the same time, the private sphere will tend to create spaces for the expansion of market dynamics while civil society will seek to develop co-regulation processes, increasing its capacity to contribute to the strategic choices of the service system.

A third process relates to the consolidation of formal processes alongside other more informal processes. Haveri (2008) makes an interesting distinction in this regard, between real processes and the rhetoric of governance popular in local contexts. The author uses the concept of the wall of rhetoric in order to represent 'the huge distance between the intentions expressed at rhetorical level and what characterizes real decision-making processes' (p. 142). This distinction between rhetoric and practice can also be seen as the distance between legislative change and the phenomena change concerning practices actually adopted by actors in building governance processes.

When these elements combine, they give rise to considerably different forms of governance.

We can therefore speak of different approaches or regimes even when discussing forms of governance. Enjolras (2009) proposes a classification of forms of governance, referring to:

1. Public governance. In this case institutional actors are public and directly manage governance decisions. Policies are developed using a technocratic approach. Civic meaning is linked to public interests and the rules of governance are defined by social rights, by the users' charter and by the ethics of the public service. Voice dynamics refer to political subjects. And lastly, those benefiting from services are seen as passive subjects and defined as users.

2. Corporate governance. Institutional actors are public but there is also some involvement of non-profit actors. Policy implementation is based on the regulation of protection (guarantees for citizens) and on payments to third-party subjects (suppliers). The process of policy definition uses a corporative approach. Civic meaning is aligned to collective interests. The ethics underlying voluntary work occupy a key role alongside social rights and the charter of people demanding such rights. In this case the voice of the public is directed towards those representing the interests at stake. Lastly, those using the services are seen as beneficiaries.

3. Competitive governance. Institutional actors are both public and private (profit and non-profit). Policy implementation is based on the construction of supply contracts and incentivizing actions. Policy development is based on network dynamics. In this case the idea of civic meaning is absent and regulatory activities are limited to protecting consumers and managing complaints.

4. Institutional partnership. In this case too actors are both public and private (profit and non-profit) but regulation is based on diversified strategies according to an almost market-oriented approach focusing on controlling prices and the behavioural expectations demanded of participants. Policies are constructed through the institutionalization of the partnership processes between the various actors involved. Civic meaning is based on processes of participation and solidarity between the actors. Great importance is given to citizenship rights and to the empowerment of citizens.

The first type of governance is typical of welfare state systems, but following the development of mixed systems in European countries, greater importance is given to the other three types of governance. What characterizes these three types is the simultaneous presence of different actors with different values and governance cultures who are required to work together. The presence of different approaches to regulation has led to the development of forms of hybrid governance combining the different rationales and cultures of the actors involved in different ways.

4.   MULTILEVEL GOVERNANCE AND THE CENTRALITY OF THE LOCAL DIMENSION

A central aspect shaping forms of governance at local level is related to the distribution of responsibilities. This aspect has two implications: on the one hand, it defines the actors involved, and on the other it relates to the distribution of power and of the relations linking the various levels of the governance processes. Although the European Community has produced various guidelines for welfare policies, governance processes are the responsibility of the single states and their regional and local authorities. Moreover, when analyzing discrete policies, it soon becomes apparent that the different levels of governance are not structured in a uniform manner. In many countries, for example, central power plays a greater role in the management of health or pension policies, while local authorities play a greater role in the development of socio-welfare or housing policies. In other words, the organization of the competences in developing discrete policies does not develop consistently through the different levels of the system. Some policies are therefore still tied to a multilevel hierarchy. The state is called upon to govern while the local authorities implement central decisions. In other cases, responsibilities may be delegated to the local level. This situation raises the issue of consistency between levels of governance, an aspect taking on particular relevance when we focus on the need to integrate the different welfare policies. In a hierarchical system, sub-system decisions enable decisions made at central level to be implemented at local level. Here, the governance function lies in the process controlling the coherence between central decisions and local actions. This situation is hard to pursue within a context of network systems which develop on multiple levels. In this regard, Hooghe and Marks (2001) claim that multilevel governance shapes the results of policies through intersections between networks that are present at the different levels of governance. This description reveals the complexity of the process by highlighting the existence of multiple networks acting on different levels. An interesting aspect of great importance in governance processes concerns the relationships which develop between members of a network who are present at local level and other members of the same network present at central level. In this case, we need to establish whether we can refer to a single global network or whether it would be better to adopt Hooghe and Marks' proposal (2001) suggesting that there are different intersecting networks in which the subjects connecting them make strategic use of their positions to acquire power to use in internal exchanges in their own networks.

The presence of different actors and networks connecting with each other puts pressure on the hierarchical rationale characterizing the multilevel structure of welfare state systems. Sellers and Lidström (2007) maintain that the welfare state has been identified with centralized state hierarchies. For these authors the universalistic, egalitarian tendencies of welfare systems lead us to expect a greater concentration of power in the central level of the system.

Another factor driving centralized governance is related to the growing demand for better control of resources through strict monitoring of expenditure. This tendency is particularly marked in the management of health policies in a number of European countries where the risk of continually rising costs prevails over the need to focus on the specificities of local areas and the integration of policies and services.

The transformation processes taking place in welfare systems across Europe and this increased complexity have led to the need to rethink the links between the different levels of welfare systems. This is particularly the case in countries with centralized governance. This tension between centralization legitimated by the need to respond to the quest for equity and control of expenditure and decentralization legitimated by the need to take account of and respond to the specificities of policy priorities at local level and policy integration has led to differentiated forms of multilevel governance. Sellers and Lidström (2007) suggest using two indicators to analyze forms of multilevel governance. The first indicator, 'Local Governance Capacities', represents the level of autonomy of local governance. This indicator is based on two sub-dimensions relative to politico-administrative capacities. The first relates to the presence of constitutional protections for the autonomy and representation of corporations in local government and to levels of employment at local government level as a proportion of all government employment. In addition, this indicator relates to the fiscal dimension with reference to local public expenditure as a proportion of total public expenditure and to local taxation as a proportion of total taxation.

The second indicator, 'Supervision of Local Government', represents the degree of control and supervision that a local authority exercises over the peripheral levels of the system. This indicator comprises politico-administrative supervision which is made up of an explicit supervision function at local level and formal controls on the way local governance and local authority services are operationalized. This indicator also includes fiscal supervision, which includes local fiscal autonomy and funding which supports local services. The analysis of the values assumed by the single member states relative to these indicators and their classification with respect to variability allows us to represent member states, in relation to their capacity to manage welfare services, through decentralization processes while permitting local autonomy.

Table 8.1   Welfare systems and multilevel governance (based on Sellers and Lindström, 2007)

		Supervision of local government			
		Low	Medium low	Medium high	High
	Low	-	Italy, Ireland	-	-
Local governance capacities	Medium low	Switzerland	-	France, Germany, Netherlands, Great Britain	Belgium, Greece, Spain
	Medium high	-	-	Norway, Portugal	Austria
	High	-	Denmark, Finland, Sweden	-	-

It is interesting to observe how the different forms of multilevel governance depend only partly on the characteristics of the welfare regimes concerned (see Table 8.1). Exemplifying this, when we analyze European states which are classified as having liberal systems of welfare we can see how this approach is associated with 'weak governance' both at local level and relative to control mechanisms between centre and periphery. This type of multilevel governance seems consistent with the decentralized approach and market rationale which characterizes Switzerland's welfare policies. It differs from the governance in Great Britain which has a more liberal welfare regime yet a more structured system of control by central government. These differences are also the result of the presence of welfare policies with markedly different forms. If we consider national health systems, we notice that the state plays a strong role of governance in the national health care system in Great Britain.

Greece and Spain both have highly developed centralized control systems paired with low local government capacities, while Portugal is distinguished by a reasonable focus both on the development of local governance capacities as well as central government control. The situation in Italy and Ireland appears particularly critical with each state having low capacity in relation to local governance combined with weak control mechanisms of central government. The Italian situation does not result from the decision to refer to the market as an approach to regulating dynamics between welfare actors but rather from a weakness intrinsic to public administration and from a regionalization process which lacks a clear definition with regard to governance dynamics and roles of actors. European countries which reveal a governance approach based on the control of central bodies are usually present in social democratic welfare systems. In this case too there are differences between the various states within social democratic welfare systems. Norway, for example, has a better balance between the autonomous capacities of local government and central control.

The differences emerging between the multilevel governance processes studied probably result from the differences within the single policies (health versus employment or pensions, and so on), from the politico-institutional history of the distinct states, and from the characteristics that have inspired the development of the institutional characteristics of PAs within the countries analyzed. In this regard Hesse and Sharpe (1991) offer a historical analysis situating the cultural development of specific PAs within the context of major political and social transformations within each nation state. Here, they refer to the 'Napoleonic' model in reference to France and the majority of Southern European countries, to the English model in reference to Great Britain and Ireland, and to the central-northern European model in reference to the welfare policies of social democratic and corporative regimes.

Although the welfare models, institutional characteristics and governance processes within the European countries considered have emerged from different starting points, they have all launched review processes with regard to their welfare systems with a large number moving towards the consolidation of mixed welfare systems. The complexity inherent within these transformations has forced the distinct European states to review the relationship between the centre and periphery, while tending to shift decision-making processes towards a more local dimension. This process is difficult because it demands a redistribution of power between centre and periphery. The centre must reduce its influence on local decisions and review the mechanisms that it uses to reproduce its position of power.

A clear example of such changes can be observed when we analyze the service funding strategies adopted by subjects operating at central level. Specific funding allocated directly to service users or to clearly defined services reduces the decision-making autonomy of the periphery, increasing the power of those operating in the centre. On the contrary, funding disbursed for inhabitants of areas with pro-capita quotas requires local authorities to define their use, increasing the autonomy of actors operating at local level. Adopting this perspective means agreeing to a redefinition of the rules consolidating power, seen in a dialectical light and centred on result-sharing (the development of community).

In a centralized system, relationships of power between actors are based on their position in the hierarchy and exchanges with citizens. In a decentralized system, on the other hand, power is linked to the legitimation of the roles of actors and their capacity to contribute to the functioning of the network (institutions and legitimated authority). In addition, power within a decentralized system is linked to the role played in information exchanges, to the position of actors in relational dynamics both within and outside the network, to participation in processes constructing meaning and to the activation of reflexivity dynamics.

Bevir and Richards (2008) also stress the importance of the local dimension in complex systems. They claim that the local dimension makes it possible to bring real governance dynamics and concrete processes closer together. The emphasis on decentralized processes results from the conviction that network dynamics are rooted in processes of exchange between actors whose actions are guided by their preferences. These actors are involved in symbolic processes and connected by communicative interactions. These interactive processes determine the functioning of networks and contribute to designing the pathways of policy development. These elements reveal the complexity of the system, which derives from the simultaneous presence of different actors and from their reflective dynamics. Consequently, the order cannot be imposed top-down; instead, hierarchical dynamics conflict with the network processes. The final result depends on these interactive dynamics so deeply rooted in the local level. Adopting a similar approach, Bovaird and Loeffler (2007, p. 294) define local governance as 'the way in which local stakeholders interact with each other in order to influence the outcomes of public policies' focusing on 'the interplay of structures, processes and other mechanisms which link networks of stakeholders'. In their definition of local governance, they start out by emphasizing that the local dimension is distinguished by the presence of a network of social actors who interact with each other and influence – or rather, contribute to influencing – the development of public policies.

5.   HYBRID GOVERNANCE: INNOVATIVE PRACTICES GOING BEYOND THE REGULATORY STATE

The main thread running through changes in governance processes is the development of practices tackling the discrepancy between regulatory cultures built on the central role of government bodies, the increased complexity of welfare systems and the hierarchical codes which accompany organizational actions.

The practices intended to reduce this discrepancy have adopted different strategies. In an initial phase, bureaucracies have attempted to tackle this growing complexity by co-opting external actors to become involved in their own decision-making processes. This attempt was intended to maintain relationships of power and to allow the system governing the services to remain at the vertex of governing processes.

In a second phase, in response to these processes, there was an attempt to overcome the criticalities intrinsic to the bureaucratic nature of the welfare state by using corporate methodologies in service management. Here 'New

Public Management' became the default approach for numerous processes of change. At the level of service regulation, this approach gave rise to the age of the regulatory state. The welfare systems of European countries have also been faced with these processes of change which must be analyzed in order to understand current trends.

5.1   Evolution of Regulatory Models: Managerial State and Regulatory State

In highly centralized states, or states where a third sector has developed to supply services on behalf of the state, the change in governance processes tends to confirm the hierarchical approach typical of public planning. In these cases, the state maintains its central role with regard to the governance function, constructing prescriptive regulatory processes in order to control performance quality and guide strategic choices.

The co-option of different actors dilutes and hybridizes the regulatory approaches, which remain tied to the centrality of the state and to the mainte-nance of the hierarchical relationships connecting it to the other actors in the system. This approach emerges mainly in social democratic regimes but also in corporative regimes, in which the third sector acts on behalf of the state by supplying services to the citizen. Here, using the classifications of forms of governance present in the literature we may refer to Public Co-management or Hard Regulation.

The presence of different actors supplying services on behalf of the state induces the PA to activate regulatory mechanisms aimed at guaranteeing user access to quality services (see Table 8.2). The state pursues these aims by defining quality indicators and evaluation criteria and by constructing public structures which ensure compliance with the standards that are set. Service suppliers may be involved in defining initial quality indicators and evaluation criteria. However, decision-making and monitoring processes remain firmly in public hands. The approach is similar in the local planning process. Although there are some forms of planning that involve the third sector, voluntary bodies are considered suppliers and are usually only co-opted within the analysis phase, rarely in the ideation phase. The decision-making process is carried out internally in the PA.

This defensive approach to the hierarchy of decision-making typical of bureaucracies is based on a number of premises that have recently been challenged by the new context in which welfare systems are situated across European member states. These aspects can be traced back to:

1.   The monopoly of the resources put into the system. Here, the more a PA tends to be the only actor investing resources in welfare policies, the

Table 8.2   Hierarchical model and complexity of welfare systems

Governance processes	Mechanisms	Processes
Guarantee the quality of services supplied to clients	• Certification schemes audit • Certification schemes	• Quality criteria are defined by the state, which is also responsible for monitoring quality • Control of autonomous (public) agencies
Guide the actions of the single actors	• Laws and permits • Hierarchical planning • Standards, formal standard-setting and standards scores	• The actions of actors are guided by means of normative processes implemented by the state, which establishes what is permissible • The state defines standards, which must be respected by the actors wishing to become part of the system, and monitors compliance
Govern available resources	• Taxation • Fees • Cap-and trade schemes • Common pool resources	• Acquisition of resources takes place through general taxation and the state. Defines collaboration schemes intended to influence the way in which resources are used (also by voluntary organizations)

greater its capacity to influence the actions of the actors wishing to take on the role of service supplier.

2. The legitimation of the state as an impartial actor capable of representing the popular will and of governing a system of actors in order to provide concrete responses to emerging social needs. Factors legitimizing the hierarchical role of the PA include the fairness of its actions, its capacity to have a vision of change and to represent the demands of citizens, and its capacity to make the best possible use of resources collected by means of general taxation.

3. The third sector's complete dependence on the resources which are distributed as a result of the operationalization of strategic measures by the PA is directly correlated to its capacity to move autonomously with regard to the acquisition of the resources necessary to act. Thus, the more the third sector acts exclusively to operationalize measures at the behest of PAs, the more it reduces its capacity to play an active role in the governance of welfare systems.

The economic crisis and the reduction of resources allocated to welfare policies together with the crisis of representative democracy, the bureaucratization of services and the difficulties involved in providing effective, efficient responses to new socio-economic needs has weakened the central role of PAs across European states. This has opened avenues for experimentation with new innovative forms of governance which differ from previous traditional models of governance and administration characterized by inherently hierarchical forms of organization.

The emergence of the idea that PAs should follow models and processes typical of private companies represented a radical criticism of the hierarchical culture of bureaucracies. Some sectors, including health, housing, employment and education have seen the rise of a paradigm of 'New Public Management' introducing the managerial culture to PAs. As far as the regulation of the processes producing public policies are concerned, the new reference code is inspired by the idea of regulatory state and can be traced back to the so-called private regulation model. In this scenario, the state is called upon to dismantle the direct management of services, which are devolved to private subjects (profit and/or non-profit), and to define the system of rules within which these subjects must operate. This process of change is also pushed forward by a process known as 'depoliticization'. In various European countries, criticism of the bureaucratization of PAs is accompanied by criticism of the impact of politics upon decision-making. In other words, the progressive de-legitimation of the actions of PAs is due, on the one hand, to excessive hierarchization and, on the other, to the erosion of the capacity of political forces to represent citizens. This has led to the widespread belief that political decisions have encroached upon the technical sphere in the actions of PAs. The imposition of the regulatory state is seen as a solution to the inability of bureaucracies to manage public services efficiently and effectively. Here, the regulatory state is viewed as an appropriate response to the increase in the growing number of independent actors and as a way of clarifying the general tasks of welfare systems within the context of representative democracy. Here also, the regulatory state is viewed as offering an effective vehicle for the operationalization of concrete actions which rely on the managerial capacity of single actors within welfare systems.

The regulatory state approach has been experienced in many countries, particularly those tending towards liberal regimes. One such example emerges from the latest reforms of the British health service, which provided a partial model for other contexts. In Italy, for example, we can find Lombardy using this type of approach. The clear division between buyer and health service provider and the introduction of vouchers are some of the mechanisms developed in this context.

In short, regulatory approaches were developed with the aim of increasing competitive dynamics. Interactions with the hierarchical culture of PAs has

Table 8.3   *Various regulatory mechanisms adopted by regulatory states*

Regulation processes	Regulation mechanisms	Practices
Quality guarantee	Certification schemes (standards, formal standard-setting, standards scores)	• The state defines general rules, delegates the definition of criteria and evaluation processes to the certification system • Criteria defined by private actors and stakeholders through actors responsible for certification • Certification through independent agencies
Guidance for actors' behaviour	Less pressure on business	Incentivizing competition by acting on economic variables

led to the term 'quasi-market' being coined to express the hybrid character of regulatory state practices (see Table 8.3).

This approach can also be identified in the processes guaranteeing the quality of services supplied to citizens. In this case, the PA limits itself to defining the procedures involved and leaves the definition of quality assessment criteria and establishment of verification processes to market dynamics.

The reviews of the role of PAs and of regulatory processes inspired by the approach of the regulatory state have drawn attention to various critical areas resulting from:

1. The debate on the perverse effects of the spurious nature of the quasi-market. Consider, for example, the informational asymmetries complicating the actions of citizens or the risk of creating monopolies in supplying various forms of health care (new-generation pharmaceuticals, for example). We may also consider the debate on the market's inefficient production of common goods highlighted in Ostrom's work (2005).
2. The debate on the self-regulating capacity of welfare service production systems, which highlights the risk that services providing fewer returns with respect to the capital invested in them would be subject to inadequate supply, resulting in inequalities in the degree of social protection of individuals.
3. The specificity of the relational character intrinsic to welfare services. For example, it is hard to apply market logic or a supply-and-demand reasoning to such areas.
4. The progressive autonomation of the third sector and its two-fold role as service provider and advocate. Moreover, alongside the legitimation of

public action, social actors have often been capable of activating private resources and channelling them into welfare policy production. These experiences have caused the third sector to become increasingly autonomous with respect to public governance actions, allowing it to acquire a less subordinate role – becoming a partner rather than a mere service provider. The function of third-sector actors is to help interpret needs and autonomously activate actions to resolve these needs.

These criticalities have contributed to the experimentation of governance practices intended to go beyond the concept of regulatory state by developing new forms of hybridization of the regulatory codes of the single actors (hierarchy, competition and collaboration). Here, the roles of single actors and the way in which they integrate their actions within governance practices have been redefined.

5.2   Meta-governance: Practices Going Beyond the Regulatory State

Attempts to develop neo-liberal approaches and experiences of 'New Public Management' have often faced resistance to change driven by the culture of the bureaucracies seeking to maintain and confirm existing power dynamics. This resistance to change has produced regulatory systems formally inspired by the regulatory state which simultaneously seek to maintain the central role of PAs in governance. One example of these hybrid regulatory approaches can be found in the construction practices of systems controlling the quality of the services supplied to citizens. The definition of quality standards and the governance of control processes remain the responsibility of the PA. Here, the inherent resistance to change exhibited by bureaucracies and poor levels of redistribution clearly reveal the limitations of this governance within complex welfare systems. In other words, systems based on a combination of the regulatory codes of hierarchy and of competition have given rise to hybrid systems lacking the capacity to guide the development of welfare policies.

We are also seeing the emergence of regulatory processes inspired by aims of cooperation, thanks also to the encouragement of the European Community, which has underscored the central role of participatory processes and the involvement of actors – both public and private – in governance processes.

The encounter between these different propensities has also led to the emergence of different forms of hybrid governance which depend on a range of factors including:

1.   The ideological culture of the dominant group and the tendency for bureaucratic dynamics to be replaced with market-oriented dynamics.

2. The capacity of bureaucracies to manage power and to incorporate hierarchical approaches into new forms of regulation.
3. The characteristics of the third sector and its capacity to negotiate an active role instead of being limited to supplying services to state bureaucracies.

We can therefore include these perspectives in an approach of co-regulation. One of the key aspects of this approach is undoubtedly the development of processes of co-production, but this logic also extends to the forms assumed by the regulatory mechanisms designed to guarantee the quality of the services supplied to citizens and/or guide the action of actors towards the overall objectives of individual welfare systems.

When forms of co-regulation are actually applied, they reveal highly differentiated characteristics. In this regard, Steurer (2013) maintains that 'Co-regulation is an umbrella term for co-operative forms of steering in which actors from different societal domains aim to achieve common objectives or supply public services jointly' (p. 397). Despite this differentiation we can nevertheless affirm that all of the approaches used begin with the specificity of the dynamics characterizing the network systems. Sørensen and Torfing (2009) examine the problem of how they can be regulated, defining networks as

> a stable articulation of mutually dependent, but operationally autonomous actors from state, market and civil society, who interact through conflict-ridden negotiations that take place within an institutionalized framework of rules, norms, shared knowledge and social imaginaries; facilitate self-regulated policy-making in the shadow of hierarchy; and contribute to the production of "public value" in a broad sense of problem definitions, visions, ideas, plans and concrete regulations that are deemed relevant to broad sections of the populations. (p. 236)

This definition of the dynamics of the networks begins by confirming the autonomy of the actors interacting with negotiation processes and contributing to producing public value. The different types of dynamics developing between the actors are oriented towards self-regulation but at the same time they are also steered by hierarchical-type dynamics. The hybrid character of these processes results from the presence of processes of cooperation, hierarchy and self-regulation.

Lægreid and Rykkja's (2015) research into procedures coordinating and resolving conflict in organizations highlights the presence of hierarchically based coordination approaches alongside other processes typical of governance networks. In their studies, these authors point out that 63 per cent of interviewees refer to administrative dynamics typical of hierarchies while 58 per cent underline the presence of negotiation dynamics between work groups jointly participating in the decision-making process. In some cases, such dynamics are integrated, while in others there is a lack of correlation between them and the presence of hierarchical dynamics seems to disincentivize the activation of network dynamics (and vice versa). This research shows that hierarchy continues to be a strong component in public systems even in the presence of dynamics of network coordination participating in the production of care services. The authors conclude that 'Coordination by networks tends to develop in the shadow of hierarchy' (Lægreid and Rykkja, 2015, p. 977).

Despite this plurality of hybrid experiences, we can refer to public co-regulation when PAs continue to play a central role in activating processes coordinating and integrating the action of the single actors, and to tripartite governance when regulatory experiences move towards self-regulation, challenging the need for a regulatory agent taking on the task of activating and integrating the action of single actors (Teubner, 2015; Sabel and Zeitling, 2008).

Although they differ in terms of the role assigned to the PAs, the paths of public co-regulation and of tripartite regulation are both based on the recognition of the centrality of participatory processes and the active involvement of all of the actors participating in producing welfare services (see Table 8.4).

The approaches adopted in regulatory processes include:

1. The co-responsibilization of actors in inducing public value. This approach involves the activation of sense-making processes based on shared reworking of experiences.
2. The participation of actors in the construction of a shared vision capable of serving as a vehicle for coordinating and steering the actions of the single actors.
3. Negotiation and formalization of shared commitments by members of the network.
4. The co-determination of criteria for the evaluation of the quality of services and expected results; the construction of self- and hetero-evaluation schemes; and the involvement of all actors in evaluation processes and the redefinition of improvement actions.

CONCLUSION

The increased complexity of welfare systems has resulted in the review of governance systems across Europe. These changes have taken on different forms depending on the nature of the welfare regimes, the regulatory culture characterizing them and the dynamics between the different social actors involved in producing welfare policies. Here it may be argued that the different governance regimes are the result of three central factors related to the role played by the state and other actors.

Table 8.4   Mechanisms and practices

	Regulatory mechanisms	Practices
Quality guarantees	• Audit certification schemes (standards, formal standard-setting, standards scores)	• Co-definition (state and network actors) of rules that everyone must respect • Control through third-party public and/ or private subjects (agreed self- and hetero-evaluation schemes)
Guidance of actors	• Codes of conduct and stakeholder management • Negotiation agreement partnerships (private-private partnerships, or public-private) • Strategic • Business partners impose restraints on a firm • Studies, campaigns, websites • Public voluntary programmes • Hybrid instrument as labels • Community strategic planning • Integrated self- and hetero-evaluation plans	• Self-determination of behaviours • Formalization of shared commitments among network members • Responsibilization of actors • Pay attention to clients, involving them in evaluation • Give stakeholders an active role and steer network • Inclusion of actors in decision-making processes • Involvement of stakeholders in evaluation

Firstly, although welfare systems throughout Europe are made up of different actors interacting in networks of systems, the morphology of these networks takes different forms. The centrality of the state and the relative marginality of the other actors in some or the presence of networks based on peers in others are all premises for the development of different regulatory systems.

Secondly, distinct forms of welfare governance are forged by the degree of involvement of actors in constructing and managing governance processes. Regardless of the presence of centrality, the process and verification of rules of behaviour may either take place entirely within the administrative apparatus of the state or through highly participatory processes. The forms and intensity of involvement will determine the decision-making arena within which actors engage in defining the rules which steer the dynamics of the network. The organizational cultures of single actors and systems are also influential in shaping the dynamics of interaction within distinct forms of governance.

A third factor of differentiation relates to the types of rules and processes which shape welfare system regulation. In this case too it is possible to imagine numerous blended positions lying between two extremes. At one extreme we can place processes characterized by the persistence of a tendentially prescriptive hierarchical culture. At the opposite extreme we find cooperative cultures with proscriptive regulatory mechanisms.

Despite the undeniable complexity of such dynamics, it is fair to say that all European countries are experiencing the development – albeit in different forms – of types of hybrid regulation distinguished by a number of transversal characteristics, whether consolidated or experimental. In particular, hybrid regulation across distinct European welfare states involves the construction of mechanisms of co-regulation achieved through participatory processes involving actors from different sectors. Here, actors are also involved in the creation of self-regulation spaces requiring direct interaction between actors and the specification of rules underlying the functioning of networks. Importantly, PAs are no longer regarded as residing at the axiom of welfare systems in Europe. A central function of PAs within the governance of welfare within European societies is to act as a link between citizens and service providers and to facilitate the actions of other network members.

Crucially, as this chapter has evidenced, recent developments in the governance of welfare systems have crystallized around experimentation in forms of social innovation and technologies useful for the governance of health and welfare systems. Lying at the heart of social innovation, locally driven place-based approaches rely upon flexible forms of governance and the co-responsibilization of actors in constructing health and welfare systems. Given the profound challenges we now face as a result of the Covid-19 health pandemic, it may be argued that these flexible and participatory forms of governance will be particularly vital in facilitating the innovative policy approaches which will be so critical in shaping a future European Social Model and economy of well-being which is fit for purpose.

REFERENCES

Alderwick, H., and Gottlieb, L. M. (2019). Meanings and misunderstandings: a social determinants of health lexicon for health care systems, *Milbank Quarterly*, **97** (2), 407.

Aliu, A., Parlak, B., and Aliu, D. (2015). Hybrid structures: innovative governance, judicial and sociological approaches, *Quality and Quantity*, 49, 1747–1760.

Artiga, S., and Hinton, E. (2019). Beyond health care: the role of social determinants in promoting health and health equity, *Health*, **20** (10), 1–13.

Bauman, Z. (2000). *Liquid Modernity*. Cambridge: Polity Press.

Beck, U. (1986). *Risk Society*. Sage: London.

Bevir, M., and Richards, D. (2008). Decentring policy networks and prospects, *Public Administration*, **87** (1), 132–141.

Bicchieri, C. (2006). *The Grammar of Society*. Cambridge: Cambridge University Press.

Bovaird, T., and Loeffler, E. (2007). Assessing the quality of local governance: a case study of public services, *Public Money & Management*, September, 293–300.

Bovaird, T., Löffler, E., and Parrado-Díez, S. (2002). *Developing Local Governance Networks in Europe*, Vol. 1. Baden-Baden: Nomos.

Castells, M. (2004). *The Network Society*. Cheltenham, UK, and Northampton, MA: Edward Elgar Publishing.

Crozier, M., and Friedberg, E. (1980). *Actors and Systems*. Chicago, IL: University of Chicago Press.

Enjolras, B. (2009). Between market and civic governance regimes: civicness in the governance of social services in Europe, *Voluntas*, **2009** (20), 274–290.

Gottlieb, L., Fichtenberg, C., Alderwick, H., and Adler, N. (2019). Social determinants of health: What's a healthcare system to do? *Journal of Healthcare Management*, **64** (4), 243–257.

Habermas, J. (1984). *The Theory of Communicative Action*. Cambridge: Polity Press.

Habermas, J., and Luhmann, N. (1973). *Teoria della società o tecnologia sociale*. Milan: Etas Kompass.

Haveri, A. (2008). Evaluation of change in local governance: the rhetorical wall and the politics of images, *Evaluation*, 14, 141–155.

Hesse, J. J., and Sharpe, L. J. (1991). Local government in international perspective: some comparative observations, in: Hesse, J. J. (ed.), *Local Government and Urban Affairs in International Perspective*. Baden-Baden: Nomos.

Hooghe, L., and Marks, G. (2001). *Multilevel Governance and European Integration*. Lanham, MD: Rowman & Littlefield.

Howlett, M., and Rayner, K. (2007). Design principles for policy mixes: cohesion and coherence in 'new governance arrangements', *Policy and Society*, **26** (4), 1–18.

Hustinx, L., Verschuere, B., and De Corte, J. (2014). Organisational hybridity in a post-corporatist welfare mix: the case of the third sector in Belgium, *Journal of Social Policy*, **43** (2), 391–411.

Jochim, A. E., and May, P. J. (2010). Beyond subsystems: policy regimes and governance, *Policy Studies Journal*, **38** (2), 303–327.

Lægreid, P., and Rykkja, L. H. (2015). Hybrid collaborative arrangements: the welfare administration in Norway – between hierarchy and network, *Public Management Review*, **17** (7), 960–980.

Marmot, M. (2020). *Health Equity in England: The Marmot Review 10 Years On*. London: Institute of Health Equity.

Merton, R. (1968). *Social Theory and Social Structure*, enlarged edition. New York, NY: Free Press.

Ostrom, E. (2005). *Understanding Institutional Diversity*. Princeton, NJ: Princeton University Press.

Sabel, C. F., and Zeitling, J. (2008). Learning from difference: the new architecture of experimentalist governance in EU, *European Law Journal*, **14** (3), 271–327.

Sassen, S. (1998), *Globalization and its Discontents*. New York, NY: New Press.

Seibel, W. (2015). Welfare mixes and hybridity: analytical and managerial implications, *Voluntas*, 26, 1759–1768.

Sellers J.M., and Lidström A., (2007), Decentralization, Local Government, and the Welfare State, *Governance, International Journal of Policy, Administration, and Institutions*, **20** (4), 609–632.

Simon, H. (1983). *Reason in Human Affairs*. Stanford, CT: Stanford University Press.

Sørensen, E., and Torfing, J. (2009). Making governance networks effective and democratic through metagovernance, *Public Administration*, **87** (2), 234–258.

Steurer, R. (2013). Disentangling governance: a synoptic view of regulation by government, business and civil society, *Policy Science*, 46, 387–410.

Teubner, G. (2015). *Ibridi e attanti*. Milan: Mimesis edizioni.
World Health Organization Commission on Social Determinants of Health (2008). *Closing the Gap in a Generation: Health Equity through Action on the Social Determinants of Health: Commission on Social Determinants of Health Final Report*. Geneva: World Health Organization.

9. 'Building a European home': mechanisms for the construction of a common social space within the European Union

Giuseppe Moro

INTRODUCTION

The construction of a common social space within the European Union was not the result of a project which can be considered as being entirely legitimate from a legal and political perspective. From a legal point of view, since its foundation social policies have never been the responsibility of the European Union. From a political perspective, the Union's interventions in the social field have been the subject of great resistance from some member states and stakeholders who considered them as unwanted interference attempting to make changes to consolidated traditional structures. The construction of a social Europe has often been the unintentional result of a confrontation or clash between institutions and social groups having deeply contrasting political visions. An important role in this process has been played not so much by classical legal rules, but rather by 'softer' social mechanisms through which the central institutions of the Union in particular have attempted to influence and condition the behaviour of other socio-political key actors, with the aim of increasing the Union's areas of social intervention and to build common policies among member states. The concept of a social mechanism takes on different meanings depending on how abstractly we wish to consider it.

Assuming an analytical approach to sociology, the idea of a mechanism is important as it allows us to explain how the various elements of social reality are linked and, in particular, how they can 'cause' each other. From this perspective a mechanism may be defined as the set of elements and their causal links that lead from a certain initial state to a subsequent one (Demeulenaere, 2011): it is the causal process, situated at the level of the interaction system, which explains how a phenomenon has been generated (Barbera, 2004). The concept of a mechanism implies that attention is focused on the social actions responsible for change: the same macro-social phenomena can be fully explained only if we are able to connect them to beliefs, tendencies, resources and to the interrelationships existing between individuals. It is necessary to focus on the causal processes that occur at the level of social action, assuming a practical role for each participant involved in order to bring about social change.

From the perspective of evaluative research, the concept of a mechanism is used above all in realistic evaluation (Pawson and Tilley, 1997) and identifies the regularities that account for the micro and macro processes which make up a programme and which demonstrate how its outputs derive from the choices made by stakeholders and their ability to put these choices into practice. Evaluation focused on mechanisms is an alternative to the counterfactual approach in that it attempts to shed light on the causal relationships between a programme and its outputs, explaining how individuals and their actions contribute to the realisation of such outputs. Mechanisms help the researcher to understand that the results of a programme derive from the behaviours implemented by the key players involved using the resources made available by a programme and by those existing in the social context in which it is carried out. For this reason, it is important to reconstruct the theory of change underlying the programme (Funnel and Rogers, 2011): because a programme will be able to produce changes if it contributes to generating a chain of interim results which lead to the achievement of desired results.

Finally, in the more specific field of the analysis of public policy, mechanisms can be considered as the actual means and tools used by decision makers to implement policy (Howlett and Ramesh, 1995). These are tools which can also be classified depending on how much the state is involved. Therefore, at one end of the scale we may find voluntary tools such as the involvement of families in the local community, and at the other direct provision by the state and regulation by laws; while in the middle of the scale we find instruments such as subsidies, incentives and information. Majone and La Spina's (2000) thesis on this subject is particularly important. They argue that, starting from the end of the 1970s, European governments changed their traditional approach to governing, reducing the role of the interventionist state and placing more importance on the role of social regulation. In other words, the state took on the role of governing society through the external provision of rules in the public's interest and for the well-being of all. A set of political coordination and regulation mechanisms which are particularly important for our analysis are those which Jacobsson (2004) has defined as 'discourse regulation mechanisms': mechanisms which refer to the use of language and to the production of knowledge and which, as a consequence, lead to a better understanding of problems and solutions in specific policy fields.

These three meanings of the mechanism concept are interrelated: public policies are increasingly implemented without a legal or direct provision, but instead attempt to influence the choices made by the various key social actors involved with the use of increasingly 'softer' tools of a discursive nature, in such a way as to trigger a course of action which may not be entirely possible to predetermine, but nevertheless generates social changes which are equally difficult to determine in advance.

Since the 1980s, also in the specific field of social policy, the transition from the use of mechanisms for the direct provision of goods and services to regulatory mechanisms aimed at influencing the choices of stakeholders not only through traditional legal regulation, but also through the use of 'softer' mechanisms such as information, exhortations and the production of common cultural references, has been particularly important.

This process has also developed within the 'European Social Space' and in the relationship between the institutions of the European Union and the nation-states. Social policy, although formally constituting an area of policy in which nation-states have maintained their autonomy, has also been involved in the process of soft regulation. Legally non-binding agreements and expectations have gradually become politically and socially binding and have been perceived as legislation, not only by nations, but also by many national key actors. The agreements themselves have been internalised and considered as the correct way to develop national social policies and to place limitations on the freedom of action formally enjoyed by nation-states. Naturally, this has not been a homogeneous and conflict-free process (indeed, in the years following the great economic crisis of 2007–2008 conflicts spread and became more intense), although in any case, the European social protection systems have had much in common. As a consequence, since they had different beginnings, these systems have become hybrids highlighting, on the one hand, aspects of mutual adaptation and conformity and, on the other, the conservation of initial positions and prevailing interests in each national context.

In the following pages we will attempt to identify the mechanisms which have contributed to changing the behaviour and the choices made by the key actors in the field of social policy, generating the process of hybridisation and political change. We will focus, in particular, on the functioning of three mechanisms which have operated at different levels in the field of social policy.

The first is social dialogue; in many ways a traditional tool which was widely employed in European countries for decades from the end of the last to the beginning of the present century to coordinate policies of various kinds with the most influential key social actors in order to promote citizens' active participation.

The second mechanism is the Open Method of Coordination (OMC), a rather innovative process which has acted above all in the relationships between member states and the central institutions of the Union, particularly the Commission. Through this mechanism an attempt was made to coordinate European and national social policy, particularly when faced with the contradictions and social conflict that emerged with the monetary integration following the Maastricht protocol, the Stability Pact and the Fiscal Compact.

The final tool is constituted by the introduction and use of social indicators: a discursive regulatory mechanism through which a common reading and interpretation of some relevant social problems, such as poverty, has been proposed. An attempt has been made to construct a database that might lead to the development of evidence-based social policies.

SOCIAL DIALOGUE

In its official papers (European Commission, 2012), the European Union has recognised that social dialogue (intended as discussions, consultation, negotiation and joint actions between employers' and workers' organisations) is a mediating process through which differences between social partners can be resolved and innovation in social and labour market policies can be promoted, mainly through the exchange of information (Euwema et al., 2015).

Social dialogue has been the culmination of a process of European economic integration. In triggering a complex political game between the Commission, member states, trade unions and entrepreneurs, it has been possible to partially get around the various sticking points involved in the implementation of European social legislation by promoting further European integration in an area which had for a long time been formally excluded from treaties and vetoed by a number of member states (Johnson, 2005).

The presence of social dialogue on the European agenda and the agreement to use it as an alternative to the community regulation method was not simply due to various member states expressing a preference in this direction. Without the full and active involvement of the European Commission in creating opportunities for the involvement of social partners in European institutions and also the innovative ability of Jacques Delors, who was President of the European Union between 1985 and 1995, to propose a new governance tool based on collective bargaining, social dialogue would not have been introduced at a European level.

Another institutional factor which has led to the introduction of social dialogue is that it has been difficult to arrive at a unanimous agreement or qualified majority of votes inside intergovernmental institutions when discussing the issue of social policy due to the use of vetoes, above all during the phase of profound change and enlargement of the Union by the British government during the 1980s and 1990s. The strengthening of social dialogue at a European level, already experimented with by numerous member states for decades, has therefore served to circumvent stalling on social policy in the European Council (EC).

A third factor has been the fact that social forces such as employers' organisations and trade unions have understood that, faced with the Commission's desire to extend the method of approval by qualified majority to regulations concerning social questions, social dialogue could be a way to pass resolutions which take into account individual preferences and mitigate the damage that the adoption of these resolutions might cause to those same interests. Various governments along with the European Commission have considered social dialogue to be an alternative way to introduce legislation on social policy, given the blocking of the majority of social legislation in the EC.

The participation of social partners in European governance has a long history and has almost always seen the Commission play a leading role. As early as the mid-1970s, the Commission organised a series of tripartite conferences to discuss topics such as vocational training, youth unemployment, equal opportunities and the reintroduction of the long-term unemployed into the labour market. In the early 1980s a number of advisory committees were set up to discuss issues of social policy, such as the reduction of working hours in order to create new jobs. An attempt to use the findings of these committees to introduce regulations at European level was blocked by the objections of both entrepreneurs and governments, so much so that during the 1980s employers' organisations (represented by UNICE, the Union of Industrial and Employers' Confederations of Europe) were opposed to participation in the tripartite talks because they feared that the results of these discussions could be used as a basis for European social legislation.

Dialogue officially became a tool for the regulation of social policy from the beginning of the 1990s, in the period that led to the signing of the Maastricht protocol, the birth of the single European currency and the strengthening of the powers of the Union with the introduction of qualified majority voting in intergovernmental bodies. The Commission intended that social dialogue would not only serve to force the launch of social legislation at European level, but also to involve the social partners in the implementation of agreements at national level. It was also reiterated that if an agreement were not reached, the European institutions would have intervened in order to achieve social regulation following the traditional route of regulatory intervention. Social dialogue was therefore accepted and its value appreciated by even the most reluctant European partners (by both nation-states and entrepreneurs) since it was perceived as a way to prevent the risk that social legislation be approved by qualified majorities within intergovernmental conferences.

Ultimately, social dialogue has been experienced in a rather ambiguous fashion: on the one hand as a way to counter the resistance of some states towards European social legislation; on the other, as a tool used to actively intervene in the formulation of such dialogue in an attempt to limit the scope and ability to intervene in both national legislation and market dynamics. Indeed, social dialogue was included in the so-called Maastricht protocol as a tool for the negotiation and implementation of European social legislation, with the commitment that the Commission should consult the social partners before proposing social policy interventions, in order to give them the possibility to negotiate.

In fact, in the second half of the 1990s, social dialogue was used in an experimental way in areas in which there was a lack of agreement inside the EC and was therefore seen as an alternative route to social regulation in a field in which some member states would have been able to exercise their power of veto. Indeed, it became evident that the EC, although formally having the power to do so, would have great difficulty amending the agreements made by the social partners involved, and would be limited to the simple choice of either approving or rejecting agreements. Two important agreements reached by social partners, which then became directives unanimously approved by the Council, concerned the regulation of the labour market: one in 1994 concerned parental leave and the other, in 1997, regarded social protection as a way to provide security for various forms of non-standard employment, in particular part-time employment. The national impact of these agreements and their following directives was naturally greater in those countries (for example, Great Britain) in which there was a lower level of protection for this type of job. Furthermore, social dialogue has been the tool used, albeit in a gradual and largely unplanned manner, to increase the role played by the European Union in areas previously unforeseen by treaties.

The concrete effects of social dialogue have been profoundly influenced by the national contexts which existed prior to the framework agreements and successive directives of the EC. The concrete effects of social dialogue in Europe have therefore been influenced by variables such as traditions of welfare, welfare preferences, the strength of unions and entrepreneurs, and traditions of bilateral and/or tripartite bargaining at a national level. However, European social legislation resulting from social dialogue has had, paradoxically, its most profound effects in the very countries which were opposed to the extension of Europe's role in the social field, leading therefore to a further hybridisation of national social policies with standards deriving from supranational agreements.

THE OPEN METHOD OF COORDINATION

The second mechanism identified, the OMC, can in some ways be considered as a method which developed out of social dialogue. It may be defined as a set of policy tools which includes codes of conduct, benchmarking and the cooperation between states rather than the construction of formally binding laws. The OMC commits countries to the adoption of a reflective approach with regard to their own programmes in a number of policy areas. Further, the OMC is supported by guidelines, targets and resources enabling national comparisons of policies which exist in distinct European states.

The OMC is made up of four key elements (Wincott, 2003):

1. The establishment of guidelines by the European Union accompanied by specific timetables to achieve short-, medium- and long-term objectives.
2. The determination of quantitative and qualitative indicators and benchmarks used as a means to determine so-called best practices.
3. The establishment of specific targets and measures for individual national and regional policies which follow general guidelines taking into consideration the various regional and national differences involved.
4. The monitoring and periodic evaluation of the results achieved.

In the two decades during which this method was used it can be stated that in some policy areas the method was given a more binding interpretation, with the central bodies of the Union setting the objectives and drawing up the general outline of the programmes through which objectives were to be achieved and determining the indicators used to measure results. However, in other policy areas a more bottom-up approach prevailed with the identification of best practices and the comparison between various policy models at national and regional levels with a view of a convergence towards identified benchmarks. In the field of social policy, an example of the first approach are labour market policies and pensions, whereas the second approach has been used in the field of insurance and social assistance, and in policies relating to families and health care.

The OMC, as a method of coordination between nation-states and institutional cooperation, was established at the Lisbon Summit (March 2000), extending the experience of the European Employment Strategy (EES) launched in the second half of the 1990s, beginning from the Employment Title included in the Treaty of Amsterdam (1997). The OMC has elevated the governance regime developed by the EES to the general method of cooperation to be adopted in areas in which the supremacy of European legislation is not stipulated; for example, in the area of social policy.

The OMC was formally proposed as the governance tool to implement the Lisbon Strategy, which sought to combine and mutually strengthen economic development, employment and social policies.

The method is made up of a few fundamental phases: the Commission and the Council approve the guidelines on a specific policy, the member states provide a report on the national situation, the Commission and the Council examine the report and the Commission proposes recommendations to guide national policy according to the indications present in the guidelines.

Since the beginning of the twenty-first century, in the field of social inclusion and protection the OMC has created:

1. National Action Plans (NAPs) and Strategic Reports in which member states explain how they have pursued common objectives in their national policy and what results have been achieved.
2. Common Reports from the Commission and EC analysing the progress of member states, focusing on areas in need of greater attention and identifying priorities for future work.
3. Peer-review exercises in which civil servants, representatives of non-governmental organisations (NGOs), academic experts and other stakeholders discuss key topics and learn from each other's experiences.

The central institutional body of the OMC is the Social Protection Committee (SPC), which is made up of senior managers who report directly to the national ministries and to the EC. The SPC has the mandate to monitor the development of social protection policies; to promote the exchange of information, experiences and best practices; and to prepare reports, especially the annual report on social protection, to be submitted to the Council. The Social OMC has been implemented with regard to important issues such as social inclusion, pensions, healthcare and long-term care.

The Social Agenda adopted at the Nice Summit (December 2000) established a timetable for the implementation of the OMC in the field of social policy; this summit saw the approval of an initial set of common objectives aimed at fighting poverty and social exclusion. During the summit of the summer of 2001 the two-year report cycle began with the member states launching the first NAP, while the first eighteen indicators for the measurement of social inclusion were approved at the Laeken European Council. In 2002 the Commission launched an action programme to fight social exclusion to be carried out through the OMC process, which was first tested by peer review on social inclusion beginning in 2004.

The second application of the OMC involved pensions and began in 2001. Worries concerning the financial sustainability of European pension systems were at the forefront due to demographic transformations across European societies which were related to ageing processes already highlighted in the conclusions of the Lisbon Summit. The OMC on pensions was officially launched by the Laeken Summit and had the general objective of ensuring the long-term sustainability of the pensions system, safeguarding the ability to achieve social goals but also maintaining financial stability and meeting new social needs. In the spring of 2002, the member states prepared the first

National Strategic Plans on pensions, on the basis of which the Commission produced the first synthesis report containing assessments of national strategies and the identification of good practices. In 2005 the member states prepared a second strategic plan on the basis of which the Commission produced a new synthesis report in 2006. The OMC on pensions has contributed towards the implementation of a series of similar reforms across Europe, including extending the duration of the working life, reducing the weight of pensions on the state, promoting supplementary private pensions and ensuring that all social groups have access to pensions.

The third case of OMC intervention related to health and long-term care. However, the results achieved here were not as satisfactory as in the first two cases.

After the redefinition of the Lisbon Strategy in 2005, characterised by its greater focus on economic growth and employment, a new process of the Social OMC 2006–2010 was launched which aimed to integrate all the previously initiated processes. The Spring 2006 EC adopted twelve common objectives of the new Social OMC inspired by general principles such as social cohesion; equality between men and women and equal opportunities for all; the interaction between economic growth, new and better jobs and social cohesion; transparency; and the involvement of stakeholders in the planning, implementation and monitoring of social policy. Since 2006 the member states have produced two national reports on social protection and social inclusion (2006–2008 and 2008–2010). During the intervening years studies of different types have been carried out on specific topics, such as the reduction of child and housing poverty and the effectiveness and efficiency of spending on healthcare. Every year the Commission has prepared reports on social protection and inclusion based upon national reports, European statistics, documents drawn up by networks of experts or resulting from peer-review exercises, and on the answers given by member states to questionnaires on various subjects. These reports were approved by the SPC and the EC, but unlike other European political processes, did not generate formal recommendations.

In addition to the institutional aspect, the OMC has also had a mutual learning dimension which aimed to promote and support the exchange of evidence and experience through peer reviews, networks of experts, discussions with NGOs, events of various kinds and conferences. Indeed, it was thought that these various forms of mutual learning might provide empirical evidence and build deliberative forums which would help key political actors to change their visions and preferences in order to work together to achieve common goals. Firstly, the experiences of peer review were carried out within the SPC, whose members analysed and discussed strategic national reports. Furthermore, numerous peer reviews were organised in various countries with the participation of officials, independent experts and representatives of NGO networks.

European networks of thematic experts in the various fields of social policy have also been set up, often on the Commission's initiative.

In the second decade of the century the Lisbon Strategy was replaced by the Europe 2020 Strategy, which further strengthens the Union's commitment towards social cohesion, introducing, for example, new targets and guidelines aimed at reducing poverty and social exclusion. Of the ten integrated guidelines of the Europe 2020 Strategy, the tenth is specifically aimed at promoting social inclusion and fighting poverty; in addition, one of the flagship initiatives of the Strategy is the European Platform against Poverty (EPAP). The central objective of the EPAP is to ensure that the benefits of growth and employment are shared widely and that people who are affected by poverty and social exclusion are given the possibility to live a dignified life. The choice to include the social dimension directly within the Strategy ensures that the reporting cycle, linked to the European Semester, also includes the social dimension which is part of the National Reform Programmes (NRPs) prepared by each member state and the specific recommendations for each country approved by the EC. At the same time, at the initiative of the SPC, the member states are also invited to draw up the National Social Report (NSR) in cooperation with the stakeholders of civil society and local authorities, therefore continuing the OMC experience. In addition, a performance-monitoring system on social protection has been developed and peer reviews continue to be carried out on specific topics, including the most important social issues of Strategy Europe 2020, such as active inclusion, child poverty and the efficiency of social security systems. Therefore, the Social OMC is now both part of the main process of the Europe 2020 Strategy, being included in reports of the European Semester as an autonomous strategy with its own agenda, methods and results continuing the experience which began in the previous decade.

The success or otherwise of this political coordination strategy has been contested. There remains a clear division between those scholars and politicians who consider the OMC to be nothing more than a purely formal exercise and those who regard it as an important vehicle which has promoted progressive reform and supported mutual learning between countries while also giving a voice to civil society.

For those who consider it in a positive light, the OMC has been a useful tool, tackling common European problems while at the same time respecting legitimate national differences, as it commits nation-states to working together to reach common objectives without having to homogenise their traditional policies and institutional frameworks (Hemerijck and Berghman, 2004). It has also been claimed that the OMC is a cognitive and regulatory framework enabling the development of a consensus around the European Social Model. The OMC also guides a progressive 'recalibration' of national welfare systems to respond to new challenges and social risks (Vandenbroucke, 2002; Ferrera,

2009). In addition, the OMC has been considered as a mechanism to promote experimental learning and deliberative problem solving, as well as being a platform to give a voice to the relevant key actors of civil society by involving them in the planning of social policies at both a European and national level.

Critics of the OMC focus primarily on its lack of legitimacy and effectiveness. A frequently made criticism is that the OMC's soft procedures are considered to be a threat to the community legislative method in which binding laws are proposed by the Commission, approved by Parliament or by the EC and enforced by the Court of Justice. In addition, it is argued that the OMC is not democratically legitimate as it is subject to neither authorisation from the European Parliament nor scrutiny from other national democratic institutions, although critics fail to identify effective alternative mechanisms for civil society participation (Dawson, 2011). On a more strictly political level, the OMC is accused of being a kind of Trojan Horse used to dismantle national welfare states and promote new neo-liberal policies (Offe, 2003). Furthermore, it is claimed that the OMC is a means to concentrate power in the hands of the European Commission and to illegitimately undermine the principle of subsidiarity by allowing the European institutions to invade the domains that the Treaties reserve for the member states (Syrpis, 2002; Smismans, 2008). On the contrary, it is asserted that the OMC is not able to make a significant impact at either a European or national level and is only a symbolic policy in which governments reintroduce existing national policies in order to display their apparent adherence to European objectives. This is also because the institutional conditions for mutual learning are lacking and incentives to support the transfer of policies between member states are too weak.

An empirical analysis of OMC processes is problematic for a number of reasons. First of all, the causal impact of an interactive process based upon collaboration between member states and the European institutions is difficult to determine since the boundaries between independent variables (in theory European policies) and dependent variables (national policies) are not clear. OMC processes do not necessarily produce new legislation and neither is it easy to isolate the influence of the OMC on national policies from other processes at a European level (for example, the Growth and Stability Pact or Structural Funds) or from that exercised by other international organisations or from changes in the national political context (Zeitlin, Barcevičius and Weishaupt, 2014).

The history of the Social OMC shows that it does not proceed according to predetermined standards, but it is rather a process of learning in progress and of self-reflection in which mistakes will be made and consequences may be unexpected. The OMC can influence national policies in two ways: in a substantive and in a procedural way (Weishaupt, 2014). From a substantive point of view, its influence can be ideological (producing changes in the position of key political players regarding a particular issue), in the formation of the political agenda (giving priority to certain issues rather than others) and programmatic (influencing the creation of new laws and administrative rules). Procedural influences regard the changes produced in governance and in the policy-making process, including: the strengthening of coordination and integration between various political fields, the improved ability to collect and to use data in order to better direct policy, the improvement of vertical coordination between the various levels of governance, greater involvement of non-state actors in the process of policy production and the development of national and transnational networks of non-state and local actors, leading to a consequent greater involvement in the processes of European policy production.

There is ample evidence not only that the OMC has contributed directly to specific political reforms in the member states, but that it has also directly contributed to framing national political thinking in a new way by including European concepts and categories within the national political debate. Moreover, the Social OMC has played an important role in the inclusion of new themes in the European and national political agenda and in increasing awareness that national social policies would have to deal with new problems. On a procedural level, the OMC has produced important changes in governance and in the procedural framework of social policy. For example, it has promoted horizontal coordination between different policies enhancing the ability of national governments to control, monitor and improve vertical coordination between various levels of government, thereby enabling networks of state and non-state actors to develop networks and become actively involved in European and national policy making.

In some ways, these effects were common to all states, although in others they were very different. Each member state, including those considered leaders in the field of social policy, has been forced to modify, albeit to a different extent, policies involved in the OMC processes (Johnson, 2005). However, the impact has been greater in those states which have less experience and weaker institutional frameworks in each specific policy. In negative terms, the benchmarking method applied to social policies has meant that some states have been subjected to continual criticism and forced to review policies. At times this has led to the development of processes of passive adjustment and resentment which has become ever more manifest.

The factor which best explains the OMC's impact in national contexts is the involvement of various social and political actors in their desire/ability to make use of data and resources strategically made available. The role played by traditional welfare regimes as a mediating factor appears to be much more limited and less systematic. This is not to say that institutional factors have had no weight, but that their weight depends on other characteristics than welfare models. For example, where there have been weaknesses in models of govern-ance due to poor involvement of NGOs, the OMC has helped their voices to be heard and has put them online; where the systems of data collection have been weak, the OMC has promoted their improvement.

SOCIAL INDICATORS

A European monitoring system operationalised through the use of social indicators was instigated by the Lisbon Strategy as one of its most important implementation mechanisms (Atkinson et al., 2002). The fundamental purpose of the European Union's social indicators is to monitor progress towards the achievement of social protection and inclusion agreed by the member states in 2001.

The system of indicators adopted by the EC of 2001 was developed and extended in following years as part of the OMC on social protection and social inclusion.

In December 2001 the EC adopted a set of indicators which were intended to play a central role in monitoring the performance of member states in the promotion of social inclusion. It was believed that these indicators would allow the states and the European Commission to monitor national and European progress towards the achievement of objectives regarding social inclusion set out by the Nice Council of 2000. The system of social indicators was developed to support mutual learning and the sharing of good practices in the field of social policy across Europe. The definition of these indicators was meant to ensure that the report on social inclusion, which the Commission was entrusted with preparing on the basis of NAPs (probably the core purpose and most important purpose of the OMC), was not only descriptive in nature, but also based on statistically relevant data. It was believed that the opinions expressed by each member state, based on country ranking in relation to social inclusion indicators, would effectively exert peer pressure on members, thereby advancing the implementation of necessary reforms. For each element of social inclusion, the Commission singled out those states with the best performance, encouraging others to follow suit and learn from their experience (Atkinson et al., 2002).

The Laeken objectives referred to social inclusion and led to the adoption of the first eighteen indicators (the so-called Laeken indicators). These objectives were followed by others on pensions, healthcare and long-term care; a total redefinition of objectives was decided by the European Council of Ministers for Social Affairs and Labour in 2011. The operational definition of the indi-cators is entrusted to the sub-group for indicators (ISG) of the SPC. The ISG's role is to develop and to define the European Union's social indicators in order to monitor progress made by member states towards the achievement of agreed social objectives, carry out analysis based on agreed indicators, develop an analytical framework to support social policy reviews carried out by the SPC and contribute to the improvement of social statistics on a European level, particularly with regard to EU Statistics on Income and Living Conditions (EU-SILC) (Social Protection Committee Indicators Sub-Group, 2015).[1]

The use of indicators is essential in order to support reports made by the member states and the preparation of the annual report on the social situation of the European Union by the SPC. Four sets (portfolios) of indicators have been developed: one comprehensive indicator on the social situation and the other three regarding the specific issues of inclusion, pensions and health. Each of these sets constitutes a monitoring tool which is sufficiently concise in its evaluation of the social situation in each country with regard to the reference objectives.

The indicators have been used in various contexts: to monitor the Union's social situation, to prepare NRPs on the occasion of the European Semester's deadlines regarding social reports, to prepare the annual report of the SPC and to write reports on relevant issues such as the adequacy of pensions or poverty and children's welfare. Furthermore, the social indicators are widely used by scholars, policy makers and stakeholders for both international and national comparisons. Inside each portfolio the indicators are divided into three categories: European Union indicators (which have a more normative meaning and contribute to the evaluation of progress made by the member states towards the achievement of common European objectives on social protection and inclusion), national indicators and context indicators.

The indicators are divided into two levels: primary indicators (a small number which cover the fields considered as being most important for the measurement of social exclusion) and secondary indicators. The member states are encouraged to include third-level indicators in their NAPs illustrating particular areas deemed as being specific to a country. Naturally, according to the principle of subsidiarity, while agreeing the indicators upon which their performance will be judged, countries are formally left free to choose the methods used to achieve these objectives.

The basic reason for the introduction of indicators was the idea that their use would allow policy makers to know which criteria are used to judge progress made. It would also favour the implementation of the most suitable promotional policies for social inclusion: the multidimensional nature of exclusion, clarified by the indicators, would underline the need for greater collaboration between the various government agencies and between the different levels of government. The OMC would therefore be employed not only between states, but also within each state. There has been great improvement in the use of indicators as a tool for social policy governance since the adoption of the Europe 2020 Strategy.

The first draft of the Strategy was published on 3 March 2010 and proposed the target of a 25 per cent reduction in poverty by 2020. The Commission proposed that the calculation of poverty be made using a single measure (number of people living on less than 60 per cent of the equivalent median national income). The achievement of this target was to be supported by the EPAP, whose objective was to strengthen the OMC on social exclusion in a platform of cooperation, peer review and the exchange of good practices.

The target contained in the final approved strategy is, however, the synthesis of three different poverty measures. The first indicator identifies the people living in families with an equivalent income equal to less than 60 per cent of the national median income and is the classic measure of poverty, adopted since the beginning of the Lisbon Strategy. The second component of the target, however, focuses more on lifestyle standards and refers to a concept of deprivation upon which there has been much disagreement ever since the Lisbon Summit. The material deprivation indicator identifies the people who live in families to which at least four of the following items apply: cannot avoid late payment of mortgages, loans, utility bills, rent; cannot afford to heat their home adequately; cannot deal with unforeseen expenses; eat a protein meal every two days; cannot afford a week's holiday a year far from home; do not own a colour television, a washing machine, a car or a telephone. The third dimension (being a member of a family in which the adults aged up to 59 worked for 20 per cent of their potential working time) is instead a measure of economic activity.

While the European target is composed of a combination of these four indicators, the individual member states are free to choose the indicator which they consider to be most appropriate for them, and also the composition. This contradiction between, on the one hand, the setting of ambitious targets which indicate the will to achieve great integration of the social policies of European countries and, on the other, the possibility to choose has attracted the criticism of those who claim that the construction of such complicated indicators essentially allows the continuation of a model in which countries maintain the freedom of initiative and to choose à la carte which ideas of social Europe to share (Copeland and Daly, 2012).

The progress made during the negotiations on the Europe 2020 Strategy regarding social exclusion poverty and social indicators has, however, made it possible for member states to agree upon a definition of poverty on a European level which is compatible which each national structure. The three dimensions of poverty have the merit of combining both the various aspects which go to constitute poverty across Europe and the cultural and political preferences existing in the continent.

However, the setting of global targets at a European level (the number of poor people to be reduced by twenty million in ten years), and the setting of European thresholds for each of the three components of poverty, points to the emergence of a European norm or benchmark to which member states must aim to adhere and indicates that there is a growth of European Union influence and involvement in this sphere. While these may be overarching pre-determined targets which are objectively set, member states still retain a great deal of freedom in terms of how policy responses to these targets are shaped (Copeland and Daly, 2012).

In any case, from the Commission's standpoint the targets tend to be inter-preted as measures of performance, even though it has never been clear exactly which mechanisms would be used to introduce targets which could influence the political priorities of individual member states and how these might be aggregated together in such a way that the final targets set at European Union level would be achieved. Once the target was set, the European Commission began to monitor the progress of member states using a 'dashboard' which uses European summary frameworks and national profiles (European Commission, 2013) and which focuses on outcome data and on transnational comparison. The dynamic relationships between income poverty, material deprivation and low household work intensity, and substandard employment are also moni-tored: relationships which constitute the most relevant political element of this approach (Ayllón and Gábos, 2017).

An important role is played here by the SPC, which in the preparation of its annual report on social Europe starting from 2012 has used a tool called the 'Social Protection Performance Monitor', which is utilised by the Committee to identify the main social trends and key positive developments across the European Union (European Commission, 2013). These trends are identified using indicators which are annually monitored to capture statistically signif-icant changes, with 2008 as the reference year, in order to reveal progress made by Strategy Europe 2020. Following the identification of the main trends which require monitoring, the SPC produces theme-based reviews of possible causes and solutions for each trend; it also produces specific forms for each country in the European Union.

The target related to poverty and social exclusion may be considered as a particular type of compromise within the European Union. With regard to this target each member state was given the option of choosing the level of their national target as well as the target indicator which is most easy to achieve or more relevant to their own political-institutional tradition. Therefore, in some ways the target indicators are 'hard' tools which enable the European Commission to exert control over national policies; on the other hand, they are also a 'soft' tool because the Commission does not provide specific national recommendations and therefore the forms of pressure exerted are limited to peer review, lobbying by NGOs and monitoring carried by the Commission (Copeland and Daly, 2012). Flexibility continues therefore to be the key to understanding the development of social policy within the Union. The voluntary nature of the targets continues the path begun by the OMC which was strongly promoted by the Lisbon Strategy, inherently institutionalising the OMC in a number of ways. It is confirmation that the fate of proposals which advocate the coordination of European social policies is associated with their ability to be part of a flexible relationship with the various national models of social policy, hybridising rather than standardising them.

Naturally, this approach based upon compromise brings with it costs, regarding both the indicators' ability to measure phenomena and in terms of its effectiveness as a tool for policy governance, even though the inclusion of non-monetary indicators may be considered as a step forward in the monitoring of the achievement of targets regarding poverty across Europe.

From the very start, the central limitation of the composite indicator of multidimensional poverty was that it was not conceived as a tool for the measurement of a clear European social policy programme or founded on theoretical work analysing the relationship between income poverty, material deprivation and low household work intensity (Gábos and Goedemé, 2016), but instead, was rather the result of a political decision motivated by the different points of view and interests of the member states (Maître et al., 2013). As a consequence, over the years there has been some criticism regarding methodological approaches and proposals to revise this system of indicators. For example, there has been opposition to the rigid indications of items making up material deprivation, particularly with regard to the idea that deprivation is not so much the absence of resources, but rather that resources available cannot adequately satisfy needs which might change greatly over time, in space and depending on class and status. The set of items has also been considered as being rather limited and unable to cover the most relevant spheres of life or as being too culturally influenced and more representative of certain countries and population groups than others (Ravillion, 2011).

CONCLUSION

The three mechanisms for the creation of a 'European Social Space' described in this chapter are undoubtedly different from each other due to the social level in which they operate. The OMC operates above all in the macro-context of the relationship between the member states and the community institutions, whereas social dialogue is found at the meso-level of relationships between institutions, civil society and active citizenship. Finally, social indicators are largely knowledge-producing mechanisms which act upon the ways in which individuals who are usually experts, and consequently institutions, interpret reality.

However, as mechanisms of governance of social policy within the European Union they seem to underlie the same theory of change, a common idea regarding how to produce innovation within the countries of the European Union which will lead to a greater sharing of social policy principles and practices and which allows for an exchange and hybridisation between systems which are traditionally very different from each other. In particular, the logical model which helps to outline the three mechanisms' mode of action seems to be Everett Rogers' diffusion of innovations theory, first proposed in the 1960s (Rogers, 1995; Funnel and Rogers, 2011, pp. 335–339).

According to this theory, diffusion is a process in which innovation is communicated over time, through communication channels among the participants of a social system. These participants are not passive recipients of communication, but it is the participants themselves who create and share information. In our case, a key role is played by the central institutions of the Union, above all the Commission and the SPC, although they search constantly for allies among the states, NGOs, citizens and intellectuals who are asked to play an active role, particularly in the production of so-called best practices.

The relevance of the diffusion theory is even more evident if we closely examine its key concepts.

It is believed that an innovation can be more easily adopted if certain specific attributes are perceived. The innovation must be considered as being: more advantageous than current tools or procedures, compatible with the pre-existing system, not over-complex, and capable of producing easily observable results. Finally, the innovation must be amenable to testing a limited period of time without obligation before being adopted indefinitely. The ways in which these three mechanisms (the OMC, social dialogue and social indicators) work to produce social innovation seem to possess these attributes. Here, proposals are gradual in nature and they are tested out in specific areas and then eventually readapted or generalised to other contexts. In addition, they are seemingly almost never binding, but instead allow key actors great leeway, particularly with regard to the member states who may partially adopt or reproduce them in an original way. Finally, social innovations emerging from these three mechanisms seem to work more on the improvement of pre-existing practices (updating statistical reporting systems, making relations between different social partners more fluid and transparent) rather than changing them dramatically.

The process of diffusion of innovation is facilitated the more the communication channels are varied and can combine a vertical orientation with a more circular and interpersonal one. Mass media is an efficient way to reach the greatest number of possible users (adopters) of the innovation. However, interpersonal contacts are also important, particularly between individuals with the same socio-economic status and educational level, in order to increase the potential for acceptance. Above all, the active involvement of opinion leaders is fundamental, as they are potentially the most innovative and more likely to generate a trickle-down process. It has been seen how the communicative process of the three mechanisms examined is an alternative to the community method of regulation which adopts the legal means of communication. Even the OMC, which involves the state institutions directly, focuses greatly on the interpersonal meetings that also occur in conferences, working groups, scientific and professional networks; the involvement of public opinion; and the leadership role played by some politicians, intellectuals or stakeholders who recognise the need for a common European direction on specific social policies.

An innovation spreads more easily if we take into account the complexity of the social system which is to adopt it and if there is an awareness that the process is influenced by the social structure, the regulatory system, opinion leaders and other agents of change. Hence the understanding that it is necessary to take into account above all the values and traditions of national systems of welfare with which it is necessary to engage in dialogue and to arrive at compromises if a common path is to be built. At the same time, there emerges the idea that a real process of change cannot be implemented without a modification of traditional systems and values; therefore the proposed European Social Model has specific characteristics (often deriving from the welfare traditions that are considered as being 'best') which are grafted onto national models.

Finally, the three governance mechanisms are characterised by a strong temporal dimension. They act as tools for the diffusion of innovation along a path that lasts many years, if not decades. We may identify agents of innovation, the early adopters, those who come in late, those who are slower and those who resist innovation. For example, as illustrated in this chapter, the European Commission has played the role of innovation agent, and some countries, historically those of northern and continental Europe, were early adopters, whereas others such as Great Britain have been more reluctant to become fully involved in social dialogue and open coordination.

Critically, however, the three governance mechanisms central to the creation of a 'European Social Space' also share limitations inherent within the theory of diffusion, first established in the 1960s when processes of change could often take longer. The EU's community method, which involves long processes of coordination, dialogue and the promotion of new cognitive concepts, has appeared to be in difficulty, particularly since the financial crisis of 2007–2008. The European Union has been confronted new problems and emergencies with ever greater regularity. The response to these problems and emergencies has appeared slow and ineffective. This has been compounded by accusations that the EU has given greater consideration to the opinions of 'late-comer' states than to the needs of those hit by the crisis in European welfare across all member states. The current Covid-19 health emergency is perhaps the most profound and challenging crisis that the European Union has ever faced. It may be argued that this crisis has brought urgency to the creation and consolidation of a common 'European Social Space'.

NOTE

1. EU-SILC collects cross-sectional and longitudinal data in all the member states and contains detailed information on the socio-economic and demographic condition of family units. Data are not based on a standard questionnaire but on a common set of variables and rules, while each country decides upon its own method of data collection. The population consists of all the private housing units present in each national territory; therefore the most-needy individuals (the homeless, those living in reception facilities) are not included in the analysis.

REFERENCES

Atkinson, A., Cantillon, B., Marlier, E., and Nolan, B. (2002), *Social Indicators: The EU and Social Inclusion*, Oxford, Oxford University Press.
Ayllón, S., and Gábos, A. (2017), The interrelationships between the Europe 2020 Poverty and Social Exclusion Indicators, *Social Indicators Research*, 130, 1025–1049.
Barbera, F. (2004), *Meccanismi sociali. Elementi di sociologia analitica*, Il Mulino, Bologna.
Copeland, P., and Daly, M. (2012), Varieties of poverty reduction: inserting the poverty and social exclusion target into Europe 2020, *Journal of European Social Policy*, **22** (3), 273–287.
Dawson, M. (2011), *New Governance and the Transformation of European Law: Coordinating EU Social Law and Policy*, Cambridge University Press, Cambridge.
Demeulenaere, P. (ed.) (2011), *Analytical Sociology and Social Mechanisms*, Cambridge University Press, Cambridge.
European Commission (2012), *Social Dialogue Guide*, European Union, Luxembourg.
European Commission (2013), *Social Europe: Current Challenges and the Way Forward – Annual Report of the Social Protection Committee*, European Union, Luxembourg.
Euwema, M., Garcia, A. B., Munduate, L., Elgoibar, P., and Pender, E. (2015), Employee representatives in European organizations, in Euwema, M., et al. (eds), *Promoting Social Dialogue in European Organizations*. Springer Open, Berlin. DOI 10.1007/978-3-319-08605-7.
Ferrera, M. (2009), The JCMS Annual Lecture: national welfare states and European integration – in search of a 'virtuous nesting', *JCMS: Journal of Common Market Studies*, **47** (2), 219–233.
Funnel, S. C., and Rogers, P. J. (2011), *Purposeful Program Theory: Effective Use of Theories of Change and Logic*, Jossey-Bass, San Francisco.

Gábos, A., and Goedemé, T. (2016), The Europe 2020 social inclusion indicators: main conclusions of the ImPRovE project on validity, methodological robustness and interrelationships, ImPRovE Working Paper No. 16/13, Herman Deleeck Centre for Social Policy, University of Antwerp.

Hemerijck, A., and Berghman, J. (2004), The European social patrimony: deepening social Europe through legitimate diversity, in Sakellaropoulos, T., and Berghman, J. (eds), *Connecting Welfare Diversity within the European Social Model*, Intersentia, Antwerp, pp. 9–54.

Howlett, M., and Ramesh, M. (1995), *Studying Public Policy: Policy Cycles and Policy Subsystems*, Oxford University Press, Oxford.

Jacobsson, K. (2004), Soft regulation and the subtle transformation of states: the case of EU employment policy, *Journal of European Social Policy*, **14** (4), 355–370.

Johnson, A. (2005), *European Welfare States and Supranational Governance of Social Policy*, Palgrave Macmillan, London.

Maître, B., Nolan, B., and Whelan, C. T. (2013), A critical evaluation of the EU 2020 poverty and social exclusion target: an analysis of EU-SILC 2009, GINI Discussion Paper No. 79, AIAS, Amsterdam.

Majone, G., and La Spina, A. (2000), *Lo Stato regolatore*, Il Mulino, Bologna.

Offe, C. (2003), The European model of 'social' capitalism: can it survive European integration? *Journal of Political Philosophy*, **11** (4), 437–469.

Pawson, R., and Tilley, N. (1997), *Realistic Evaluation*, Sage, London.

Ravillion, M. (2011), On multidimensional indices of poverty, Policy Research Working Paper 5580, World Bank Development Research Group, Washington D.C.

Rogers, E. M. (1995), Lessons for guidelines from the diffusion of innovations, *Joint Commission Journal on Quality Improvement*, **21** (7), 324–328.

Smismans, S. (2008), New modes of governance and the participatory myth, *West European Politics*, **31** (5), 874–895.

Social Protection Committee Indicators Sub-Group (2015), *Portfolio of EU Social Indicators for the Monitoring of Progress Toward the EU Objectives for Social Protection and Social Inclusion*, European Union, Luxembourg.

Syrpis, P. (2002), Legitimising European governance: taking subsidiarity seriously within the Open Method of Coordination, EUI Working Papers Law 2002–10.

Vandenbroucke, F. (2002), Foreword: sustainable social justice and 'open co-ordination' in Europe, in Esping-Andersen, G., Gallie, D., Hemerijck, A., and Myers, J. (eds), *Why We Need a New Welfare State*, Oxford University Press, Oxford, pp. viii–xxiv.

Weishaupt, J. T. (2014), The social OMCs at work: identifying and explaining variations in national use and influence, in Barcevičius, E., Weishaupt, J. T., and Zeitlin, J. (eds), *Assessing the Open Method of Coordination: Institutional Design and National Influence of EU Social Policy Coordination*, Palgrave Macmillan, Basingstoke, pp. 203–233.

Wincott, D. (2003), Beyond social regulation? New instruments and/or a new agenda for social policy at Lisbon? *Public Administration*, **81** (3), 533–553.

Zeitlin, J., Barcevičius, E., and Weishaupt, J. T. (2014), Institutional design and national influence of EU social policy coordination: advancing a contradictory debate, in Barcevičius, E., Weishaupt, J. T., and Zeitlin, J. (eds), *Assessing the Open Method of Coordination: Institutional Design and National Influence of EU Social Policy Coordination*, Palgrave Macmillan, Basingstoke, pp. 1–15.

10. Conclusion: towards a progressive transformation of the European economic and social model

Giovanni Bertin, Marion Ellison and Giuseppe Moro

In conclusion, as this book has evidenced, divergent conceptual and empirical understandings of the ideational notion of a 'European Welfare System', more broadly conceptualized as a 'European Social Model', have emerged from distinct analytical perspectives. Moreover, the debate regarding the potential development of a unified and coherent European Welfare System is not a recent phenomenon. Illustrating this, a number of concrete indicators have been devised to inform this debate within previous analytical studies of national welfare systems, particularly during the expansionary period of welfare systems in Europe. From this perspective, as a number of authors contend, there are unifying characteristics emerging from social solidarity underpinning the historical development of welfare systems across Europe (Ellison, 2011; Genschel and Hemerijck, 2018; Hemerijck, 2002; Houtepen and Ter Meulen, 2000; Keating, 2020; Laitinen and Pessi, 2014; Larsen, 2006; Stjernø, 2004; Wilde, 2007).

As Hemerijck (2002) argues, these unifying characteristics can be traced back to three fundamental factors. The first is welfare solidarity, which is realized by the provision of full employment and adequate welfare provision, including comprehensive and equitable health and education services combined with a social security safety net during illness, old age, unemployment and disability. In addition, welfare solidarity is demonstrated by measures directed at reducing poverty and marginalization. It is argued that the concept of welfare solidarity is widely accepted and shared by the population who support the institutional programs and collective taxation to fund welfare provision.

The second unifying characteristic underlying the development of European welfare systems is the presence of policies committed to the notion of social justice as an important factor contributing to development and progress of European societies. No contradiction between economic competitiveness and social cohesion is seen to exist here. Social cohesion is a factor that facilitates economic and social development and an ideal shared by individual countries as well as more generally across the European Union.

The final unifying characteristic concerns the pervasive influence of organizations from across a range of sectors within each country. Welfare systems are evidenced as emerging through participatory processes and negotiations between these organizations (Hemerijck, 2002).

These unifying elements reveal that every nation has taken up the idea that certain social risks cannot be an individual problem for individual actors, but each nation must find a response that comes from a position of solidarity. The differences between and within individual countries must be related to the ideological affiliations of the key players, to their dynamics in relation to power and negotiation, to the cultures of belonging and to their concrete practices as these have determined the processes by which national (and internal) welfare systems have been constructed (Blekesaune and Quadagno, 2003; Healy et al., 2018; Lahusen and Grasso, 2018; Lim and Endo, 2016). The processes of social change, the financial crisis of 2007–2008 and the legitimization of public policies have contributed to the start of transforming welfare systems. In parallel, the European Union has also contributed to the development of debates surrounding welfare system reorganization. The phase of revisiting the welfare system that is in place has significantly altered the structure of all national welfare systems and also the differences that have developed. This transformative process can be analyzed from three different points of view.

A first perspective concerns the economic and social rights that can be claimed and the degree of social protection European citizens are afforded. From this standpoint, there are significant differences among nations as well as within them where social spending and the presence of services highlight these (Mussida and Parisi, 2020; Otto, 2018; Spasova et al., 2017; Spasova and Ward, 2019). The composition of social spending with respect to the different social risks (new and old) and the spread of services targeting different population sectors present significant differences (Aaberge et al., 2017; Abrahamson et al., 2019; Fresno et al., 2019; Muir, 2017; Rechel, 2018; Sainsbury et al., 2017). These are attributable to the history of the welfare systems in individual countries as well as to cultural, political and economic factors that have marked the expansion phase. From this point of view, it is easy to say that significant differences remain between nations as well as within individual countries and to conclude that to speak of a European Welfare System is a contrivance.

In the face of these differences, however, it is useful to underscore how the distance between welfare regimes has been reduced. This is an issue that is still discussed in literature dealing with the comparison of welfare systems. It seems, however, that a route which highlights their hybrid character and the presence of what had been considered an alternative logic has been identified (Bleses and Seeleib-Kaiser, 2004; Kujala and Danielsbacka, 2019). Today almost all welfare systems are accompanied by policies that refer to the logic of the welfare state alongside processes that recover market logic or stimulate interventions based on the consolidation of solidarity networks and community-type dynamics. In short, the re-engineering phase of welfare systems has led to a reduction in the differences in political production processes and in the roles played by the different actors involved in their realization.

A second perspective concerns the legitimacy of the idea of building a Europe based on the sharing of a homogeneous welfare system among all countries. These aspects have still not been extensively researched, but from the analysis of the works present in literature and from the European Union surveys (Bonasia and De Siano, 2019; Kiess et al., 2017; Zeilinger and Reiner, 2020), two trends have emerged. On the one hand, there are countries with more fragile welfare systems which wish to build a European Welfare System capable of spreading the same level of protection from economic and social risks throughout the Union. This tendency is particularly present in those countries which have recently joined the Union and which previously orbited in the area of the Soviet Union. In these cases, the difficulties of economic systems in profound but still fragile transformation and development coexist alongside recently established welfare systems. Conversely, there are other countries that have a more consolidated welfare system and see the homogenization of welfare systems and the growth of the European Union's role in their management as a possible threat to acquired fundamental economic and social rights, fearing a return to greater individual exposure to possible social risks.

A third, and perhaps most compelling aspect has to do with the cultural and territorial practices that have been concretely affirmed in individual nations. In this perspective the important role played by the European Union in orienting the internal debate within each single country is manifested. Not having a direct role in defining concrete welfare policies, the Union has tried to influence the action of individual nations in a number of ways. Firstly, work groups have been created to develop a culture of practice and broad policy measures to be adopted to combat social risks. Through open coordination, the action of the actors involved in welfare policies has been oriented and a method of governing the new welfare systems proposed. Further, projects involving collaboration among nations have been financed. These cultural and territorial practices aim to facilitate the introduction of innovative practices in the management of welfare policies. In this way the creation of networks of actors, who have compared experiences and homogenized the practices of production of welfare policies, has been encouraged. Further, the exchange of best practice has enabled improvements in welfare measures and practices across European states emphasizing the importance of social innovation skills.

The dissemination of good practice has enabled countries with weaker, more recent and, consequently, less consolidated welfare systems to compare themselves with countries exhibiting more innovative practices. This has been done in order to understand whether and to what extent these experiences could be useful in constructing concrete responses to new social risks and the limitations of fiscal resources that characterize the internal debate within each individual country. In other words, effective forms of social innovation disseminated through the Social Open Method of Coordination (OMC) have been proposed not as models to be rigidly adopted by member states, but as positive practices to be understood through comparative assessment of the effectiveness of social innovations within distinct territorial spaces and diverse national contexts.

These three actions also highlight a logic of governance that overcomes the dynamics of a multilevel hierarchy. In doing so, these actions break new ground in relation to the potential construction of a European Welfare System through the creation of shared cultural and governance practices. These, in turn, are based on participatory processes, on the construction of cooperative networks and on the comparison and dissemination of good practices.

These brief considerations make it possible to reach a first important conclusion, which is that a Social Europe exists and has a greater consistency than is often stated within politically polemic rhetoric. Of course, there is no 'European Social Model' if by this term we mean a unified welfare system designed in a rational way and then implemented uniformly in the different nations of the continent. But the long history of building a united Europe, begun after the great tragedy of the Second World War, cannot be reduced to just an economic dimension, be it the creation of a common market or a single currency. European identity is also achieved by widespread adherence to a number of fundamental political values, such as limiting inequality, thereby necessitating the forging of political regimes and policies consistent with these egalitarian values. This would entail interventionist states with redistributive policies and regulatory instruments across a broad range of areas, including income, housing, education, the labour market and social protection. Critically, it may be argued that adherence to these principles goes beyond the formal borders of the European Union, whether we refer to the citizens of nations that do not belong to the Union, but are willing to do so, or to the citizens of the countries that have decided not to be part of the Union or even to abandon it.

Building a common 'European Social Space' has been the ever-transitory result of an incremental process forged by unstable compromises between the many actors who have played a part in its creation. A number of these have been delineated in this volume. The most significant players are, first of all, the central European institutions of the European Commission and the European Court of Justice. These have constantly tried to widen the too tightly woven legislative links and agreements between nations to promote common social policies or at least promote principles and tools that allow national social policies to find a common ground. Other actors are identified as the national governments and, above all, their political forces which have seen Europe as a resource to strategically modify consolidated welfare structures or, in some cases, as a constraint which has forced them to heavily reform their welfare systems to adapt to European requirements.

Other actors are recognized in the large vested organizations such as those representing entrepreneurs and trade unions. After an initial period of distrust, united European participatory organizations have been created and these have played both a crucial role in the construction of social policies alongside making habitual use of European policies to strengthen their mutual contractual position on a national level as well as with their national governments. Further, recent years have seen the proliferation of new national and transnational civic society actors. These range from protest movements and advocacy associations to third-sector companies and have not only constituted a forceful presence for the construction of a Social Europe, but have acted as protagonists for a radical organizational transformation of European welfare states.

A final group of actors are the intellectuals who have found in the European space a new playing field and who have become European welfare thinkers elaborating analyses and concepts together with proposing hypotheses for reform that have quickly spread through each country with a transnational impact that would have been unthinkable a few years ago.

From the close of the last millennium to the beginning of the new one, a range of concepts, underpinned by principles of 'new welfare', have been established and advanced by social, political and cultural forces across European societies. These principles and concepts have led to significant transformations across European welfare systems. Central principles underpinning 'new welfare' include: the integration of the public and private sectors; targeting and sanctioning beneficiaries of social assistance; the notions of individual responsibility, workfare, activation, social investment and social innovation; and, in terms of policy management, multilevel governance and strategic planning. These concepts have been widely debated by European intellectuals and have legitimated welfare across European societies.

The fragmented, multi-actor and multidimensional process of building a European Social Space has led to the other major transformation highlighted in this volume; that is, the hybridization of European welfare systems. Traditional welfare administration was a reference point for European welfare analyses; however, this appears to have lost its heuristic value in recent decades. More specifically, if the state and its role was once the fundamental classification criteria, it is now reduced in scope both horizontally (due to the ever-increasing presence of market and community-oriented welfare producers) and vertically, with a national space which seems to be increasingly squeezed between local and global dimensions. Furthermore, each welfare system has been influenced by new principles that have resulted in heterogenous policies as well as different local territorial hierarchies, following consequent shifts in the balance of power between the public, private and third sectors within local socio-economic contexts. It has thus become increasingly difficult to find internal coherence within individual nations while, at the same time, a number of policies have unexpectedly become similar to those of all other European states. This volume has provided an in-depth analysis of common European political strategies directed at young people and elderly people; however, the same phenomenon has occurred across a number of policy areas, including labour market and employment policies and higher education policies across European societies.

The hybridization process has also been particularly significant with regard to governance. The focus is no longer on the analysis of individual policies, policy sectors and institutional actors. The traditional difference between centralist-leadership states and federal states, governed by market logic, seems to have disappeared. Instead, hybrid welfare systems have been consolidated and New Public Management techniques have been widely used in social services organization systems. From a social and political point of view, it may be relevant to ask whether the hybridization of welfare systems across European welfare states is the final outcome of a process in which common principles have been grafted onto established welfare regimes which have nevertheless retained essential aspects of original frameworks and traditional identities, or whether it is an intermediate step that can lead to a unitary conception of welfare in Europe.

During the first decade of the 2000s the unitary thrust appeared strong, moving towards the establishment of a European Social Model inspired by the principles of the so-called neo-welfarism, as discussed in Chapter 2. The years following this initial period, however, have called this evolutionary perspective into question. First of all, these principles of neo-welfarism have been operationalized within a socio-political context dominated by the financial crisis of 2007–2008 and the issue of sovereign debts and associated austerity policies across a number of European countries. The European Social Model has been perceived as a tool more for reducing welfare than reforming it. Further, the very idea of a united Europe has lost its political appeal. More recently, the Dutch and French referendums which rejected the European constitution, the outcome of the Brexit referendum and, finally, the emergence of Eurosceptic parties and governments both in the Eastern countries, which entered the Union only a few years ago, as well as in some of the founding countries like Italy and France, have served as a clamorous contradiction to notions of a united Europe. The current Covid-19 health pandemic has exacerbated economic and social problems across Europe, creating an even more fragile socio-political context in a number of European countries. While containment of the Covid-19 virus is of uppermost importance, issues relating to social cohesion are also being prioritized.

The progressive inclusion of the most disadvantaged and vulnerable social groups in European societies has been one of the characteristic features of European history over the last sixty years. The emergence of xenophobic movements, however, has called this aim into question. And, despite their many contradictions, so-called populist movements are an expression of the discomfort of the impoverished middle and working classes in need of greater protection and safeguarding. Importantly, limits of the founding principles of the neo-welfarism models have also emerged and it is, perhaps, this aspect which deserves the attention of social policy scholars. New welfare approaches based upon labour market inclusion have failed to respond effectively to challenges relating to the intensification of labour market inequalities and in-work poverty. Further, increasingly stringent targeting of people wholly or partially reliant on social security has resulted in the moral condemnation of the poor. It may be argued that the weakest and most needy social groups in society are being systematically excluded as a result of moral condemnation, sanctioning and high levels of conditionality.

Having said this, the process of social policy integration in Europe has continued despite the re-emergence of nationalistic movements or, perhaps, paradoxically, as a result of them. In effect, increased awareness of the growing fragility of the European Project has increased awareness that its survival is strongly connected to its ability to realize a shared European Welfare System.

In many ways, processes of European integration will continue in the wake of the transformations within the European economic and social sphere over the last two decades. In other respects, however, elements of innovation have emerged, which may impact on social policies across European societies. We will be able to fully assess the implications of these processes in the coming decade; however, we can make some observations from the preceding analysis.

The operationalization of major European Union policies legitimated by the European Pillar of Social Rights has taken the form of institutionalized top-down governance. On the other hand, and from a grassroots perspective, the production of welfare appears to have moved away from the state/ market dichotomy becoming increasingly meshed and integrated, while processes characterized by participation, co-production, self-regulation and co-responsibility have been affirmed. These processes are not only aimed at building activation paths, but also advocacy movements and, especially in recent times, bottom-up services which are relevant and meaningful, thereby enabling the operationalization of social rights for vulnerable groups.

The construction of social protection networks is an element that has characterized the development of nation-states in every European country. This aspect is seen as a distinctive element of the action of individual states but not yet considered as an element of European identity. The shift in responsibilities regarding the construction of welfare systems from nation-states to Europe is seen as a risk, reducing social protection and acquired rights rather than as a factor in the development of the idea of a united Europe. From this perspective the construction of a European Welfare System is probably seen as a process that must allow national histories and systems to be maintained while simultaneously activating a process that can lead to social safeguarding systems that provide the same degree of social protection within specific socio-economic contexts, political systems and diverse organizational forms. The destiny of the European community also seems to be linked to the ability of building a European identity and to activating a process that leads citizens to identify themselves with the idea of Europe. In fact, citizenship and identity are two of the founding factors within the communitarian dimension which facilitates the social solidarity in Europe (Ellison, 2011; Lehning and Weale, 2005; Nadalutti, 2015). In this perspective, the actions of the community have initiated processes that are contributing to the construction of a shared idea of welfare policies from the bottom up. Our analytical work allows us to point out some paths that can help consolidate these processes.

A first parameter regards reflecting on the meaning of 'social rights' where it is not attributable solely to state action but includes the overall action of the community and the ability to integrate formal actions with informal networks. Secondly, there is a need to avoid standardizing logic systems that claim to build a single welfare model. In fact, while similar levels of social protection should be reached, these should not be confused with the forms and organizational processes to be pursued in reaching them as the role of the actors, regulatory forms and their integrative dynamics are necessarily embedded in local cultures. A third element concerns international comparison methods and the construction of learning opportunities based on concrete experiences. In this respect the European Union has played and can play a fundamental role in providing opportunities to foster growth within the system through the dissemination of successful experiences. Finally, a fourth component can be traced back to the elements of cultural homogeneity that seem to have become consolidated alongside the process of redefining the welfare systems that have developed in every European nation. In this view, we can assume that basic values, the logic of policies, the logic of social investment, the transition from a logic of hierarchical regulation to a process of network governance, the centrality of the concept of community and the construction of its capacity to be resilient, and the need for actions that contain and activate people's resources are all aspects that, albeit with different intensities, are emerging in the cultures of the different European welfare systems.

The full realization of a Social Europe will require a renewed commitment to how it was imagined ten years ago as one that is based on the sharing of a number of values to guide the construction of welfare systems capable of guaranteeing similar levels of social protection. As the previous chapters have shown, the European Social Model today offers a flexible space for innovative, sophisticated and locally relevant solutions to emerge. This space recognizes the role and operational practices of a diverse range of actors. Critically, as this volume has evidenced, the European Union's capacity to re-invigorate and re-construct collaborative networks across European societies needs to be consolidated.

Here it is contended that social solidarity in Europe is strengthened by the consolidation of existing networks of mutual responsibility and by the creation of new relevant networks within and across European societies. As this book has also revealed, these networks are also strengthened by the principles of universal rights legally enshrined in the Charter for Fundamental Human Rights and the social rights enshrined in the European Pillar of Social Rights.

In this volume we recognize that there are still great differences between European nations; however, it should also be emphasized that in the last three decades in which the cultural and political hegemony of the neo-liberal paradigm emerged with greater force, a European approach to tackling and solving social problems has remained. This approach is not only theoretical, but rather a recognition of a number of social rights at European level. These rights include: the free movement of people and workers, the right to social security and the creation of a set of standards aimed at balancing social rights in areas such as health and safety in the workplace.

In essence, to neglect the social fabric of Europe is to neglect a central unifying premise of the European Social Project itself (Amato et al., 2019; Cantillon, 2019; Garben, 2019; Vesan and Corti, 2019). The European Pillar of Social Rights recognizes that 'Economic and social progress are intertwined.'[1] Yet the austerity and retrenchment of welfare states that characterized the response to the financial crisis of 2007–2008 have undoubtedly weakened the capacity of public health social protection systems to respond to the current Covid-19 crisis (Bedford et al., 2020; Hosseinpoor et al., 2018; Marmot, 2020; ONS, 2020). Moreover, inadequate public health infrastructures and public pharmaceutical capabilities have also been revealed by the differential impact of the pandemic and concomitant strategic response in different European countries (EAPN, 2020; Marmot, 2020; Mavragani, 2020; Urali and Oyebode, 2004). Austerity policies and welfare reforms have exacerbated poverty and social exclusion for vulnerable groups across Europe. Emerging evidence reveals that the economic impact of the Covid-19 pandemic will be most felt, as with the financial crisis of 2007–2008, by the most vulnerable people in society, particularly in poorer regions of Europe. Exemplifying this recent epidemiological evidence from the UK has revealed that this has had a direct impact on levels of mortality related to Covid-19 among vulnerable groups (ONS, 2020). At the time of writing the Office for National Statistics (UK) found that people living in the most deprived areas in England and Wales were dying at twice the rate of those living in the least deprived areas of England and Wales (ONS, 2020). A number of commentators have called for a renewed focus on policies directed at reducing health inequalities and related economic and social inequalities (Torales et al., 2020). It is argued that substantial and continued investment in European health care systems is a fundamental requirement if we are to guarantee equality of access and ensure the responsiveness public health care to all people who live and work in Europe. More broadly, the imposition of harsh austerity policies, including welfare reforms, the deregulation of labour markets and strict monetary measures, across a number of European countries has reinvigorated debates concerning the future of the European Social Model itself (Ferrera, 2020; Hartlapp, 2020; Romano and Punziano, 2016; Sciarra, 2020; Zeitlin and Vanhercke, 2014). For one in four living and working in the European Union, the lived experience of multiple and complex forms of poverty and social exclusion means enduring precarious lives (Eurostat, 2020). However, as this book has evidenced, the European Social Model has the potential to provide the flexible and complex architecture required for the development of collaborative, innovative, relevant and locally responsive policy measures.

Critically, however, this book has also argued that a reconfiguration of the relationship between economy and society is crucial to the continued relevance and effectiveness of the European Social Model, particularly with regard to its capacity to support collaborative and locally responsive measures which make a meaningful difference to the well-being of people living and working in Europe. Moreover, the Covid-19 health crisis has clearly exposed the urgent need to re-configure the existing relationships between economy and society across Europe. A number of commentators have argued that this requires the replacement of the primacy of the market economy as a system for producing, exchanging and consuming substitutable commodities according to price, with a 'foundational economy' which focuses on the equitable distribution of universal basic services (UBS) as an entitlement granted to all who live and work in European societies (Barbera et al., 2018; Bowman, 2014; Coote and Percy, 2020; Earle et al., 2018; Engelen et al., 2017; Froud and Williams, 2018; Heslop et al., 2019; Plank, 2020).

Evidence in this volume has also provided an evidence-based rationale for place-based community partnerships involving diverse models of ownership supported by access to services as a social right. The primary aim of these place-based community partnerships within distinct European societies is to promote the quality of life. The recent Covid-19 crisis has led to the emergence of spontaneous social solidarity in the form of local community-based solutions aimed at ensuring equitable and inclusive food distribution while supporting people who are most vulnerable and isolated across European societies (ESPON, 2020). These solutions contrast markedly to market-based economic and distributive approaches which focus on boosting private consumption by delivering economic growth.

The architecture of the foundational economy is based upon access to UBS as a human right (Earle et al., 2018; Froud and Williams, 2018; Heslop et al., 2019; Plank, 2020). Exponents of this approach argue that UBS will also facilitate place-based local control and diverse models of ownership and that this approach is more equitable, efficient and sustainable than an economic approach which focuses on market transaction (Coote and Percy, 2020; Froud and Williams, 2018; Heslop et al., 2019; Plank, 2020). Evidencing this, the current Covid-19 crisis has exposed the depth and extent of inequities in labour markets across Europe. In particular, as recent evidence reveals, many people working in health and social care professions across Europe are poorly paid and have to suffer poor employment conditions (Mai et al., 2019; Matilla-Santander et al., 2020; Wagner et al., 2019). Issues of distributive justice emerge across Europe as we reflect on the value and recognition given to those people employed in caring professions who have risked and given their lives to save others during the Covid-19 health crisis. In the UK, for example, a significant number of people working in health and social care professions are low-paid and have poor employment conditions (Andersen and Westgaard, 2015; Mai et al., 2019; Matilla-Santander et al., 2020; Trydegård, 2012; TUC, 2020; Wagner et al., 2019).

While issues of distributive justice and human rights are paramount, many analysts have also argued that introducing Universal Basic Income (UBI) would be a progressive way forward as the state would then be responsible for ensuring that all people who live and work in post-Covid-19 European societies have a guaranteed income (Johnson et al., 2020; Parolin and Siöland, 2020).

Critically, however, a number of commentators have critiqued this view, arguing that the operationalization of UBI may lead to the institutionalization of low pay (Chohan, 2017; Fouksman and Klein, 2019; Martinelli, 2016; McDonough and Morales, 2019; Ortiz et al., 2018; Sage and Diamond, 2017; Straubhaar, 2017). An evaluation of the recently piloted UBI Programme in Finland found that the scheme did lead to improved perception of economic welfare, mental well-being, confidence and life satisfaction (Kangas et al., 2020). As argued in this volume, policy measures such as UBI and UBS within foundational economies would be facilitated by the flexibility of the current architecture of the European Social Model and OMC. It may be argued that in the immediate aftermath of the Covid-19 crisis this flexibility and capacity to operationalize complex measures which meet local needs is critical. The architecture of the European Social Model, particularly with regard to place-based community programmes, offers a close alignment with innovative economic infrastructures such as the foundational economy. This alignment would facilitate the equitable and sustainable delivery of universal services and measures vital to the health and well-being of all who live and work in Europe.

More broadly, this book highlights the need to rethink the relationship between economy and society while acknowledging factors contributing to the recent transformation of welfare systems in Europe. These factors include the capacity of institutions to resist change, the socio-economic drive towards change, the characteristics of local socio-economic contexts, the concrete action systems rooted in segments of the welfare system, the ideologies of opposing forces and the social dynamics influencing the permanence of the culture of solidarity across Europe. It may be argued that given the gravity of the current crisis, the social dynamics shaping solidarity across Europe will be a critical determining factor influencing the future social and economic model of Europe. In post-Covid-19 Europe, the relationship between public health, work, formal care, informal care, inequality, poverty, the labour market and capital lies at the axiom of the relationship between economy and society. The tragic impact of the Covid-19 health crisis has strengthened appeals for a focus on a 'European economy of well-being' (Bauhardt and Harcourt, 2019; Chertkovskaya et al., 2019; ILO, 2018; Marmot, 2020; Patterson, 2020). Indeed, the development of a welfare economy formed the central focus of the Finnish Presidency of the Council for the European Union between 1 July 2019 and 31 December 2019. A central premise of this strategy is that macro-economic policy should be formulated upon a comprehensive analysis of its implications upon the well-being of citizens, particularly in relation to potential impacts on vulnerable groups and equitable access to quality social and health care services (Ardalan, 2019; Bauhardt and Harcourt, 2019; Chertkovskaya et al., 2019; ILO, 2018; Marmot, 2020; Patterson, 2020).

As we face the most profound humanitarian, social and economic challenge of the twenty-first century it is critical that we recognize the urgency of this task. Crucially, while policy responses and measures have been largely confined to distinct European settings there is also a palpable sense of our shared humanity, evidenced by many concrete examples of social solidarity across European borders. For example, people suffering from the Covid-19 virus have been transferred between European countries for specialist treatment, and specialist medical equipment has been distributed across countries. It is this sense of common purpose and mutuality that will be most needed if we are to find unity in diversity and repair and re-invest in the European Social Model at this time of crisis. It may also be argued that the Social OMC in its current form does provide a flexible and complex architecture for this renewed focus on the delivery of a European well-being economy which is relevant and meaningful to people who live and work across Europe. As argued in Chapter 4, a more coordinated approach to the intersection between work and welfare requires the introduction of new and relevant approaches, including the introduction of UBS and UBI as part of a foundational economy built upon a recalibration of work and well-being within a digital era (Boobier and Waterson, 2019; Gentilini et al., 2019; Gironde and Carbonnier, 2019; Hodder and Nowak, 2019; Lahusen and Grasso, 2018; Sloman, 2019).

The current global health crisis will undoubtedly exacerbate the tears in the social fabric of Europe clearly evidenced by this volume. The impact of the crisis on the economic architecture and political sphere is predicted to be extreme (Ayittey et al., 2020; Nicola et al., 2020; Ozili and Arun, 2020; Sułkowski, 2020). The fragility of European integration itself does have historical precedent, and for this reason it may be argued that if we are wise, we will learn from history. We are reminded that the European Enlightenment itself was born of economic, political and social crises across Europe (Outram, 2019; Porter, 2002). The fundamental basis of the European Enlightenment was the Age of Reason[2] epitomized by Rousseau's *Social Contract* in which he proclaimed that 'society should be ruled by the general will of the people'.[3] The evidence in this volume underlines this fundamental concept by emphasizing the importance of social and economic democracy in shaping policies that are locally relevant and meaningful for the well-being of people living and working in Europe. At the time of writing, so many people are living in tragic circumstances, with loss, poverty and social isolation being commonly experienced across Europe. Surely it is time to repair and re-invent the European social and economic model by moving towards a European economy of well-being.

NOTES

1. European Commission (2017), Article 11, p. 7. https://ec.europa.eu/commission/priorities/deeper-and-fairer-economic-and-monetary-union/european-pillar-social-rights_en.
2. The Age of Enlightenment, also known as the Age of Reason, was a philosophical and intellectual movement which was characterized by progressive ideas between 1715 and 1789. Influential intellectuals and philosophers included Thomas Paine, Francis Bacon, Thomas Hobbes, René Descartes, Galileo Galilei, Johannes Kepler, Isaac Newton, John Locke, Jean-Jacques Rousseau and Gottfried Wilhelm Leibniz.
3. *The Social Contract* (1762) was written by the French philosopher and writer Jean-Jacques Rousseau (1712–1778). His central argument was that that laws are binding only when they are supported by the general will of the people. Rousseau challenged the traditional order of society with his notion that 'Man is born free, but he is everywhere in chains.'

REFERENCES

Aaberge, R., Langørgen, A., and Lindgren, P. (2017). The distributional impact of public services in European countries. Eurostat Working Paper. https://ec.europa.eu/eurostat/documents/3888793/5857249/KS-RA-13-009-EN.PDF.

Abrahamson, P., Greve, B., and Boje, T. (2019). *Welfare and Families in Europe.* London: Routledge.

Amato, G., Moavero-Milanesi, E., Pasquino, G., and Reichlin, L. (2019). *The History of the European Union: Constructing Utopia.* Oxford: Hart.

Andersen, G. R., and Westgaard, R. H. (2015). Discrepancies in assessing home care workers' working conditions in a Norwegian home care service: differing views of stakeholders at three organizational levels. *BMC Health Services Research,* **15** (1), 286.

Ayittey, F. K., Ayittey, M. K., Chiwero, N. B., Kamasah, J. S., and Dzuvor, C. (2020). Economic impacts of Wuhan 2019-nCoV on China and the world. *Journal of Medical Virology,* 92, 473–475.

Barbera, F., Negri, N., and Salento, A. (2018). From individual choice to collective voice: foundational economy, local commons and citizenship. *Rassegna Italiana di Sociologia,* **59** (2), 371–398.

Bauhardt, C., and Harcourt, W. (2019). *Feminist Political Ecology and the Economics of Care: In Search of Economic Alternatives.* London: Routledge.

Bedford, J., Enria, D., Giesecke, J., Heymann, D. L., Ihekweazu, C., Kobinger, G., Lane, H. C., Memish, Z., Oh, M. D., Schuchat, A. and Ungchusak, K. (2020). COVID-19: towards controlling of a pandemic. *The Lancet,* **395** (10229), 1015–1018.

Blekesaune, M., and Quadagno, J. (2003). Public attitudes toward welfare state policies: a comparative analysis of 24 nations. *European Sociological Review,* **19** (5), 415–427.

Bleses, P., and Seeleib-Kaiser, M. (2004). *The Dual Transformation of the German Welfare State.* Basingstoke: Palgrave Macmillan.

Bonasia, M., and De Siano, R. (2019). Financial crisis and the convergence of European welfare provision. MPRA Paper 97509, University Library of Munich, Germany.

Boobier, T., and Waterson, M. (2019). *Advanced Analytics and AI: Impact, Implementation, and the Future of Work.* [Audiobook]. www.overdrive.com/search?q=C82A8829-8794-4B91-8914-5FAFD6E098B7.

Bowman, A., Ertürk, I., Froud, J., Johal, S., and Law, J. (2014). *The End of the Experiment? From Competition to the Foundational Economy.* Manchester: Manchester University Press.

Cantillon, B. (2019). The European Pillar of Social Rights, in M. Ferrera (ed.), *Towards a European Social Union: The European Pillar of Social Rights and the Roadmap for a Fully-fledged Social Union.* Torino: Centro Einaudi.

Chertkovskaya, E., Paulsson, A., and Barca, S. (2019). *Towards a Political Economy of Degrowth.* Lanham, MD: Rowman & Littlefield.

Chohan, U. W. (2017). Universal Basic Income: a review. Available at SSRN 3013634.

Coote, A., and Percy, A. (2020). *The Case for Universal Basic Services.* Bristol: Polity Press.

EAPN (European Anti-Poverty Network) (2020) EAPN statement on Covid-19. www.eapn.eu/wp-content/uploads/2020/03/EAPN-E2a.-EAPN-Statement-on-Covid-19-4163-4194.pdf.

Earle, J., Froud, J., Johal, S., and Williams, K. (2018). Foundational economy and foundational politics. *Welsh Economic Review*, **26**, 38–45.

Ellison, M. (ed.) (2011). *Reinventing Social Solidarity across Europe*. Bristol: Policy Press.

Engelen, E., Froud, J., Johal, S., Salento, A., and Williams, K. (2017). The grounded city: from competitivity to the foundational economy. *Cambridge Journal of Regions, Economy and Society*, **10** (3), 407–423.

ESPON (European Spatial Planning Observation Network) (2020). Collecting experiences and evidence on local and regional responses to COVID19. European Union. www.espon.eu/covid19.

Eurostat (2020). Living conditions in Europe: poverty and social exclusion. https://ec.europa.eu/eurostat/statistics-explained/index.php/Living_conditions_in_Europe_-_poverty_and_social_exclusion

Ferrera, M. (2020). More solidarity than meets the eye? Challenges and prospects for Social Europe, in R. Careja, P. Emmenegger and N. Giger (eds), *The European Social Model under Pressure: Liber Amicorum in Honour of Klaus Armingeon*. Wiesbaden: Springer VS.

Fouksman, E., and Klein, E. (2019). Radical transformation or technological intervention? Two paths for Universal Basic Income. *World Development*, 122, 492–500.

Fresno, J. M., Meyer, S., and Bain, S. (2019). The future of social services in Europe. *Public Policy*, **4** (1), 64–76.

Froud, J., and Williams, K. (2018). *Foundational Economy: The Infrastructure of Everyday Life*. Manchester: Manchester University Press.

Garben, S. (2019). The European Pillar of Social Rights as a revival of Social Europe, in M. Ferrera (ed.), *Towards a European Social Union: The European Pillar of Social Rights and the Roadmap for a Fully-fledged Social Union*. Torino: Centro Einaudi.

Genschel, P., and Hemerijck, A. (2018). Solidarity in Europe. School of Transnational Governance Policy Brief 2018/01. https://cadmus.eui.eu/handle/1814/53967.

Gentilini, U., Grosh, M., Rigolini, J., and Yemtsov, R. (2019). *Exploring Universal Basic Income: A Guide to Navigating Concepts, Evidence, and Practices*. Washington, D.C.: World Bank Publications.

Gironde, C., and Carbonnier, G. (2019). *The ILO @ 100: Addressing the Past and Future of Work and Social Protection*. Leiden: Brill.

Hartlapp, M. (2020). European Union social policy: facing deepening economic integration and demand for a more social Europe with continuity and cautiousness, in S. Blum, J. Kuhlmann, and K. Schubert (eds), *The Routledge Handbook of European Welfare Systems*. Routledge: London.

Healy, S., Borowiak, C., Pavlovskaya, M., and Safri, M. (2018). Commoning and the politics of solidarity: transformational responses to poverty. *Geoforum*. DOI: 10.1016/j.geoforum.2018.03.015.

Hemerijck, A. (2002). The self-transformation of the European Social Model(s). *Internationale Politik und Gesellschaft*, 4, 39–67.

Heslop, J., Morgan, K., and Tomaney, J. (2019). Debating the foundational economy. *Renewal*, **27** (2), 5–12.

Hodder, A., and Nowak, P. (2019). *The Future of Work and the Future of Unions*. Bradford: Emerald.

Hosseinpoor, A. R., Bergen, N., Schlotheuber, A., and Grove, J. (2018) Measuring health inequalities in the context of sustainable development. *Bulletin of the World Health Organization*, **96**, 654–659.

Houtepen, R., and Ter Meulen, R. (2000). New types of solidarity in the European welfare state. *Health Care Analysis*, **8** (4), 329–340.

ILO (International Labour Organization) (2018). *Care Work and Care Jobs for the Future of Decent Work*. Geneva: ILO. www.ilo.org/wcmsp5/groups/public/---dgreports/---dcomm/--publ/documents/publication/wcms_633135.pdf.

Johnson, M., Johnson, E., Webber, L., and Nettle, D. (2020). Mitigating social and economic sources of trauma: the need for Universal Basic Income during the Coronavirus pandemic. *Psychological Trauma: Theory, Research, Practice, and Policy*, **12** (S1), S191–S192.

Kangas, O., Jauhiainen, S., and Simanainen, M. (2020). *Suomen perustulokokeilun arviointi*. Finland Government, Institutional Repository for the Government. https://julkaisut.valtioneuvosto.fi/.

Keating, M. (2020). Beyond the nation-state: territory, solidarity and welfare in a multiscalar Europe. *Territory, Politics, Governance*, 1–15. DOI: 10.1080/21622671.2020.1742779.

Kiess, J., Norman, L., Temple, L., and Uba, K. (2017). Path dependency and convergence of three worlds of welfare policy during the Great Recession: UK, Germany and Sweden. *Journal of International and Comparative Social Policy*, **33** (1), 1–17.

Kujala, A., and Danielsbacka, M. (2019). The modern welfare state, in *Reciprocity in Human Societies: From Ancient Times to the Modern Welfare State*. Cham: Palgrave Macmillan.

Lahusen, C., and Grasso, M. T. (2018). *Solidarity in Europe: Citizens' Responses in Times of Crisis*. London: Palgrave Macmillan.

Laitinen, A., and Pessi, A. B. (2014). Solidarity: theory and practice – an introduction, in A. Laitinen and A. Pessi (eds), *Solidarity: Theory and Practice*. Lanham: Lexington Books.

Larsen, C. A. (2006). *The Institutional Logic of Welfare Attitudes: How Welfare Regimes Influence Public Support*. Farnham: Ashgate.

Lehning, P. B., and Weale, A. (2005). *Citizenship, Democracy and Justice in the New Europe: Political Theory and the Integration Process*. Florence: Taylor & Francis.

Lim, S. H., and Endo, C. (2016). The development of the social economy in the welfare mix: political dynamics between the state and the third sector. *Social Science Journal*, **53** (4), 486–494.

Mai, Q. D., Hill, T. D., Vila-Henninger, L., and Grandner, M. A. (2019). Employment insecurity and sleep disturbance: evidence from 31 European countries. *Journal of Sleep Research*, **28** (1), e12763.

Marmot, M. (2020). *Health Equity in England: The Marmot Review 10 Years On*. London: Institute of Health Equity.

Martinelli, L. (2017). Assessing the case for a universal basic income in the UK. IPR Policy Brief. Institute for Policy Research, University of Bath. www.bath.ac.uk/publications/assessing-the-case-for-a-universal-basic-income-in-the-uk/attachments/basic_income_policy_ brief.pdf.

Matilla-Santander, N., Martín-Sánchez, J. C., González-Marrón, A., Cartanyà-Hueso, À., Lidón-Moyano, C., and Martínez-Sánchez, J. M. (2020). Precarious employment, unemployment and their association with health-related outcomes in 35 European countries: a cross-sectional study. *Critical Public Health*, 1–12.

Mavragani, A. (2020). Tracking COVID-19 in Europe: infodemiology approach. *JMIR Public Health and Surveillance*, **6** (2): e18941. DOI: 10.2196/18941.

McDonough, B., and Morales, J. B. (2019). *Universal Basic Income*. New York: Routledge.

Muir, T. (2017). Measuring social protection for long-term care. OECD Health Working Paper No 93. https://doi.org/10.1787/a411500a-en.

Mussida, C., and Parisi, M. L. (2020). Risk of poverty in Southern Europe. *Metroeconomica*, **71** (2), 294–315.

Nadalutti, E. (2015). *The Effects of Europeanization on the Integration Process in the Upper Adriatic Region*. Cham: Springer.

Nicola, M., Alsafi, Z., Sohrabi, C., Kerwan, A., Al-Jabir, A., Iosifidis, C., ... and Agha, R. (2020). The socio-economic implications of the coronavirus and COVID-19 pandemic: a review. *International Journal of Surgery*, 78: 185–192.

ONS (2020). Note: age-standardised mortality rates, all deaths and deaths involving the coronavirus (Covid-19), Index of Multiple Deprivation, England, deaths occurring between 1 March and 17 April 2020. London: ONS.

Ortiz, I., Behrendt, C., Acuña-Ulate, A., and Anh, N. Q. (2018). Universal Basic Income proposals in light of ILO standards: key issues and global costing. Available at SSRN 3208737.

Otto, A. (2018). A benefit recipiency approach to analysing differences and similarities in European welfare provision. *Social Indicators Research: An International and Interdisciplinary Journal for Quality-of-Life Measurement*, **137** (2), 765–788.

Outram, D. (2019). *The Enlightenment*. Cambridge: Cambridge University Press.

Ozili, P. K., and Arun, T. (2020). Spillover of COVID-19: impact on the global economy. Available at https://ssrn.com/abstract=3562570.

Parolin, Z., and Siöland, L. (2020). Support for a universal basic income: a demand–capacity paradox? *Journal of European Social Policy*, **30** (1), 5–19.

Patterson, K. (2020). It's a virus, and this isn't a war. Social Europe. 28 April. www .socialeurope.eu/its-a-virus-and-this-isnt-a-war.

Plank, L. (2020). Reframing public ownership in the foundational economy: (re)discovering a variety of formsm, in: Barbera, F., and Rees Jones, I. (eds), *The Foundational Economy and Citizenship: Perspectives on Civil Repair*. Bristol: Bristol University Press.

Porter, R. (2002). *Enlightenment: Britain and the Creation of the Modern World*. London: Penguin.

Rechel, B. (ed.) (2018). Organization and financing of public health services in Europe: country reports (No. 49). World Health Organization. www.euro.who.int/ en/publications/abstracts/organization-and-financing-of-public-health-services-in -europe-country-reports-2018.

Romano, S., and Punziano, G. (2016). *The European Social Model Adrift: Europe, Social Cohesion and the Economic Crisis*. London: Routledge.

Sage, D., and Diamond, P. (2017). *Europe's New Social Reality: The Case Against Universal Basic Income*. London: Policy Network.

Sainsbury, R., Lawson, A. M. M., and Priestley, M. (2017). Social protection for disabled people in Europe: synthesis report. Academic Network of European Disability Experts (ANED). www.disability-europe.net/theme/social-protection.

Sciarra, S. (2020). How social will Social Europe be in the 2020s? *German Law Journal*, **21** (1), 85–89.

Sloman, P. (2019). *Transfer State: The Idea of a Guaranteed Income and the Politics of Redistribution in Modern Britain*. Oxford: Oxford University Press.

Spasova, S., Bouget, D., Ghailani, D., and Vanhercke, B. (2017). *Access to Social Protection for People Working on Non-Standard Contracts and as Self-Employed in Europe: A Study of National Policies*. Brussels: European Commission.

Spasova, S., and Ward, T. (2019). *Social Protection Expenditure and its Financing in Europe: A Study of National Policies*. Luxembourg: Publications Office of the European Union.

Stjernø, S. (2004). *Solidarity in Europe: The History of an Idea*. Cambridge: Cambridge University Press.

Straubhaar, T. (2017). On the economics of a universal basic income. *Intereconomics*, **52** (2), 74–80.

Sułkowski, Ł. (2020). Covid-19 pandemic; recession, virtual revolution leading to de-globalization? *Journal of Intercultural Management*, 12, 1–11.

Torales, J., O'Higgins, M., Castaldelli-Maia, J., and Ventriglio, A. (2020). The outbreak of COVID-19 coronavirus and its impact on global mental health. *International Journal of Social Psychiatry*, **66** (4). https://doi.org/10.1177/0020764020915212.

Trydegård, G. B. (2012). Care work in changing welfare states: Nordic care workers' experiences. *European Journal of Ageing*, **9** (2), 119–129.

TUC (Trades Union Congress) (2020). Testing and tracing for Covid-19: how to ensure fair access and manage monitoring in the workplace. www.tuc.org.uk/research -analysis/reports/testing-tracing-covid-19.

Urali, V., and Oyebode, F. (2004). Poverty, social inequality and mental health. *Advances in Psychiatric Treatment*, 10, 216–224.

Vesan, P., and Corti, F. (2019). New tensions over Social Europe? The European Pillar of Social Rights and the debate within the European Parliament. *JCMS: Journal of Common Market Studies*, **57** (5), 977–994.

Wagner, A., Rieger, M. A., Manser, T., Sturm, H., Hardt, J., Martus, P., ... and Hammer, A. (2019). Healthcare professionals' perspectives on working conditions, leadership, and safety climate: a cross-sectional study. *BMC Health Services Research*, **19** (1), 1–14.

Wilde, L. (2007). The concept of solidarity: emerging from the theoretical shadows. *British Journal of Politics and International Relations*, **9** (1), 171–181.

Zeilinger, B., and Reiner, C. (2020). Trajectories of reforming European welfare state policies under the post-2008 socio-economic governance regime, in Wöhl, S., Springler, E., Pache, M., and Zeilinger, B. (eds), *The State of the European Union*. Wiesbaden: Springer VS.

Zeitlin, J., and Vanhercke, B. (2014). Socializing the European Semester? Economic governance and social policy coordination in Europe 2020. Swedish Institute for European Policy Studies. doi: 10.2139/ssrn.2511031.

Index